INTELLECTUAL ROMANTICS
A Study in Modern English Poetry

THATTARATHODI RAGHAVAN

ATLANTIC PUBLISHERS AND DISTRIBUTORS

Published by
ATLANTIC PUBLISHERS AND DISTRIBUTORS
B-2, Vishal Enclave, New Delhi-27
Phone 5413460, 5429987

Sales Office
4346/4C, Ansari Road, Darya Ganj,
New Delhi-110 002
Phone 3273880, 3285873
Fax 91-11-3285873

ISBN 81-7156-444-5

Typeset at
APD Computer Graphics
B-2, Vishal Enclave, New Delhi-110 027
Printed in India at
Mehra Offset Press
New Delhi

DEDICATED TO

The Memory of Prof. V.S. Seturaman, who was a revered teacher, unswerving idealist and scholar *par-excellence*

ACKNOWLEDGEMENTS

The credit for moulding my clay into the shape suggested by this study should go to the late Prof. V.S. Seturaman (Formerly Head of the Department of English and Dean, Faculty of Arts, Sri Krishnadevaraya University, Anantapur, Andhra Pradesh), who belonged to a fast-vanishing order of idealist-teachers. To me he has not been just a research supervisor: he has been a sobering, sensitizing and humanizing influence in a profound sense. The gratitude I feel towards him is too deep for words. Next only to him I owe a debt of gratitude to Dr. T. Sriraman of the C.I.E.F.L., Hyderabad, for the invaluable help he has rendered in curbing the waywardness of my linguistic expression. I am also deeply indebted to Prof. Jack Stillinger of the University of Illinois, U.S.A., Prof. S. Viswanathan of the Central University of Hyderabad, Prof. C. Subba Rao of the Sri Krishnadevaraya University, and Mr. R.A. Jayantha of the Sri Venkateswara University for their expert comments on the theory presented in this study. I am beholden to Dr. (Miss) C.T. Indra of the University of Madras and Smt. Sivagami, Research Scholar in the University of Illinois, for their generous gestures. And I owe much to my beloved colleagues Sri M.V. Subba Rao and Dr. C. Krishna Murthy for various kinds of help I have received from them in the course of a long-drawn effort. My thanks are also due to Mr. E. Ramachenna Reddy for his assistance in typing out this work.

I place on record my gratitude to the A.S.R.C., Hyderabad, for allowing me a grant to facilitate the use of the impressive collection of books available at the Centre.

Thattarathodi Raghavan

PREFACE

The topic for this study has perhaps been rather ambitious in its range. It was, in fact, decided on after deep deliberation. The choice of it was influenced primarily by a hope of being able to arrive at some fresh insights.

The most formidable challenge posed by the choice of a wide-ranging field has been of reducing the scope of the work to viable dimensions. It has entailed certain arbitrary omissions. Another baffling problem has been the inaccessibility of a good part of the contributions made by critics in both the U.K. and the U.S.A., particularly in recent years. And, with all the generous help received from the A.S.R.C., Hyderabad, and the British Council Library, Madras, it has imposed a severe limitation on the work. The effort might well have been far more rewarding and satisfying in its absence.

The study is focused on some of the major poets of the twentieth century in whom Romantic propensities have gone hand-in-hand with acute sceptical tendencies. A large number of poets whose Romantic leanings are more pronounced have had to be pushed to the side-lines in the process most apologetically.

The study is divided into seven chapters:

Chapter I presents the argument in three parts dealing respectively with its general, theoretical and technical aspects. *Chapter II* discusses the Romantic affinities of Edward Thomas. *Chapter III* is meant to highlight the intellectual strain in the 'facile' Romanticism of Walter de la Mare. *Chapter IV* is on the early poetry of W.B. Yeats and is meant as an introductory to the more important chapter that follows. *Chapter V* is devoted to the later poetry of Yeats. *Chapter VI* concerns itself with the contribution of T.S. Eliot to the Romantic tradition. *Chapter VII* sums up the argument after a brief survey of the post-modernist trends affecting the prospects of the Romantic tradition.

Thattarathodi Raghavan

[illegible]

[illegible] devoted [illegible] held [illegible]

[illegible]

[illegible] the scope of the work [illegible]

[illegible] and the [illegible]

[illegible] a dissertation on the work. The editor [illegible]

[illegible]

[illegible]

Contents

CHAPTER I

GENERAL, THEORETICAL AND TECHNICAL ASPECTS

I

The progress of poets down the ages till modern times has been presented in a nutshell by Peter Viereck:

From the Sublime to the Meticulous in Four Stages

Dante	:	We were God's poets
Burns	:	We were the people's poets
Mallarme	:	We were poet's poets.
Today (preening)	:	Ah, but we are critics' poets.[1]

'Meticulous' in the context echoes 'ridiculous' and the implication seems rather ominous. The epigram humorously highlights the pathetic plight of the modern poet in the wake of his subordination to the analytic critic. The bardic and the long-haired poets have disappeared. Their modern counterparts are much-too-trim.

Writing for the critic, thus, becomes a feature of contemporary self-consciousness, as remarked by John Bayley.[2] And the new poetry seems to assume the characteristics of a machine that can be dismantled at will into its constituent parts without losing anything, thanks to critical canons that expect us "to extract, squeeze, tease and press every drop of meaning" out of poetry.[3] Cerebration and analysis have tended to suppress the Romantic Imagination for quite some time. Its withdrawal and reassertion in modern poetry perhaps sum up the history of the Romantic tradition in the twentieth century.

---

1. Quoted in Bayley, John, *The Romantic Survival: A Study in Poetic Evolution* (London: Chatto & Windus, 1957, Paperback, 1969), pp. 68-69. Henceforth referred to as *RS*.
2. *Ibid.*, pp. 69-70.
3. Eliot, T.S., "The Frontiers of Criticism" in *On Poetry and Poets* (London: Faber and Faber, 1957), p. 113. Henceforth referred to as *OPP*.

A survey of the fluctuating fortunes of Romanticism in the century may involve a curious exploration of a series of conflicting stances and ironic assertions. For one thing, as Harold Bloom puts it, "modernist poetry in English organized itself to an excessive extent, as a supposed revolt against Romanticism, in the mistaken hope of escaping its inwardness."[4] As has been widely acknowledged, what the *soi-disant* enemies of Romanticism like T.E. Hulme, Ezra Pound and T.S. Eliot were reacting against in the early part of the century was Romanticism *in its decline*. And they "read their objections to its tone, conventions and world-view back on to the high Romantics."[5] It sounds rather incredible that these eminent men should have had so much difficulty in distinguishing the shadow from the substance. However, as it appeared, their mistaken labours brought about a rejuvenation of the Romantic tradition in the century.

The faint-hearted adherence of the poets of the *fin-de-siacle* to worn-out Romantic modes had brought much odium on the tradition at the turn of the century. The feeble tone of its Georgian practitioners had also done it harm. Lascelles Abercrombie, for one, would appear to have simplified the matter a little too much, by opposing Romanticism to realism, making no allowance for realities other than physical. His definition of Romanticism as a tendency to rely on inner experience, however, links it up with psychological realities.[6] Traditional critics like F.L. Lucas deprived Romanticism of its charm. Romanticism tended to lose its identity too in the ocean of subjective definitions. In such a context, the fate of Lovejoy's attempt at identifying the common aspects of Romanticism is hardly surprising.[7] The definitions in most cases betrayed the obsessions of the individual critics rather than the true nature of

---

4. Bloom, Harold, "The Internalization of Quest-Romance" in Bloom, Harold (ed.) *Romanticism and Consciousness: Essays in Criticism* (New York: W.W. Norton & Co., 1970), p. 6. Henceforth referred to as *RC*.
5. Bornstein, George (ed.) *Romantic and Modern – Revaluations of Liberty Tradition* (1977), Introduction, p. x. Henceforth referred to as RM.
6. Abercrombie, Lascelles, *Romanticism* (London: High Hill Books, 1926, Reprint 1963), p. 95.
7. Lovejoy, Arthur O., "On the Discrimination of Romanticisms", *English Romantic Poets: Modern Essays in Criticism*, ed. M.H. Abrams (London, Oxford, New York: Oxford University Press, 1960), pp. 3-24. Henceforth referred to as *ERP*.

Romanticism. In other words, we may say that the various definitions served as objectives-correlative for expressing the emotions of critics.

The popular fallacy of identifying Romantic poetry with nature-poetry has been much commented on. The fact that the great Romantics were essentially humanists is often lost sight of. But Harold Bloom goes to the other extreme, when he calls Romantic poctry 'anti-naturc poctry'.[8] For substantiating his argument Bloom points out that even "Wordsworth managed to have a reciprocity or dialogue with nature only in flashes." But surely, Wordsworth's attempt at subordinating the interests of nature to the concerns of man does not amount to an anti-nature stance. Geoffrey H. Hartman reveals a commendable grasp of the process, when he observes that "Wordsworth subdued poetry to the theme of nature's role in the growth of the individual mind." "The dream of nature in Wordsworth", he adds, "does not lead to formal romance, but is an early developmental step in converting the solipsistic into the sympathetic imagination; it entices the brooding soul out of itself, toward nature first, then toward humanity."[9] Hartman, thus, traces the progress from 'naturalization' to 'humanization' – from the self-conscious to the anti-self-conscious level of the mind – that marks out the great Romantics from lesser men.

The modernists' aversion to Romanticism may be attributed, partly at least, to their misunderstanding of the kind of interest the great Romantics brought to bear on man and nature. Eliot, for example, says:

> "...there may be a good deal to be said for Romanticism in life, there is no place for it in letters...."[10]

The "impulse to the spirited phrase" evidenced here seems rather surprising in Eliot. Perhaps it also yields hints of an apathy for life and suggests an unwitting attempt at driving a wedge between life and literature. Obviously, this is one of Eliot's early statements that disturbed him later. T.E. Hulme's objection "even to the best of the Romantics" sounds equally unconvincing.

---

8. *RC.*, p. 9.
9. Hartman, Geoffrey, H., 'Romanticism and Anti-self-consciousness' from *Beyond Formalism*, reprinted in *RC.*, p. 55.
10. Eliot, T.S., *The Sacred Wood* (London: Methuen & Co. Ltd., 1920, University paperback, 1966), p. 32. Henceforth referred to as *SW*.

The humanitarian concerns of Wordsworth and the relevance of the Romantic poetry for the modern man have been impressively brought out by Jane P. Tompkins, when she says of Wordsworth:

> He believes that the need for poetry's refining influence has been created by the "increasing accumulation of men in cities", which has "blunted the discriminating powers of the mind...the uniformity of occupation", moreover, "produces a craving for extraordinary incident, which the rapid communication of intelligence hourly gratifies." Wordsworth affirms that his poetry will counteract this trend by enlightening the understanding, strengthening and purifying the affections, and enlarging the mind's capacity to become excited "without the application of gross and violent stimulants.[11]

She also points out how, after the French Revolution, the sensibility, cultivated for its own sake earlier, turns into an effort to show that "poetry's power over the feelings can bind men together by appealing to their deepest human sympathies."

The enormous strides in discursive learning witnessed in the present century do not appear to have undermined the validity of Romantic perceptions by any means. Nor have they blotted out the Romantic instincts of the modern man. What we have been witnessing is only "an accelerating increase in the pigeonholed knowledge by individuals, of more and more about less and less."[12] The need for the more inclusive knowledge yielded by the poetic imagination is only accentuated in the context. The modern psycho-analysts' attempts to delve deep into the infra-rational faculties of the human mind have done signal service to Romanticism.[13] They have provided the Romantic poet with a credible base for his claims on the mode of functioning of the sub-conscious mind. Of course, it is true that there has been, as yet, no successful attempt at distinguishing between the infra-rational and the supra-rational. The Coleridgean view of the coalescence of subject and object, which happens because of a sense of shared awareness, is misread by the positivist critics like I.A. Richards. And, as for Coleridge's insistance that the secondary imagination "dissolves, diffuses, dissipates, in order to

---

11. Tompkins, Jane P. (ed.), *Reader-Response Criticism: From Formalism to Post-Structuralism* (Baltimore and London: The Johns Hopkins University Press, 1980), p. 216. Henceforth referred to as *RRC*.
12. Barfield, Owen, *Saving the Appearances: A Study in Idolatry* – A Harbinger Book (New York: Harcourt, Brace & World, Inc.), p. 145.
13. See *RC*., p. 5. Prof. Bloom seems to hold the contrary view.

recreate",[14] many suspect the authenticity of the process. The Freudian depth-psychology has now assured us of a different level of inner activity that falsifies the pretences of man. Truth has, thus, been conceived of as psychological rather than objective.[15]

The Romantic creed had no doubt been narrowed and simplified in the early years of the twentieth century to a ridiculous extent. Poetry had become a vehicle for simple-minded emotions and lost all intellectual bearings. A.E. Housman's confession on the process of poetic composition and the way poetry physically affects the reader takes us to one extreme.[16] Thomas Hardy's use of poems for giving vent to his overwhelming emotions without having resort to distancing devices exposed him to the charge of sentimentality. Yet, the credit for giving eloquent expression to the agony of the disinherited mind for the first time in English poetry should perhaps be his. Hardy's contribution towards shifting the centre of interest from the external world to the poet's own consciousness has been nearly Wordsworthian.[17] The theological questionings of Hardy perhaps befogged the significance of his contribution for quite some time. The lovely phantasies of de la Mare's early verse seem to have forced even his admirers to miss the profound symbolism of his later work. The Georgian week-end poets did not fight shy of their escapist leanings and easy emotions. Their bid to breathe a new life into English poetry was pitifully feeble. An understandable partiality for 'Englishness' seems to have resulted in the exclusion of Edward Thomas, a gifted poet of the Wordsworthian school, from the Georgian fold. Edward Thomas was, in fact, "distinctively modern"[18] both in sensibility and mode of expression. Yet, he suffered a long neglect.

---

14. Shawcross, J. (ed.) *Biographia Literaria* (London: Oxford University Press, 1907, reprint, 1939), Vol. I, p. 202. Henceforth referred to as Shawcross.
15. Spears, Monroe K., *Dionysus and the City: Modernism in Twentieth Century-Poetry* (New York: O.U.P., 1970), p. 55. Henceforth referred to as *DC*.
16. Housman, A.E., "The Name and Nature of Poetry", *A.E. Housman — Poetry and Prose: A Selection* ed. F.C. Horwood (London: Hutchinson Educational, 1971—reprint, 1972), pp. 243-248.
17. Pinto, Vivian de Sola, *Crisis in English Poetry 1880-1940* (London: Hutchinson University Library, 1951, reprint 1967), p. 51. Henceforth referred to as Pinto.
18. Leavis, F.R., *New Bearings in English Poetry: A Study of Contemporary Situation* (London: Chatto & Windus, 1932, reprint 1959), p. 69. Henceforth referred to as *New Bearings*.

The literary scene witnessed by the self-styled anti-Romantics in the early part of the century was indeed depressing. And the *Coup d'etat* they effected was apparently called for. T.E. Hulme's bid to classicize poetry had a salutary impact on prevailing modes. Of course, in that process, he reduced man to a pitiful thing by reckoning him as "an extraordinarily fixed, limited animal". His suspicion about the infinite was perhaps justified. But we are only amused when we find him count out Keats from the Romantics:

> Verse strictly confined to the earthly and the definite (Keats is full of it) might seem to them to be excellent writing, excellent craftsmanship, but not poetry....[19]

Hulme, however, draws a useful distinction between the two types of languages when he says:

> The direct language is poetry, it is direct because it deals in images. The indirect language is prose, it uses images that have died and become figures of speech.[20]

The distinction plays a vital role in the resuscitation of the Romantic tradition in the twentieth century. Hulme was evidently the spirit behind the Imagist revolt spear-headed by Ezra Pound. But Pound, surely, was not allergic either to personal emotion or to the infinite as much as Hulme. His definition of Image as an "intellectual and emotional complex in an instant of time" and his prescription for the "direct treatment of the 'thing', whether subjective or objective,"[21] suggest that he had an open mind in the matter. His silence on the intrusion of the infinite seems significant in the context of Hulme's obsession with it. But a rigorous adoption of the Imagist ideals turns out to be far from desirable. A typical Imagist poem like Pound's 'Metro', for all its concentration, brevity and vitality, does not transform the object. Such poems perhaps epitomize the extreme feelings of their authors against the presence of the discursive element in poetry. Imagism was virtually French Symbolism shorn of its magical and mystical pretensions. But the Imagists appeared

---

19. Hulme, T.E., "Romanticism and Classicism", David Lodge (ed.), *Twentieth Century Criticism* (Longman, 1972), p. 99. Henceforth referred to as *TCC*.
20. Quoted in Read, Herbert, *The True Voice of Feeling* (London: Faber and Faber, 1947, Papercovered edition, 1968), p. 107. Henceforth referred to as *TVF*.
21. Eliot, T.S., (ed.) *Literary Essays of Ezra Pound* (London: Faber and Faber Ltd., 1954), p. 3.

unaware of their debt to the great Romantics from whom the Symbolists had drawn their technique and carried to an extreme. When T.S. Eliot allowed himself to be schooled by the French Symbolists in his early phase, he, too, revealed little awareness of their debt to the Romantic tradition.

Symbols have always had a vital role in Romantic poetry. Coleridge, for instance, says:

> In looking at objects of nature, I seem rather to be seeking, as it were asking for something within me that already exists than observing anything new.[22]

As remarked by Bateson, symbols served the great Romantics as "objectives-correlative to their subjective experiences"[23] and testified to a conscious cerebral control in their poetry. With the lesser Romantics it was indeed a different matter. The "rationalization of Romanticism"[24] became a crying need because of them. Hulme's insistence on classical virtues in poetry (while, ironically enough, warming to Bergson's Coleridgean view of the artist's function)[24a] signalled a movement in that direction. Eliot's aggressive attempt to depersonalize poetry had also a salutary impact on the Romantic tradition. But the 'escape' from personality and emotions that he advocated had allowed scope for a good deal of misunderstanding. But a closer look at his theory of objective correlative might well have helped to clear the air, as it was meant to objectify the emotions of the poet while sharing them with his readers. Eliot's rapport with the Romantic idea of poetry as an emotive language was thus suggested. While his belief in the poet's ability to control the responses of his readers hinted at here might have amused quite a few, the therapeutic value of the objective correlative as a self-disciplining device could hardly be questioned. What he had opposed

22. Quoted in Frye, Northrop, "The Drunken Boat: The Revolutionary Element in Romanticism", in Frye, Northrop (ed.), *Romanticism Reconsidered: Selected Papers from the English Institute* (New York and London: Columbia University Press, 1963), p. 11. Henceforth referred to as *RR*.

23. Bateson, F.W., *English Poetry: A Critical Introduction* (London: Longmans, Green, 1950), p. 87.

24. *Ibid*., p. 89.

24a. See Krieger, Murray, *The New Apologists for Poetry* (Connecticut: Greenwood Press, Publishers, 1956, reprint by the University of Mennesota Press, 1977), pp. 32-35.

was the indulgence of emotions, as observed by Eliseo Vivas.[25] His theory of dissociation of sensibility has been critically examined by many in recent times. Frank Kermode, for one, shows how there is little historical propriety in treating the dissociation as a seventeenth century phenomenon.[26] While tracing an imagistic link between the Romantics and the moderns, he also observes how Donne actually lacked the qualities which Eliot valued most. He says:

> Miss Tuve's now famous demonstration that Donne's images have a logical, or at any rate a pseudological function was a direct affront to the basis of the theory that he was a poet of the modern Image. Eliot himself veered round to such a view when he prophesied the demise of Donne....[27]

Kermode also points out how Donne's poems reveal the note of passion, the true voice of feeling, characteristic of the great Romantics.[28] It was the same note that had made the Romantic a *persona-non-grata* to Eliot. Kermode's findings seem formidable, though his comments suggest a bias in Milton's favour. Eliot's dissociationist argument, substantial as it is, has obviously been not so sound in its implications.

All the same, it may be unfair to suspect the sincerity of Eliot's anti-Romantic protestations in his early phase, though the means he adopted to cure himself of his Romantic affiliation were odd indeed. What he sought to achieve was a proper distancing between the poet and his audience on the one hand and the man that suffers and the poet that creates on the other. The popular opinion that holds him guilty of hunting with the hound and running with hares at the same time has not perhaps been wholly discriminating. The significant distinction he has drawn between 'verse' and 'poetry' in his essay on Rudyard Kipling may perhaps go a long way towards clearing the confusion.[29] And the views he has expressed in his later essay on "The Three Voices of Poetry" may clinch the issue once

---

25. Vivas Eliseo, *Creation and Discovery: Essays in Criticism Aesthetics* (New York: The Noonday Press, 1955), p. 175.
26. Kermode, Frank, *Romantic Image* (London: Routledge and Kegan Paul, 1957), p. 142. Henceforth referred to as *RI*.
27. *Ibid*., p. 147.
28. *Ibid*., p. 148.
29. Eliot, T.S., *OPP*., pp. 228-251.

for all in favour of Romanticism.[30] They will be discussed in the chapter on T.S. Eliot.

The rhetorical discontinuity brought about by the symbolist obsession of the moderns made the modernist idiom, "dry, oblique, learned and extremely compressed".[31] And a proper corrective for the malaise turned out to be beyond the reach of the modernists at the moment, thanks to the crying need they felt to keep themselves abreast of the times. Yeats' achievement in steering clear of the modernist excesses, while making use of the Symbolist methods was singular. Broadly speaking, the emphasis in the first half of the twentieth century was on the process of tightening the poetic modes and on delving into the darker recesses of human consciousness. Such tendencies are reversed only in the post-modernist phase that started in the mid 1950s.

This process of 'tightening' has often been taken for an anti-Romantic revolt. The way in which some original minds have deluded themselves into such a notion, perhaps, makes 'irony' and 'paradox' the ruling phrases of the century. The extent to which the great Romantics have been unacknowledged legislators for most of the prominent critics and poets of the modern literary arena should prompt us to attempt a reappraisal of Romanticism in its relation to the modernist poetry.

II

The devaluation of Romanticism outlined earlier resulted largely from the absence of a proper understanding and assessment of its concepts. First of all, as hinted at already, the humanistic implications of Romanticism got entirely obscured, while its negative aspects were highlighted by both its friends and enemies. F.L. Lucas, for example, in his full-length study of Romanticism, had hardly anything to say about its positive aspects. Yet he seems to have done a real service to the Romantic tradition, when he pinpointed how the Freudian viewpoint "links together various characteristics of Romanticism, some healthy and some morbid, that hitherto seemed

30. *Ibid.*, pp. 89-102.
31. Perkins, David, *A History of Modern Poetry: From the 1890s to the High Modernist Mode* (Cambridge, Massachusetts and London, 1976), p. 7. Henceforth referred to as *HMP*.

arbitrary and disconnected".[32] Edmund Wilson also stresses the negative aspects of Romanticism, when he brands both Eliot and Yeats as escapists.[33] George Bornstein has rightly observed that the Blakean view of Romanticism, favoured by Northrop Frye, serves as a corrective to the notions of critics like Edmund Wilson.[34] Wilson's partiality for science and ordinary life, which were slighted by the Symbolists, need not have prompted him to take a dim view of the achievements of Eliot and Yeats. For the Symbolist technique adopted by them has not, after all, rendered them blind to the realities of life. The inclination of many modernist critics and poets to treat Romanticism as a disease perhaps suggests a fear that it might open the flood-gates of emotions submerging all intellectual barriers.

The anti-Romantic tide that swept the modern arena had apparently gained its vital force from the unfair insinuations of Matthew Arnold. He maintained, among other things, that the "Romantics did not know enough".[35] Perhaps, we have reason to be happy about their comparative ignorance, as excessive learning might well have "deadened or perverted"[36] their poetic sensibility (as it perhaps happened in Arnold's own case). Arnold himself was certainly aware that true poetry was made in the soul, and not in the wit, and an over-abundance of information could hardly help in the process.[37]

Romanticism had, in fact, come as a breath of fresh air. Historically speaking, it had brought about an internalization – "the shifting of the centre of gravity of consciousness from the cosmos

---

32. Lucas, F.L., *The Decline and Fall of the Romantic Ideal* (Cambridge University Press, 1936, reprint 1963), pp. 233-34.

33. Wilson, Edmund, *Axel's Castle: A Study in the Imaginative Literature of 1870-1930* (New York, London: Charles Scribner's Sons, 1935).

34. Bornstein, George, *Transformations of Romanticisms in Yeats, Eliot and Stevens* (Chicago and London: The University of Chicago Press, 1976), p. 20. Henceforth referred to as *TR*.

35. Arnold, Matthew, "The Function of Criticism in the Present Time" in *Matthew Arnold's Essays in Criticism* (First and Second Series, Dent, London, Every Man's Library, 1906, Dutton: New York, reprint 1966), p. 13. Henceforth referred to as *EC*.

36. *SW*., p. 52.

37. Arnold, Matthew, "The Study of Poetry", *EC*., pp. 235-260.

around him into the personal human being himself".[38] It had helped man to cleanse the doors of perception and see into the life of things. As Blake puts it –

> " To see a world in a grain of sand
> And heaven in a wild flower,
> Hold infinity in the palm of your hand
> And eternity in an hour."
>
> (William Blake, "Auguries of Innocence")

And what the great Romantics conceived of and achieved was far from escape or intoxicated dreaming. Theirs was indeed a culture of feelings, but not feelings divorced from thoughts, as the modernist critics apparently believed. Imagination had helped the great Romantics to achieve a fusion of thoughts and feelings and to effect "a coalescence of the subject and the object", as Coleridge calls it. R.A. Foakes puts the Coleridgean theory in perspective:

> Coleridge's theory of the imagination as the supreme unifying and the creative power in the poet, was one aspect of a transcendentalism much less emphasized by modern writers who base their critical outlook on his; the imagination for Coleridge was that faculty which idealizes and unifies, the faculty by which he may perceive the unity of the universe, and apprehend God. It is not through Reason and self-knowledge that we approach the divine, but through the highest form and principle of all our possible self-knowledge. It is through the individual consciousness represented at its highest in the creative act of the imagination which repeats the external act of creation of God, that we perceive God.[39]

The fusion of thoughts and feelings occasioned in the process is evidently an achievement of the imagination. And it amounts to the transcendental faculty taking charge of poetry. Denis Donoghue aptly describes imagination as "that mental power which finds unnecessary the strict separation of conscious and unconscious life, of primary and secondary processes, in Freud's terminology; which deals with contradictions not by subordinating one to another but by accommodating all within a larger perspective; and which entertains feelings and motives before they have been assigned to categories or organized into thoughts, attitudes, statements, values or commit-

---

38. Barfield, Owen, *History of English Words* (London: Faber and Faber, 1953, Reprint 1969), p. 165.

39. Foakes, R.A., *The Romantic Assertion: A Study in the Language of Nineteenth Century Poetry* (London: Methuen & Co. Ltd., 1958), p. 42. Henceforth referred to as Foakes.

ments".[40] It is implied that the poem resulting from such a deeper awareness is the product of the total personality. And we may safely assume that the poetry of the first voice or impersonal voice referred to by Eliot,[41] at its best, results from a similar process. The Inner Voice mentioned elsewhere by Eliot[42] has to be distinguished from this impersonal voice. As maintained by C.K. Stead, the former is the voice of conscious individualistic thought,[43] and is taken care of by the self-conscious level of the mind. And, though it may pass for the personal voice in the Eliotian terminology, its affinity to the 'character' of the poet is obvious.

The highest form of self-consciousness has to be identified with the transcendental faculty and associated with the imaginative process that achieves the unifying vision expressed in a poem. This process has at times been misconstrued by the positivists. To I.A. Richards, for example, imagination is "a word like any other and is put to work without special privileges". The Coleridgean conception of unity is thus construed as a 'composure'.[44] As observed by Gerald Graff, "whereas Coleridge invoked the transcendentalist spiritualism in order to assert that the imagination yields truth, Richards invokes a materialism in order to assert that imagination can never be false".[45] If Richards has taken the Romantic harm out of the word 'imagination' as observed by Denis Donoghue,[46] he seems to have thrown out the baby, as it were, with the bathwater.

Obviously, this highest form of self-consciousness is distinct from human awareness in its popular sense. We may call that inspired consciousness or the common consciousness working in submission to the higher, so that it takes on voluntarily the spontaneity of the latter. The unity achieved in the process marks the moment

---

40. Donoghue, Denis, *The Sovereign Ghost: Studies in Imagination* (U.S.A., 1976, London: Faber & Faber Ltd., 1978), pp. 25-26. Henceforth referred to as *SG.*
41. *OPP*., p. 100.
42. Eliot, T.S., *Selected Essays* (London: Faber & Faber Ltd., 1932, reprint 1958), pp. 27-29. Henceforth referred to as *SE.*
43. Stead, C.K., *The New Poetic: Yeats to Eliot* (1964, Penguin Books by arrangement with Hutchinson of London, 1967), p. 143. Henceforth referred to as *NP.*
44. *SG*., p. 1.
45. Graff, Gerald, *Poetic Statement and Critical Dogma* (Chicago and London : The University of Chicago Press, 1970, Paperback, 1980), pp. 58-59.
46. *SG*., p. 3.

of knowing which is also the moment of poetic creation. "The knower, then, ceases to exist as subject at all", as remarked by Owen Barfield. And, conversely, when he comes fully to himself as subject, he ceases to know. Barfield adds that "imaginations are generated in the poet's consciousness as he passes from the former state to the latter, and the difficulty is to retain them in the memory".[47] The anti-self-consciousness referred to by Geoffrey H. Hartman may be identified with that state of 'knowing'.[48] In the Blakean terminology what it yields is an 'organized innocence' that is akin to man's original state of innocence and harmony. It is craved for by the Romantic poet as a possible means of getting over dialectical tensions. It is indeed a momentary achievement. The vital force that helps in the process was earlier associated with inspiration and attributed to the whims of the Muse. The poet "himself hardly knew what it was – a kind of wind perhaps, which blew where it listed and might fill his sails at some odd moment after he had whistled for it all day in vain." But "today, we are more inclined to think of inspiration as a mood – a mood that may come and go in the course of a morning's work."[49] We may also liken it to a cerebral stroke, as indicated by Abrams.[50] The new perspective, surely, does not alter the substance of the resultant poetic achievement. And the effort, when it is of a high order, does not reveal any escapist tendency, as the insight afforded thus enables the poet to see not only with but through the natural world to what may lie beyond it. And, as Allen Tate insists, "an insight of that order never begins at the top; it carries the bottom along with it, however high it may climb."[51] In other words, it involves the apprehension of the essential unity without neglecting exteriorities. Gerard Manley Hopkins calls it "the dearest freshness deep down things" ("God's Grandeur").

Such a view, however, brings in its train several new complications.

---

47. Barfield, Owen, *Poetic Diction: A Study in Meaning* (London: Faber & Faber, 1928, reprint 1957), p. 209. Henceforth referred to as *PD*.

48. Hartman, Geoffrey, H., *RC*., pp. 45-46.

49. *PD*., p. 109.

50. Abrams, M.H., *Natural Supernaturalism: Tradition and Revolution in Romantic Literature* (London: Oxford University Press, 1971), p. 414.

51. Tate, Allen, "The Symbolic Imagination" in *The Man of Letters in the Modern World: Selected Essays: 1928-1955*. London: Meridian Books, Thames and Hudson, 1957), p. 112.

At the self-conscious level the mind is apt to be over-conscious of its 'esemplastic power' and may, thus, promote 'egotistical' tendencies on the part of poets. What Keats named 'the egotistical sublime' instances such a tendency, albeit in a sublime form. His own negative capability perhaps provided an effective means of controlling such a trend. But in its unrestrained, decadent forms it has brought much odium on the Romantic tradition. Yeats' father goes, understandably enough, to the extent of equating personal utterance with egotism and warns his son against falling a prey to it.[52] He favoured dramatic expression as it helped in the objectivization of personal feelings. But after his early experiments with the dramatic mode Yeats finds that only personal utterance is after his heart. He believes that it could be as fine an escape from rhetoric and abstraction as drama itself. For holding his emotions in leash he has resort to other methods too. They will be dealt with in the chapters on Yeats.

Subjectivity in its extreme form at times assumes the dimensions of a malady, though Geoffrey H. Hartman, for one (as noted by Harold Bloom), regards it as an inevitable stage in the progress of the mind towards a more humanized imagination.[53] The curbing of it is apparently the concern of the self-conscious level of the human mind. It seems to be one of "the craftsman's problems", in the words of T.S. Eliot.[54] The inherent tendency that promotes such a concern also seems to affect only the self-conscious level. Viewed thus, the 'negative capability' exemplified by Shakespeare and Keats would also seem to be a matter concerning the same level of the mind, although it is contrasted with the solipsistic tendency revealed by poets like Milton and Wordsworth. The distinction drawn by Coleridge between the two ways in which the poetic imagination worked in Shakespeare and Milton should go a long way towards identifying the two types:

> While the former darts himself forth, and passes into all the forms of human character and passion, the one Proteus of the fire and the blood; the other attracts all forms and things to himself, into the unity of his own IDEAL. All things and modes of action shape themselves anew in

---

52. Yeats, W.B., *Autobiographies* (London: Macmillan & Co. Ltd., 1955), p. 102.
53. *RC.*, p. 2.
54. *OPP.*, p. 238.

> the being of Milton; while Shakespeare becomes all things, yet for ever remaining himself...[55]

Ironical as it may seem, the unconscious activity of the mind occasioned by an imaginative perception is influenced by the self-conscious level. In other words, it is the outer consciousness that determines the direction and mode of the unconscious activity, though it has apparently nothing to do with the quality of the vision subsequently achieved. While the solipsistic mode of imagination, promoted either by humanistic concerns or by an unchecked self-consciousness, enables the poet to see himself in every object that he perceives, the sympathetic mode, backed up, as it is, by an inborn feeling for the objects of perception, prompts him to negate his own personality and identify himself with them. In either mode, the imagination's essential function seems to be identical. The reconciliation of the subject and the object – the percipient and the perceived – mind and nature – in the act of cognition occurs irrespective of whether the subject goes out to mingle with the object as it happens in the case of the sympathetic imagination, or the object merges itself with the subject losing its own identity, as it occurs in the solipsistic mode. Such a union of polarities affords a sense of joy and occasions a perception of unity in diversity, of harmony in conflict, of life in the lifeless, and of "something" as Wordsworth puts it:

> ... loftier, more adorned,
> Than is the common aspect, daily garb
> Of human life...
>
> (*Prelude*, Book V, 11, 575-7)

A capacity to achieve such perceptions, either negative or affirmative, may go a long way towards making life worth living. Let us hear Coleridge speak of the Wordsworthian achievement:

> The union of deep feeling with profound thought; the fine balance of truth in observing; with the imaginative faculty in modifying, the objects observed; and, above all the original gift of spreading the tone, the atmosphere, and with it the depth and height of the ideal world around forms, incidents and situations of which, for the common view, custom had bedimmed all the lustre and dried up the sparkle and the dew drops.[56]

---

55. Shawcross, Vol. II, p. 20.
56. *Ibid.*, Quoted in Hough, Graham, *The Romantic Poets* (Hutchinson of London, 1953, reprint 1976), p. 82.

But T.E. Hulme, for one, has ridiculed the Romantic tendency to think in terms of a heaven on earth and to be obsessed with the Infinite. The classical poet, he says, remembers always that he is mixed up with earth. "He may jump, but he always returns back; he never flies away into the circumambient gas."[57] We can certainly appreciate the sincerity of Hulme's feelings in the context. But his reluctance to acknowledge that the great Romantics had their feet firm on the solid earth, while their mental resources helped them to achieve transcendental perceptions, may not stand to reason. Wordsworth, for example, was keen on looking "steadily at his subject". As pointed out by Frederick A. Pottle, his assertion in this regard in the Preface to the Lyrical Ballads, paradoxical though, means "grasping objects firmly and accurately in the mode of common perceptions, and then looking at them imaginatively."[58] While tracing the progress of his inner life ever since his childhood in "Tintern Abbey", he has impressed on us that the insight he gained into the life of things is not the result of a light-hearted fancy. We are convinced that he has cared enough for the physical features of the objects of nature. The insights he gained into essential aspects were surely not at the expense of external features. His endeavour was only to see farther and deeper. H.W. Garrod has observed how the Wordsworthian mysticism was rooted in "sensationalism".[59] Coleridge has made a refreshing confession in his "Dejection – An Ode" of a fear that he is losing grip over the faculty of imagination that enabled him to 'feel' things while seeing them:

> I see them all so excellently fair,
> I see, not feel, how beautiful they are.

The confession implies that the capacity to see things in their outward aspects was very much with him earlier. In fact, he reckons it as a mark of genius:

> Like the moisture or the polish on a pebble, genius neither distorts nor false-colours its objects; but on the contrary brings out many a vein and many a tint, which escapes the eye of the common observation, thus

---

57. *TCC.*, p. 96.

58. Pottle, Frederick, A., 'The Eye and the Object in the Poetry of Wordsworth', *The Yale Review*, Vol. XI, Autumn, 1950, Yale University Press, reprinted in *RC.*, p. 283.

59. Garrod, H.W., *Wordsworth: Lectures and Essays* (London: Oxford University Press, 1923, reprint 1958), p. 105. Henceforth referred to as Garrod.

> raising to the rank of gems what had been often kicked away by the hurrying foot of the traveller on the dusty high road of custom.[60]

And obviously, there is no "inherent and inescapable conflict"[61] between the scientific and the poetic modes of apprehending realities. They are complementary and supplementary. Of course, we are apt to be carried away by Wordsworth's contempt for the "meddling intellect" which "murders to dissect", and for the "philosopher", who would "botanize on his mother's grave". As indicated by Abrams, these lines have to be read only as his "judgements against the fallacy of misplaced abstraction", and against the scientist whose "laboratory habits are so indurate that he continues to analyze where only imagination and feelings are relevant".[62] Harold Bloom has told us how the dualism in Wordsworth made Blake think ill of him.[63] Of the earlier Romantics Blake alone perhaps reveals a relative obsession with the spiritual aspects of things. Hulme's comments on the Romantics might sound tenable to a certain extent if Blake alone were meant. Of course, it may be unfair to ignore Blake's "sense of human responsibility".[64] And Shelley's visionary inclinations at times seem to obscure his revolutionary zeal and expose him to the onslaughts of critics. The note of caution sounded by some prominent critics like M.H. Abrams[65] and George Bornstein[66] against overemphasizing the transcendentalizing function of the Romantic imagination is apt to be misunderstood. We are not to lose sight of the fact that the transcendentalizing function is not an end in itself but a part of the humanizing process.

A self-conscious pursuit of a Unity of Being in the artistic productions of the present century has been typical not only of W.B.

---

60. Mackail, J.W. (ed.), *Coleridge's Literary Criticism* (1908, London: Oxford University Press, Geoffrey Cumberlege, reprint 1949), p. 122.
61. Abrams, M.H., *The Mirror and the Lamp: Romantic Theory and the Critical Tradition* (London, Oxford, New York: Oxford University Press, 1953, Oxford University Paperback, 1971), p. 308. Henceforth referred to as *ML*.
62. *ML*., p. 309.
63. *RC*., p. 8.
64. Leavis, F.R., *English Literature in Our Time and the University* (London: Chatto & Windus Paperback, 1969), p. 107.
65. *ML*., pp. 313-14.
66. *TR*., p. 8.

Yeats, Ezra Pound and T.S. Eliot, but of others like Edward Thomas and Walter de la Mare. The achievement of such a unity is perhaps the primary function of the poetic imagination as envisaged by Coleridge and Wordsworth. The fusion of thought and feeling and the elimination of the distinction between the animate and the inanimate, the personal and the impersonal, the subjective and the objective as also the coalesence of the percipient and the perceived are aspects of that unity. The theory of the 'undissociated sensibility' brought into vogue by T.S. Eliot may look rather humble in the presence of this all-inclusive theory of imagination propounded by the great Romantics. The unification referred to by Eliot in his early criticism seems to occur at the self-conscious level, which attends to the process of versification, leaving the more significant task of poetry-making to an inner, deeper, impersonal, transcendental faculty identified by him with the poet's soul. And in the Coleridgean phraseology we may call it a matter of 'fancy' that has nothing to do with the process of imagination. Eliot himself should naturally have realized the inadequacy of his theory in the light of his later convictions. Possibly, he fought shy of redefining it. We remember how, in his early essay on Marvell, he found it difficult to define the complex term 'wit'.

The Coleridgean formulation on the fusion of thought and feeling does not make the role of the conscious level of the mind in the process explicit. But his insistence on the achievement of the highest form of self-consciousness need not be construed as a denial of the role of its lesser forms. The modernists take upon themselves the task of stressing that role, without detriment to their essential affiliation to the Coleridgean thesis. Viewed thus, the difference between the two approaches would seem to be a matter of emphasis.

Borrowing a phrase from Wallace Stevens we may observe that Romanticism represents a significant effort at "present-perfecting" through gaining insights into the life of things with the help of the transcendental faculty of imagination. A cold and calculating rationalism is "a wasteland of dead mechanism and compulsive repetition, Blake's dark Satanic mills".[67] "Familiar nature is no

67. Boly, John R., "Auden and the Romantic Tradition in The Age of Anxiety", *Daedalus: Journal of the American Academy of Arts and Sciences*, Summer, 1982. p. 150.

more than a blooming, buzzing confusion until we began thinking as well as perceiving", as the narrator in Owen Barfield's *World Apart* maintains.[68] The effort is perhaps more relevant in the modern context, in view of the new stresses and strains, conflicts and contradictions that render the present far from perfect. The modern trend towards an "anarchic surrender to experience" should naturally be of vital concern to the modern Romantic. The primary concern of the Romantic artist should be to impose an order on his experience and thus make life bearable for himself and others. Coleridge's "Dejection – An Ode" gives eloquent expression to that abiding concern of the Romantic poet:

> ... would we aught behold of higher worth,
> Than that inanimate cold world allowed
> To the poor, loveless, ever-anxious crowd,
> Ah! from the soul itself must issue forth
> A light, a glory, a fair luminous cloud
> Enveloping the earth –
> And from the soul itself must there be sent
> A sweet and potent voice, of its own birth
> Of all sweet sounds the life and element.

III

The modern environment has indeed been far from congenial for the Romantic tradition to flourish. For one thing, the Romantic poet always revealed a distinctive tendency to withdraw into himself and live in a kind of self-imposed isolation. And his interest in the objects around him often seemed to be in proportion to their utility as symbols for projecting his inner awareness. Moderns could seldom brook such a stand-offish attitude. They frowned on the idea of treating the poet as a man apart and aloof. They hated the notion of a break between art and life. But, when we look back at the great Romantics with unprejudiced minds, we are bound to be convinced that there is hardly any novelty about such a stance. The attempt to unite life and art has rightly been called "the crucial point of similarity between Romanticism and the avant-garde."[69]

Monroe K. Spears has pointed out how, in the early twentieth

---

68. Barfield, Owen, *Worlds Apart* (London: Faber and Faber, Ltd., 1963), p. 87.

69. Paz, Octavio, *Children of the Mire: Modern Poetry from Romanticism to the Avant-Garde* (1974), The Charles Eliot Norton Lectures 1971-72, Translated by Rachel Phillips (Cambridge, Massachusetts and London, England: Harward University Press), p. 103.

century, I.A. Richards ridiculed the "phantom aesthetic state" and insisted that "poetry is continuous with other forms of experience, and hence open to inspection." T.S. Eliot too, as indicated by Spears, insisted that "the poet was not a mysterious outcast but a man like others."[70] It is amusing to note that the New Critics who propagated the notion of art as the creation of a heterocosm, a world parallel to, but distinct from, the real one, had drawn their inspiration from Richards and Eliot. For the notion implied an aesthetic discontinuity and a kinship with those against whom the leading lights of our century had declared a virtual war.

The Romantic tradition has revealed remarkable flexibility and vitality in adapting itself to the new situation. The major Romantic poets of the century have not shunned the atrocious facts of modern life. And poetic diction has got approximated to the language of the common man. Obviously, the new effort in this regard has virtually been a repetition of the Wordsworthian endeavour of the earlier century. But, thanks to the all-pervasive zest for democratic values that has prevailed in the new context, the need for such a change now has perhaps been all the more imperative. Of course, some major writers of the century like Pound, Eliot and Yeats did not share the moderns' concern either for the common man or for democracy. Their inability to share the ethos of the man-in-the street is apt to be taken for an anti-humanist stance. Indeed their views in the matter were largely at variance with those of the great Romantics. Yet perhaps it hardly matters for the Romantic tradition, as it concerns only the self-conscious level of their minds. Romanticism, as we understand it, depends primarily on an inner level that helps a deeper perception of the world around us. And poetry, as Jane P. Tompkins puts it, "must operate at the most profound level of human experience, rather than dissipate its force on any particular social issue, in order to achieve maximum effectiveness."[71] The conscious mental activity that determines the religious, social and political inclinations of the Romantics has been expertly analyzed by Northrop Frye, when he says:

> ...Whether the Romantic poet is revolutionary or conservative depends on whether he regards this original society as concealed by or as

70. *DC.*, p. 25.

71. *RRC.*, p. 216.

> manifested in existing society. If the former, he will think of true society as a primitive structure of nature and reason, and will admire the popular, simple or even the barbaric more than the sophisticated. If the latter, he will find his true inner society manifested by a sacramental church or by the instinctive manners of an aristocracy.[72]

The Romantic conception of a poem as a heterocosm, that makes a parallel world, seems to have given scope for a feeling that the modern Romantic has acquiesced in the idea of a divorce between life and art. Should it be the case, the tendency to take the Romantic for an escapist, would certainly be pardonable. But a Romantic poet living in our midst can hardly afford to turn a blind eye to the realities of life. He could indeed "cast a cold eye" on them. The parallel world of his making reveals only an imaginative re-ordering of his chaotic experiences in the real world. The transcendental faculty which effects that re-ordering obviously needs the assistance of the self-conscious level of the mind to make its effort relevant from the human angle. And, if the conscious mind bungles it up like a clumsy servant, we would not be justified in blaming it on the Romantic imagination. Denis Donoghue, defines the distinction between the two:

> When imagination comes under question, it is often because of its association with the licence of self-consciousness, which can easily be given a bad name as curiosity or self-regard.[73]

Donoghue also mentions how Lionel Trilling associates mind with the idea of order, even the idea of hierarchy, "the subordination of some elements of thought to others."[74]

Apparently, when the outer layer of consciousness grows stiff and impervious, it is apt to suppress the inner voice, as it perhaps happened in the case of the later Wordsworth. Obversely, when the inner voice happens to be stern and imperious or when its sources are to be traced to the infra-rational, it may refuse to yield to the manoeuvrings of the conscious level of the mind, as it seems to have happened in the case of D.H. Lawrence. In Lionel Trilling's view, imagination proposes as its ideal the direct, unmediated access to experience in preference to the distance imposed by rational categories. Donoghue says :

---

72. *RR.*, p. 13.
73. *SG.*, p. 5.
74. *Ibid.*, p. 7.

> ...The mind complains of imagination that it is wayward, irresponsible, self-engrossed. Imagination complains of mind that it is totalitarian, it demands immediate obedience, imposes its categories upon experience, it is premature in its orders and conclusions.[75]

Though mind is, thus, regarded as "a civil servant, a bureaucrat, illiberal in administrative zeal", its sobering influence is needed to guard imagination against slipping into negative, unhealthy channels.

The air of artificiality that afflicts certain poems which seek to verbalize genuine visionary perceptions may suggest either the incompetence of the conscious mind or, as in some eminent cases like Yeats', its earnest bid to regulate such perceptions with a view to achieving either a Unity of Being or other less laudable ends.

The personae and masks adopted by modern Romantics as distancing devices often tend to make the sincerity of their poetic utterances suspect. The adoption of such devices is evidently a concern of the self-conscious level of the mind. We have to look deeper to judge the authenticity of poetic perceptions. As mentioned earlier, the negative capability is also a matter of conscious artistry. It has been rightly called "a way of fending off the logic of subject and object: instead of raging for certitude, one chooses to live with doubts, question marks, divisions".[76] In other words, it involves a conscious effort on the part of the poet to gain an awareness that leads to an identity with the object without the interference of the personal element. Yet such an effort apparently needs the backing of an innate tendency in the poet, as hinted at already. While T.S. Eliot's attempt at depersonalizing poetry was perhaps born of a sincere desire to attain an identical capacity, he seemed to have been handicapped a good deal in that endeavour by the absence of such an innate tendency in him. We may identify it with his lack of imaginative sympathy.

Byron may serve as a glaring instance of a poet who managed to cultivate a negative capability to an unusual degree, in spite of his solipsistic leanings. The talent revealed thus does not, however, make Byron essentially a Romantic. René Wellek rightly says :

> A man who considers nature dead and inimical to man, who considers

---

75. *Ibid.*, pp. 8-9.
76. *Ibid.*, p. 22.

> imagination merely as a combinatory associative power, and who does not use symbolic and mythic devices is not a Romanticist..."[77]

Yet one could hardly object to an attempt at branding Byron and his likes as negative Romantics, when they reveal the intensity of the Romantic process without the accompanying vision. Obviously, they fail to cross the threshold of self-consciousness to gain access to a deeper awareness. In the words of Stuart M. Sperry they are "being cut loose from the old certainties, the old orthodoxies, without the attainment of the new insights necessary for progressing on to an organic re-integration."[78] And such a condition causes isolation and despair because it offers no cosmic explanations. The modern world perhaps makes an ideal breeding ground for such negative trends which draw sustenance from nihilistic leanings. They speak of an inability to believe in the power of imagination and of the resultant failure to exploit it.

In a Romantic poet the authenticity of the imaginative perceptions seems to be of greater significance than the sincerity of his profession. Lionel Trilling has spoken of the modern "ideology of irrationalism" which celebrates "the attainment of an immediacy of experience and perception which is beyond the power of rational mind." He pinpoints an inconvenient fact when he adds:

> ... In our day, it has become possible to claim just such credence for the idea that madness is a beneficent condition to be understood as the paradigm of authentic existence and cognition.[79]

Though Trilling's remark seems to allude to a general depravation, it speaks of a move to exalt authenticity at the expense of conventional sincerity and rational control both in poetry and life. A scrupulous care for the consistency and sincerity of professions should in any case be the concern of the self-conscious level of the mind. We may call it a matter of character in more than one sense. And, though we may associate it with the personality of a man in common parlance, the poetic personality concerns a deeper level of the human mind. Eliot, as we have noted already, calls it impersonality.

In any case, a proper co-ordination between the two levels of

---

77. Wellek, R. René, "Romanticism Re-examined", from *Concepts of Criticism,* reprinted in *RR*., p. 110.
78. Sperry, Stuart, M., "Toward a Definition of Romantic Irony in English Literature", *RM*., p. 19.
79. Trilling, Lionel, quoted in *SG*., p. 7.

the human mind would seem essential for the making of good poetry. A tendency to listen to the inner, deeper, impersonal voice and record it with the help of the conscious mind may perhaps be deemed the essential aspect of Romanticism. A poet who ignores or suppresses that voice in the name of good health or balance because of the over-assertive nature of his conscious mind, may have to be called a versifier, as implied by Eliot.

The qualities of the verse composed by such a writer may hardly be distinguishable from the "needful qualities of a fit prose", as hinted at by Matthew Arnold. He says:

> ... The men of letters whose destiny it may be to bring their nation to the attainment of a fit prose, must of necessity, whether they work in prose, or in verse, give a predominating and almost exclusive attention to the qualities of regularity, uniformity, precision and balance. But an almost exclusive attention to these qualities involves some repression and silencing of poetry...[80]

The distinction drawn by Eliot between poetry and verse seems to have been influenced in a large measure by Arnold's views on the matter.[81] It also reveals affinities with the distinction drawn by Gerard Manley Hopkins between poetry of inspiration and Parnassian verse.[82]

Such a distinction between poetry and verse is likely to present problems. For instance, a poem, particularly a long one, is bound to have patches of verse in it, as the transcendental perception effected at the unconscious level is unlikely to be long and uninterrupted. In fact, the momentary nature of such perceptions has often made their verbalization a delicate and difficult task. The problem has perhaps been particularly acute in modern poetry, owing to the tendency of visionary perceptions to grow increasingly tenuous. The impact of extreme scepticism on the modern mind may answer for that development. The lack of solidity may not, however, detract from the validity or significance of such perceptions.

D.H. Harding has pointed out how the contemporary poets "are at one with the Romantics in not treating the language as

---

80. Arnold, Matthew, "The Study of Poetry", *EC.*, p. 252.
81. See Stead, C.K., "Eliot, Arnold and the English Poetic Tradition", *The Literary Criticism of T.S. Eliot*, ed. David Newton de Molina, University of London, The Athlone Press, 1977, pp. 184-206.
82. See *TVF.*, pp. 76-77.

simply amenable to their purposes", though they are averse to the role of the poet as seer. He adds that the Romantics in this respect recovered a characteristic quality of English poetry. His observations concerning the Romantics are enlightening. He says:

> "Their exact intention could not be formulated in advance; it reached definition only in what the language actually produced when worked in it, rather as a sculptor's exact intention cannot exist apart from the materials that define it..."[83]

Harding also says elsewhere that unlike Pope and his followers who used language as a tool for their purposes, the Romantics treated it rather as a material or medium and to some extent submitted their purposes to it. In other words, what they sought to verbalize was their original perception and not ideas that existed already. And the credibility of such perceptions depended largely on the success of the verbalization attended to by the conscious mind. The problem of the Romantic poet would thus seem to be two-fold. The task of verbalizing momentary perceptions without distorting or diluting them would seem to be no less formidable than the more significant task of achieving them. For it often amounts to an attempt at expressing the inexpressible. Wordsworth's poetry at its most characteristic is found to be a struggle with the intractability of language.[84] Dorothy Wordsworth has told us of how he tired himself with seeking an epithet for the cuckoo. His effort was, as remarked by John Livingston Lowes, "to express directly what cannot be expressed directly – the sound of cuckoo's wandering voice."[85] At last, he is said to have successfully translated the cuckoo's literal voice, into terms of inner experience as evidenced by the poem "To the Cuckoo". What tired Wordsworth in this instance would seem to be the twin tasks of translating an outer experience into an inner awareness and of giving it adequate expression.

The struggles of the modern Romantics in this regard have been recorded by poets like Eliot and Yeats. Though Eliot, in

83. Harding, D.W., 'The Character of Literature from Blake to Byron' on Ford, Boris (ed.), *A Guide to English Literature*, Vol. 5, From Blake to Byron (1957, London: Cassell. The Belle Seuvage Library edition, 1962), p. 63. Henceforth referred to as Harding.

84. Beer, J.B., *Coleridge the Visionary* (Chatto & Windus, 1970), p. 22. Henceforth referred to as Beer.

85. See Lowes, John Livingston, *Convention and Revolt in Poetry* (Boston and New York, Houghton Mifflin Company, Cambridge: The Reverside Press, 1926), pp. 9-10.

particular, consciously equipped himself to tackle the problems of the craftsman, his technique apparently did not measure up to his expectations at times. A passage from "Burnt Norton" bears testimony to his struggle in this regard:

> ... Words strain,
> Crack and sometimes break under the burden,
> Under the tension, slip, slide, perish,
> Decay with imprecision, will not stay in place,
> Will not stay still...
>
> (11. 149-153)

It has been observed[86] that "scarcely a poem or fragment of the poet's exists which does not dramatize, in some significant fashion of technique or substance, his own statement that each venture into the expression of poetry

> Is a new beginning, a raid on the inarticulate
> With shabby equipment always deteriorating.
> In the general mess of imprecision of feeling,
> Undisciplined squads of emotion."
>
> ("East Coker", Lines 179-182)

In the early part of the twentieth century, the modernists showed an excessive feeling for the classical virtues of "concentration, tautness and extreme economy in poetic expression".[87] It was, partly at least, the result of their obsessive aversion to the rhetorical excesses and emotional abuses of their predecessors. The Coleridgean organisistic theory and symbolism served them eminently in the context, though they appeared unaware of their debt in that regard. The poem thus gains a meaningful shape, as observed by A.C. Partridge,[88] though, more often than not, that meaning remains beyond the grasp of the common man. Ironically enough, it happened in spite of a conscious effort on the part of the modernists to eliminate the distinction between the poet and the common man.

Inspired by Eliot's theory of Dissociation of Sensibility the modernists extolled John Donne at the expense of Milton. And they emulated his colloquial language and speech rhythms, while attempting

86. Sanders, Charles, "Beyond the Language of the Living: The Voice of T.S. Eliot", *Twentieth Century Literature: A Scholarly and Critical Journal* (Vol. 27, Winter 1981, Number 4), p. 376.

87. Partridge, A.C., *The Language of Modern Poetry*: *Yeats, Eliot, Auden* (London: The Language Library, Andre Deutsch Ltd., 1976), p. 17. Henceforth referred to as Partridge.

88. *Ibid*., p. 56.

to unify their sensibility in the light of his practice. But their desire to endow poetry with the naturalness of speech did not make it less than obscure in most cases. Their failure in this regard was partly due to the extremely complex nature of the experience they had to assimilate. Chaotic experiences were often sought to be presented in chaotic forms. And this novel imitative form that represented chaos by chaos naturally invited protests from critics like Yvor Winters. The logical disconnection and syntactical fragmentation promoted in the process brought about a rhetorical discontinuity.

Donald Davie makes rhetorical discontinuity his definition of modernism.[89] The tendency, referred to by Monroe K. Spears,[90] of certain critics to attribute it to the pernicious influence of Franco-American Modernism has been pernicious in itself, as it neglects the positive aspects of the modernist revolution. Just as the Romantic revolt was against "the conventionality and donnishness of the earlier poetic diction",[91] the modernist revolt perhaps came as a timely corrective for the excesses of the earlier phase. And it was not too radical either, as it largely affected only the forms and techniques of poetry.[92] Perhaps we are justified in calling it a peripheral revolution, inasmuch as the essential aspects of the English poetic tradition remained intact in spite of it.

It may be worth pondering as to how the conscious effort at purging poetry of its rhetoric affected the prospects of Romanticism in our century. Rhetoric in most cases seems to have come handy for concealing the vacuum caused by the failure of imagination. And a poetry that is truly imaginative can seldom be handicapped by its absence. W.P. Ker puts it succinctly:

> Imagination can use the simplest diction because it has got at the truth, found what can appeal to the right mind of man, because it is strong in life, thought and language. Rich poetic vocabulary is then unnecessary....[93]

---

89. Davie, Donald, *Articulate Energy: An Enquiry into the Syntax of English Poetry* (London: Routledge and Kegan Paul, 1955). Henceforth referred to as *AE*.
90. *DC.*, p. 20.
91. Harding, p. 60.
92. See Spender, Stephen, *The Struggle of the Modern* (Berkeley and Los Angeles: University of California Press, 1963, reprint 1965), pp. 47-49. Spender has drawn attention to the peripheral nature of the modernist revolution as also to its essential attachment to the Romantic tradition.
93. Chambers, R.W. (ed.) *Form and Style in Poetry: Lectures and Notes by W.P. Ker* (London, Melbourne, Toronto: Macmillan, 1966), p. 250.

W.B. Yeats may be a classic example of a poet whose poetry remained eminently Romantic on being purged of rhetoric although it reappeared in his later work in modified forms. When he said that "in 1900 everybody got down off his stilts" he was apparently referring to his own effort in that regard.[94] Yet he made no secret of his antipathy towards the extremist tendencies of the modernists in versification.

The modernists took to free verse and favoured speech rhythms in their quest for an organic form which Herbert Read regards as a Romantic legacy. But it resulted in a plethora of new verse by false pretenders to the gift of the Muse and tended to blur the outward distinction between poetry and prose. D.H. Lawrence evolved his own distinctive mode of free verse to give unrestrained expression to his perceptions. While it eminently suited his genius, it was apt to be abused by lesser men. Herbert Read's comment on the Lawrencian mode, however, sounds rather harsh. His view that Lawrence's was a prose-contribution implies a failure to give due credit to the essential aspects of Romantic poetry.[95] It may exemplify the general tendency to blame the faculty of imagination for the failings of the intellect. Indeed we are aware that the Lawrencian verse does not measure up to Herbert Read's idea of the greatest poetry in which "the creative power and intellectual energy wrestle as in a war-embrace".[96] Edward Thomas' distinguished mode of expression perhaps provides an ideal *via media* between the traditionalist and modernist extremes. W.B. Yeats sticks to the use of metrical verse all through his life. The traditional form serves him as "ice or salt" for packing his personal emotions, as they tend to rot.[97] He evolves a passionate syntax and manages to verbalize his perceptions in all their intensity with a distinctively Yeatsian flavour.

The mythical method adopted by Yeats and Joyce in their distinct ways has been commended by Eliot. He finds it useful in manipulating a continuous parallel between contemporaneity and

94. Yeats, W.B., *The Oxford Book of Modern Verse, 1892-1935,* chosen by W.B. Yeats (London: Oxford University Press, 1936, reprint 1972), p. XI. Henceforth referred to as *OBMV*.

95. *TVF.*, p. 100.

96. *Ibid.*, p. 160.

97. Yeats, W.B., *Essays and Introductions* (London: Macmillan & Co. Ltd., 1961), p. 522. Henceforth referred to as *EI*.

antiquity.[98] Though it affords a semblance of order to certain works, the method largely fails to deliver the goods, since the modern man has not been responding to traditional myths and metaphors as the writers do. The gap caused that way was sought to be filled by the invention of new personal myths of limited significance.

In a conscious bid to assimilate a wide variety of dreary and dreadful experiences, modern poetry has had to admit a great amount of fresh material, which had hitherto been considered unpoetic. The War poets, for example, had to find a new breed of objectives-correlative on battle-fronts, for giving vent to their unique emotions in the face of the blood-curdling scenes of war. It was indeed a far cry from the blessed forms which the great Romantics had counted on for recording their perceptions. John-Heath-Stubbs' observation that "the language of Romantic poetry is essentially an instrument for the expression of Innocence rather than Experience",[99] might be apt when we relate it to such experiences. The description of a genre of modern Romantic poetry as poetry of experience would seem particularly significant in the context.[100]

The New Critics, who may perhaps be called the unwilling inheritors of the Romantic tradition in lierary criticism, maintained that poems are autotelic and favoured close-reading to such an extent that Eliot himself could not help calling them the 'lemon-squeezer school'. Eliot could hardly have anticipated such an alarming growth from the seeds he had unconsciously sown in his early life, along with I.A. Richards. The New Critics encouraged the analysis of poetic imagery for its own sake and accorded a pride of place to metaphor by treating it as the basic unit of poetry. The presence of conflicting elements, thus, became the measure of a poem's greatness. And "structures of expression gained priority over structures of experience", as observed by Donald Davie.[101] The emphasis in the context has tended to be mainly on metaphor.

---

98. Eliot, T.S., "Ulysses, Order and Myth" in *The Modern Tradition*, (ed.) Richard Ellmann and Charles Feidelson, Jr. (New York: Oxford University Press, 1965), p. 681.

99. Stubbs, John-Heath, Introduction to the *Faber Book of Twentieth Century Verse* (London: Faber and Faber, 1953, Third edition, 1975), p. 22.

100. See Langbaum, Robert, *The Poetry of Experience: The Dramatic Monologue in Modern Literary Tradition* (1957, New York, 1963). Langbaum regards the Romantic and the modern traditions as a single unit.

101. *AE.*, p. 93.

In its commitment to the metaphor, modern poetry has perhaps reached the extreme limit of fragmentation. A poem treated in isolation, as a picture of conflicts and contradictions, may be an apt symbol for the modern man.

In such a context the Romantic imagination naturally has a challenging task. Has it risen to the occasion? R.A. Foakes, for one, seems inclined to think that modern Romantic poetry has nearly lost its integral vision.[102] But it may be unfair to suggest that even the best of moderns have pitifully knuckled down before the forces of disruption and discord.

If the Romantic sensibility has been eroded by the extreme sceptical leanings of the modern mind, the essential aspects of Romanticism have still managed to survive in our midst, as evidenced by some of the major poetic achievements of our century. The endeavour in the following pages will be to reassess them with a view to determining the authenticity and validity of modern Romantic perceptions.

102. Foakes, p. 16.

CHAPTER II

ROMANTIC AFFINITIES OF EDWARD THOMAS

The varying manifestations of Romantic instincts in the English poetry of the present century may be material enough for scores of dissertations. And an orthodox account of them may bring into focus poets like Walter de la Mare, D.H. Lawrence, Stephen Spender, Dylan Thomas and Edwin Muir. The contributions of others like Edward Thomas and the later Yeats and Eliot, whose Romantic affinities have often been disputed, are apt to be overlooked in the process, although they have been largely responsible for the resuscitation of the Romantic tradition in the modern context.

The Romantic strain in the poetry of the twentieth century has been a common strand that links up the modernists with the less aggressive moderns. Romanticism in the new context has tended to grow close to realism allowing ample scope for contradictory assertions on the affiliations of individual poets. An element of scepticism characteristic of the modern mind seems to lend a new dimension to the Romantic achievements of the century, as it seeks to establish a rapport with realism. The sceptical approach, however, does not appear to detract from the significance of Romantic perceptions, as it seems to work only at the conscious level of the mind. The impression, instead, is of Romanticism growing new teeth to chew and digest new realities. Such an approach, surely, was not wholly alien to the great Romantics of the earlier century. It was, in fact, characteristic of Keats. Jack Stillinger, for one, seems to commend it when he says:

> It is a notable part of Keats's wisdom that he never lost touch with reality, that he reproved his hoodwinked dreamers who would shut out the world, that he recognized life as a complexity of pleasure and pain, and laid down a rule for action: achievement of the ripest, fullest experience that one is capable of. These qualities make him a saner, if less Romantic, poet than his contemporaries, and they should qualify him as the Romantic poet most likely to survive in the world.[1]

1. Stillinger, Jack, "The Hoodwinking of Madeline", *English Romantic Poets: Modern Essays in Criticism*, (ed.) M.H. Abrams (London, Oxford, New York: Oxford University Press, 1960, second edition, 1975), p. 466.

And obviously, along with Keats, the 'sceptical Romanticism' that he subscribed to, has also found favour in our times.

The Georgian endeavour, initiated by Edward Marsh in the early part of the present century, to impart "a new strength and beauty to English poetry", was certainly laudable. The Georgian poetry seems to have taken off fairly well. But, ironically enough, it was weighed down by the same high-sounding ideals which had lent it motive force. It had perforce to fly low. And presumably, only when it went out of Marsh's hands, it developed a precipitously downward curve. The Georgians thus turned into a butt of ridicule. As mentioned by C.K. Stead, what appeared revolutionary in 1910 turned reactionary by 1920.[2] No wonder, Robert Graves, a Georgian himself in his early years, teamed up with his wife to ridicule them.[3]

As is widely acknowledged, the qualities the original Georgian movement had aimed at were to be found in the poetry of Edward Thomas. Yet, the interest evinced by critics like F.R. Leavis and H. Coombes to disentangle Thomas from the Georgian fold is understandable. In fact, those who have claimed him for the Georgian school seem to have wronged him much. They praise his poetry mainly for its simplicity, charm and narrow, provincial character. The latter tendency has been evidenced in recent times in the work of Jan Marsh.[4] Thomas, obviously, owed something to the Georgian aesthetic. Yet, if he has to be branded a Georgian on that score, he was a Georgian with a difference.

Evaluating the contributions of his contemporaries and predecessors as a sensitive critic, Thomas was able to develop a historical perspective which formed the core of T.S. Eliot's idea of tradition. And, in his own poetry, Thomas succeeded in avoiding the foibles he had noticed in others. His comment that Yeats would perhaps have made fewer mistakes in his poetry had he been a less curious critic, suggests the relavance of his own criticism to his poetry.[5] The "verbosity" found in the early Morris, Yeats and

2. *NP.*, p. 110.
3. Graves, Robert and Riding, Laura, *The Common Asphodel* (1949).
4. Marsh, Jan, *Edward Thomas: A Poet for his country* (London: Paul Elek, 1978).
5. Longley, Edna (ed.), *A Language not to be Betrayed: Selected Prose of Edward Thomas* (Carcanet Press in Association with Mid-Northumberland Arts Group, 1981), p. 85. Henceforth referred to as *ALNB*.

Wordsworth was perhaps a thing he guarded himself against.[6] He also drew lessons from "the exquisite unnaturalness" of Pater's style, and "the perversion of language and metre" by Swinburne.[7] Thomas' comment that unless a man wrote with his whole nature concentrated upon his subject, "he was unlikely to take hold of another man",[8] reminds us of Yeats' emphasis on the Unity of Being and Eliot's later insistence on the Unification of Sensibility. The Modernist meat, however, proved too strong for him, as remarked by Edna Longley.[9] Yet, if he did not have vinegar in his blood to the extent desired by Ezra Pound, he was, surely, not so mild as the latter believed.[10] Thomas had, in fact, found the Georgian stuff rather insipid. He was hard put to the task of evolving a new form, as none of the available forms suited his taste.[11] Hardy's numerous experiments in versification might have interested him in the context. The "middle way between dead traditionalism and frenetic modernism" adopted by Robert Frost, he heartily approved of.[12] But he was conscious of Frost's tendency to be diffuse at times.[13] Frost and Yeats had shown him how the speech of poetry could be that of life.[14] It may, however, be unfair to suggest that he owed much to them. In any case it seems likely that he was much impressed by the way in which Yeats had stripped poetry of all adornments. Though Thomas was alive to the modern revolt against the picturesque and declamatory way of writing typified by the early Yeats, he loved to be picturesque without being declamatory.[15] Edna Longley says:

> Like Yeats, Thomas participated in the battle of early 20th century literature to exorcise the later 19th century. It sometimes seems as if what he was doing, in his own theory and practice, was dismantling an ornate, outdated literary edifice brick by Pateresque brick, until it no

6. *Ibid.*, p. 76.
7. *Ibid.*, p. 161.
8. *Ibid.*, p. 160.
9. *Ibid.*, Introduction by Edna Longley, p. XII.
10. *Ibid.*, p. XII.
11. *Ibid.*, p. XV.
12. *Ibid.*, p. XII.
13. *Ibid.*, pp. 130-131.
14. *Ibid.*, p. 85.
15. *Ibid.*, p. 85.

> longer blocked the way forward. Pound and Eliot were to come along with their bulldozers, but bulldozers can inflict a lot of incidental damage.[16]

Thomas' contribution to the essential aspects of the native English tradition has also been significant. Apparently, he was traditional in the way in which Eliot was to use the word later.[17] Yet, he was not for blindly imitating even the best of his predecessors. He must have realized how the spiritual absorptions of the Romantics often hindered their physical vision. He observed:

> The distance between Nature and other writers, even Wordsworth, is very great; they have as it were, a burning glass that puts fetters on the sun.[18]

Wordsworth's ability to see the objects of nature with the outer and the inner eyes at the same time has already been commented on. But, by the exacting standards set by Edward Thomas, Wordsworth's physical vision might seem rather weak.

A comparison of Wordsworth's "To the Cuckoo" with Edward Thomas' "Sedge-Warblers" is likely to bring home the distinction between their approaches. To Wordsworth the Cuckoo is more a wandering voice than a bird –

> O BLITHE New-comer! I have heard,
> I hear thee and rejoice.
> O Cuckoo: shall I call thee Bird,
> Or but a wandering Voice?
>
> While I am lying on the grass
> Thy twofold shout I hear,
> From hill to hill it seems to pass
> At once far off, and near.
>
> Though babbling only to the Vale,
> Of sunshine and of flowers,
> Thou bringest unto me a tale
> Of visionary hours.
>
> Thrice welcome, darling of the Spring
> Even yet thou art to me
> No bird, but an invisible thing,
> A voice, a mystery;

---

16. *Ibid.*, Introduction by Edna Longley, p. XV.
17. *SE.*, p. 14.
18. *ALNB.*, Introduction by Edna Longley, pp. XVI-XVII.

The same whom in my schoolboy days
I listened to; that Cry
which made me look a thousand ways
In bush, and tree, and sky.

To seek thee did I often rove
Through woods and on the green;
And thou wert still a hope, a love;
Still longed for, never seen.

And I can listen to thee yet;
Can lie upon the plain
And listen, till I do beget
That golden time again.

O blessed Bird! the earth we pace
Again appears to be
An unsubstantial, faery place;
That is fit home for Thee![19]

But though very much a physical presence, the Cuckoo here does not seem to gain a concrete shape. In fact, the picture looks rather hazy like that of Thomas' "Unknown Bird".[20] Though Wordsworth certainly cared for the physical aspects of the objects he perceived, we find hardly anything in the poem that helps us to identify the bird, except perhaps its name. The description may suit any song-bird of the Spring. The experience sought to be expressed in the poem is perhaps too mystical and mysterious to allow enough of concreteness in its imagery. The rapturous feelings aroused by the bird's song are not sufficiently restrained, though that seeming lack of restraint perhaps creates an impression of spontaneity and sincerity in the feelings expressed.

The imagery of "Sedge-Warblers", on the other hand, appears too concrete to allow any trace of excessive sentiment. The poem is replete with sensuous details. Though the poet has apparently been overwhelmed by the beauty of the moment, his physical eye functions most efficiently. He describes the 'small brown birds' –

---

19. Wordsworth, William, "To the Cuckoo", *The Poetical Works of Wordsworth,* (ed.) Thomas Hutchinson, A New Edition, revised by Ernest De Selincourt (London, New York, Toronto: Humphrey Milford, Oxford University Press, 1904, reprint 1942), pp. 183-84.

20. Thomas, R.G., (ed.) *The Collected Poems of Edward Thomas* (Oxford: Clarendon Press, 1978), pp. 85-87. Henceforth referred to as *ETCP*.

.–. clinging so light
To willow twigs, sang longer than the lark,
Quick, shrill, or grating, a song to match the heat
Of the strong sun, nor less the water's cool,
Gushing through narrows swirling in the pool.[21]

The precision and delicacy of the imagery here suggest a firm intellectual grip over the situation. And a sobering awareness of all that the song lacks, – "all words, all melody/all sweetness almost" – constitutes a guarantee against false or exaggerated sentiments.

The example of Richard Jefferies was apparently helpful to Thomas in his endeavour to match the clearness of the physical with the penetration of the spiritual vision.[22] Robert Frost demonstrated to him how to ensure "absolute fidelity to the postures which the voice assumes in the most expressive intimate speech".[23] And he seems to have absorbed much that was Hardyan, though he could not wholly approve of what he, rather apologetically, called the 'rusticity' in Thomas Hardy.[24] Thomas attributed the Hardyan 'obsession with the blindness of Fate and the carelessness of Nature' to this rusticity, though we find similar notions creeping into his own poetry later, despite his finer sensibility.[25] His "February Afternoon", for instance, says:

God sits aloft in the array,
That we have wrought him, stone-deaf and stone-blind.[26]

Such notions bring Hardy close to Thomas and the moderns, though Thomas does not seem to have taken it thus. Also, while Thomas finds the 'blessed hope' attributed to Hardy's darkling thrush rather untenable, his own sedge warblers are heard

Wisely reiterating endlessly
What no man learnt yet, in or out of school.[27]

Thomas, like Hardy again, does not believe in any special affinity between man and Nature. He shows no inclination to attribute divinity to the presences of Nature either. Yet, we cannot

21. (a) *Ibid.*, p. 211.
22. *ALNB.*, p. 174.
23. Coombes, H., *Edward Thomas: A Critical Study* (London: Chatto and Windus, 1956, reprint 1973), p. 185. Henceforth referred to as *Edward Thomas.*
24. *ALNB.*, p. 72.
25. *Ibid.*, p. 73.
26. *ETCP.*, p. 271.
27. *Ibid.*, p. 211.

afford to be as sure as F.R. Leavis[28] that the intimations that come to him are not of immortality, when we see them in the light of his comment

> ... it is in the country more often that we become aware, in a sort of majestic quiet, of the destiny which binds us to infinity and eternity.[29]

The fact that Thomas, unlike Wordsworth, did not set much store by them, cannot, surely, nullify the significance of his tendency to yield to them, momentarily though, and to yearn to "fade far away, dissolve, and quite forget."[30]

Such intimations finding expression in poems like "Ambition", "The Glory", "Haymaking", "The Brook", "Tears", "Beauty", "October", "Liberty", and "Old Man" may have to be traced to his mystical leanings, though Thomas apparently believed that he was no mystic. Thomas' lack of pretensions in this regard may have to be attributed to his unassuming nature. He can certainly be called a mystic in the limited sense of one who attains, or believes in the possibility of attaining, insights into mysteries transcending ordinary human knowledge. And we have to regard the mystical element in his poetry as the essential aspect of his Romanticism. Andrew Motion, in his study of the poetry of Edward Thomas, has not only acknowledged his mystical leanings but has also observed that his "preoccupation with the inexpressible" links him up with the earlier Romantics on the one hand and the modernists on the other.[31]

Thomas' inability to linger in his visions for long may well be proof of his inadequacy as a mystic, and not perhaps as a Romantic poet.

Some eminent critics have, however, sought to discount the Romantic inclinations of Edward Thomas. F.R. Leavis, who has made a signal contribution towards a reassessment of Thomas' poetic achievement, for example, says:

> Edward Thomas is concerned with the finer texture of living, and here

---

28. *New Bearings*, p. 63.
29. *ALNB*., p. 200.
30. *HMP*., p. 218.
31. Motion, Andrew, *The Poetry of Edward Thomas* (London, Boston and Henley: Routledge & Kegan Paul, 1980), pp. 100-101 and 161. Henceforth referred to as *PET*.

> and now, the ordinary moments in which for him the "meaning" (if any) resides.[32]

What is only implicit in Leavis' comment is made explicit by H. Coombes when he observes, in his celebrated study of Edward Thomas, that "his final attitude is not romantic; however great his longing, for a perfect 'home' where he can find his 'rest' in beauty, he never deceives himself by excluding the painful".[33] If a man's capacity to perpetuate visionary moments to the total exclusion of the physical world earns him the title of a Romantic poet, poetry-writing may well turn into a profession of saints. For most of us, as remarked by Thomas, the visionary or God-like view is impossible except in a few particular and irrecoverable moments.[34] We remember how the same sentiments are echoed in T.S. Eliot too.[35]

Michael Kirkham has made a more assertive bid to negate the Romantic affinities of Edward Thomas. He has sought to prove that in a good number of poems, Thomas has tried to expose the pride and delusion of the Wordsworthian Romanticism.[36]

What Thomas has attempted, as a matter of conscious strategy, is the creation of a balanced picture. Such an effort apparently involved a blending of the Wordsworthian solipsistic leanings with the Keatsian capabilities. We would do well to remember that Keats had long ago attempted the exposure of the pride and delusion of the Wordsworthian egotistical sublime, without ceasing to be a Romantic. Thomas' lines

> ... But the end fell like a bell!
> The bower was shattered; far off the train roared.[37]

would seem to have drawn their inspiration from the concluding stanza of Keats' "Ode to a Nightingale" :

> Forlorn! the very word is like a bell
> To toll me back from thee to my sole self.

---

32. *New Bearings*., p. 61.
33. *Edward Thomas*, p. 211.
34. *ALNB*., p. 200.
35. See Eliot, T.S., "The Dry Salvages", *Four Quartets* (London: Faber and Faber, 1954, reprint 1959), pp. 206-207.
36. Kirkham, Michael, "The 'Desert Places' in Edward Thomas' Poetry", *University of Toronto Quarterly* (Summer 1979, Vol. XLVIII, No. 4), p. 290. Henceforth referred to as "The Desert Places".
37. *ETCP*., p. 103.

> Adieu! the fancy cannot cheat so well
> As she is fam'd to do, deceiving elf.[38]

If, as remarked by H. Coombes, Thomas was ultimately in no need of Mr. Eliot's (rather grim) warning of "the deception of the thrush", Keats was not in need of it either.[39] Thomas' comment on Frost perhaps reveals his understanding of the inadequacy of the Wordsworthian mode. He says:

> Mr. Frost knows the life of which he writes rather as Dorothy Wordsworth did. That is to say he sympathizes where Wordsworth contemplates.[40]

Thomas' bid to temper the Wordsworthian contemplation with a Keatsian sympathy would seem to be a matter of conscious poetic strategy. The resultant change, therefore, does not seem to affect the validity of his imaginative perceptions. His tendency to readjust his stance soon after the visionary moment is apparently accentuated by the burden of self-consciousness, with which he kept battling all through his life. And his agnostic tendencies may perhaps account for the lack of profundity in his transcendental experiences. Wordswoth, in fact, has a clear edge over him in that regard. The belief Wordsworth had in himself as also in the divinity manifested through the presences of nature was beyond Thomas, largely because of his sceptical bent of mind. As R.G. Thomas takes it, his intellectual detachment perhaps shied away from the unidentified unknown.[41] If we are favourably disposed towards Thomas, we may well call it an essential aspect of Thomas' "distinctively modern sensibility".

H. Coombes observes that there is always 'something' in Thomas that prevents anything like a full surrender being made.[42] We may perhaps name it the sceptical element. Elsewhere Coombes has also referred to 'something' that worked effectively against 'at-home-ness' in Thomas and has apparently identified it with the

---

38. Keats, John, "Ode to a Nightingale", *A Keats Selection* (ed.) Norman Howlings (London, Melbourne, Toronto: Macmillan, 1966), p.169. Henceforth referred to as *A Keats Selection*.
39. *Edward Thomas*, p. 211.
40. *ALNB.*, p. 130.
41. *ETCP.*, Introduction by R.G. Thomas, p. XX.
42. *Edward Thomas*, p. 210.

'dread' aroused by the presences of nature.[43] That sense of dread also perhaps has its root in the same sceptical element.

The sceptical approach has apparently promoted a wry humour in Thomas. It has already been expertly analysed by H. Coombes.[44] A sense of humour, we are aware, was wholly absent in the earlier Romantics, thanks largely to their visionary absorptions. Even in Keats, presumably, the element of scepticism was not to the extent of allowing him to indulge in humour. Melancholic tendencies had indeed made matters difficult for Keats more than for Thomas. The ironic detachment that promoted a sardonic humour has obviously been accentuated in the modern context. The modernists tend to misprize the Romantics partly for their lack of it. Edward Thomas makes up for that deficiency in his own distinctive manner.

It may be worth pondering whether the sceptical approach has made Thomas incapable of the Keatsian sense of fulfilment.[45] Thomas' endeavour to present a balanced picture, mentioned earlier, seems to have been backed up both by a conscious strategy and a sceptical bent of mind. In his "Ode to Autumn" Keats has sought to present a placid moment in all its intensity. Obviously, the feeling projected therein could not have lasted long for Keats. Moreover, a closer look at the poem may convince us that Keats' feelings were perhaps too complex to subject themselves to such a deliberate effort. For example, when he says:

> Where are the songs of spring? Ay, where are they?
> Think not of them, thou hast thy music too,[46]

the rhetorical question suggests a yearning for the intenser pleasures afforded by the Spring, and a disturbing awareness of their inaccessibility at the moment. The poet's effort in the context seems to be to make the best of a bad bargain. Such hints, far from diluting the significance of the visionary effort, may bear testimony to Keats' distinctive sensibility.

Thomas' "July" suggests a fulfilled state of being without the disturbing note of yearning we have perceived in the Keatsian Ode:

---

43. *Ibid.*, p. 206.
44. *Ibid.*, pp. 237-38.
45. *Ibid.*, pp. 199 & 201. In Coombes' opinion, it has.
46. "Ode to Autumn", *A Keats' Selection*, p. 172.

Naught moves but clouds and in the glassy lake
Their doubles and the shadow of my boat.
The boat itself stirs only when I break
This drowse of heat and solitude afloat

To prove if what I see be bird or mote,
Or learn if yet the shore woods be awake.

Long hours since dawn grew, – spread, – and passed on high
And deep below, – I have watched the cool reeds hung
Over images more cool in imaged sky:
Nothing there was worth thinking of so long;
All that the ring-doves say, far leaves among
Brims my mind with content thus still to lie.[47]

If, however, ambivalence is a characteristic of Thomas more than of Keats, it is perhaps the result of a conscious effort on the part of the former to give it poetic expression.

Thomas' complexity has at times not been properly appreciated. John Freeman's comment that Thomas felt "utterly at home" in nature perhaps amounts to an unconscious self-projection.[48] Thomas, presumably, could not have felt entirely at home even in the cosiest of heavens. Like his two pewits, Thomas tried to balance himself between the earth and the sky, though he could not share the merry mood of the birds.

For a similar reason, Michael Kirkham's comments on Thomas' "Melancholy" sound rather odd. He says that the poem induces and condones more than it presents and analyzes the strange sweetness of abandoning oneself to despair.[49] One could hardly have felt happy if the poem were to present only a picture of acute melancholy. Presumably, Thomas' "Rain" is called by Coombes "perhaps the bleakest poem of all" for no other reason.[50] Strangely enough, Michael Kirkham is much impressed by the painful expression of despair in it.[51]

Thomas' effort to analyze his melancholy while giving it poetic expression evidently helped him to grapple with it to some extent. As in the case of Keats, his regard for nature was probably heightened by his melancholy disposition. And, along with his visionary

47. *ETCP.*, p. 201.
48. Quoted in *Edward Thomas*, p. 205.
49. The Desert Places, p. 284.
50. *Edward Thomas*.
51. The Desert Places, p. 285.

leanings, his interest in natural phenomena must have helped in relieving his melancholy marginally at least.

The features of Thomas' poetry that distinguish it from the conventional Georgian stuff have been competently dealt with by Middleton Murry, F.R. Leavis, H. Coombes and others. Coombes has rightly observed that Thomas is a poet of human nature rather than nature. Thomas' eye misses nearly nothing. And he does not seek to colour the landscape like Thomas Hardy. He realizes how his distinguished predecessors, including even Wordsworth and Shelley, were at times "lured into unveracity".[52] He observes that Keats, almost alone, "entirely lacks inartistic intention". His own effort has presumably been to approximate himself to the level of Keats. His fidelity to the observation of the moment does not, however, prevent him from using the outer scene for gliding back into the inner landscape with the ease and poise of a skilled athlete. Nevertheless, "his way of saying seems to depend largely on the way of seeing", as John F. Danby puts it.[53] We remember how it has mostly been the other way round with the typical Georgians. The distinctive phrases employed by F.R. Leavis for highlighting this aspect of Thomas' achievement render a proverbial significance to his observations.[54]

Thomas' desire to be true to the outer scene does not, however, conflict with his desire to be true to himself. The exquisite integrity of his postures and the psychological subtlety of his portraits impress us as much as the delicacy and intensity of his physical perceptions. He would appear to have stolen a march over the great Romantics including Keats in all these respects. Evidently, he considers "the borrowed posture or the unfelt word a betrayal".[55] He was alive to the fact that Frost himself "shows us less of his own feelings and more of other people's ..."[56] Perhaps, that is why their ways part. His approach has indeed been too subtle, delicate and minute for Frost. Apart from Thomas' "great sensitiveness and

52. *ALNB.*, p. 181.

53. Danby, John F., "Edward Thomas", *Critical Quarterly* (Vol. I, Winter, 1959), p. 313. Henceforth referred to as Danby.

54. *New Bearings*, pp. 61-64.

55. Danby, p. 317.

56. *ALNB.*, p. 128.

integrity",[57] it is his skyward urge that marks him out from the "begetter" of his verse.

The psychological subtlety characteristic of Thomas has given room for a certain amount of misunderstanding. John Pikoulis, for example, slips into the notion that Thomas was not capable of love.[58] Possibly, Thomas' own words have encouraged such a notion. For he says:

> My eyes scarce dare meet you
> Lest they should prove
> I but respond to you
> And do not love[59]

Yet, we have hardly any reason to believe that Thomas was by any means shallow in his affections. His love involved a complex awareness of the various factors that promoted the feeling, thanks largely to his characteristic self-consciousness. He was not simple-minded enough to dote on any one. The deep humility that makes him identify himself with

> ... moon, sparrow and mouse what witnessed
> what they could never understand or alter
> or prevent in the dark house[60]

might also have complicated matters for his critics. However, if true love is to be conceived of as an emotional self-indulgence that submerges all intellectual barriers, Thomas was plainly not capable of it.

Thomas' cravings, admitted or not, are seldom unqualified. His nostalgic moods, unlike Thomas Hardy's, get shattered in no time. He knew that

> ... Recall
> was vain: no more could the restless brook
> Ever turn back and climb the waterfall
> To the lake that rests and stirs not in the nook.[61]

His urge for the sky is sobered by his love of the earth. It is perhaps

---

57. Rowlinson, D.H., "More Creation *Versus* Statement: Frost and Edward Thomas", *The Practice of Criticism* (Cambridge University Press, 1971), p. 100.

58. Pikoulis, John, "Alun Lewis and Edward Thomas", *Critical Quarterly* (Vol. 23, No. 4, Winter 1981), p. 25.

59. *ETCP*., p. 277.

60. *Ibid*., p. 369.

61. *Ibid*., p. 59.

the solidity of the earth that prompts him to be less sceptical of it. And naturally, he shows a partiality for it. But he is aware that life on the solid earth is not everything, as mentioned by John F. Danby.[62] In the words of Andrew Motion, Thomas is convinced that the time and the timeless are interdependent and moments of everlastingness "can neither exist nor remain in ignorance of their opposite for long".[63] He says:

> I could not be as the sun
> Nor should I be content to be
> As little as the bird or as mighty as the sun.[64]

Thomas himself has been aware of the probability of some people failing to appreciate such a seeming duplicity, for he says:

> Those who have always lived on firm ground
> Are quite unreal in the matter of the wind.[65]

Thomas' love for the earth has secured him from misanthropic tendencies. Michael Kirkham has rightly pointed out that "idealism–yearning for the infinite, singleness and sameness of being, free of the tangle and variety of finite life – entails misanthropy".[66] Kirkham's effort to wish away the Romantic inclinations of Thomas is perhaps influenced by a well-meaning desire to stress Thomas' wide humanity. But Romanticism, as we understand it, is impoverished in the absence of humanity, though the resultant poverty is often sought to be made up for by other means.

"The Other" provides a clue to the working of Thomas' mind. Middleton Murry calls it "the most powerful and most austerely imagined poem."[67] H. Coombes regards it as "the most extensive treatment in a single poem of the theme of self-searching". But he feels that the quest described is for the poet's deepest and real self.[68]

---

62. Danby, p. 317.
63. Motion, Andrew, "Everlasting Moments: Review of Edward Thomas' *The Chess Player and Other Essays*", in *The Times Literary Supplement* (August 21, 1981), p. 961.
64. *ETCP*., p. 181.
65. *Ibid*., p. 155.
66. "The Desert Places", p. 289.
67. Quoted in Longley, Edna (ed.), *Edward Thomas: Poems and Last Poems* (Collins Annotated Student Texts), Commentary by Edna Longley, P. Henceforth referred to as *PLP*.
68. *Edward Thomas*, p. 217.

Andrew Motion also inclines towards such a view, when he deals with the "double vision" of Thomas.[69]

Edna Longley's view of the poem sounds more perceptive. She observes that the poem is a prophetic microcosm of Thomas' whole scope and development as a poet. The quest, according to her, is for self-knowledge. She says that the complementary aspects of Thomas move towards integration. Her view that the whole action of the poem takes place inside one head sounds significant.[70]

Michael Kirkham has made a serious bid to come to grips with the poem.[71] He analyses it in the light of D.W. Harding's view that the unadmitted craving for an adequate social group was behind Thomas' most characteristic moods. He seeks to prove that the poem deals with "the solitary's need, and his inability to satisfy his need, for social connection." H. Coombes' belief that 'the other' is the poet's real self is thus deemed untenable. Michael Kirkham carries conviction up to this point. But then, he appears to tread on slippery grounds. He says that the questing self is mistaken in supposing that the casual encounters of 'road and inn' are indeed the sum of what is not forest. For a man of agnostic inclinations, we feel, that 'road and inn' may make an apt symbol for social living as opposed to the field of activity of the Romantic artist represented by 'forest' or 'solitude'. The solitary's exploratory advance towards the world of noisy activity is apt to yield nothing but dissatisfaction. And, when the quester of Thomas' poem finds the people he meets in the inn dull boors, we have perhaps no reason to be shocked. The quest, we are sure, is doomed to fail, owing to the innate limitations of the quester. He says:

> I sought then in solitude.
> The wind had fallen with the night; as still
> The roads lay as the ploughland rude,
> Dark and naked, on the hill.
> Had there been ever any feud
> 'Twixt earth and sky, a mighty will
> Closed it: the crocketed dark trees,
> A dark house, dark impossible

---

69. *PET.*, pp. 32-52.

70. *PLP.*, p.

71. Kirkham, Michael "Edward Thomas' Other Self" *Ariel : A Review of International English Literature* (Vol. 6, No. 3, July 1975), pp. 65-77. Henceforth referred to as *Ariel.*

Cloud-towers, one star, one lamp, one peace
Held on an everlasting lease:

And all was earth's, or all was sky's;
No difference endured between
The two. A dog barked on a hidden rise;
A marshbird whistled high unseen;
The latest waking blackbird's cries
Perished upon the silence keen.
The last light filled a narrow firth
Among the clouds. I stood serene,
And with a solemn quiet mirth,
An old inhabitant of earth.

Once the name I gave to hours
Like this was melancholy, when
it was not happiness and powers
Coming like exiles home again,
And weaknesses quitting their bowers,
Smiled and enjoyed, far off from men.
Moments of everlastingness.[72]

The Romantic artist's return to solitude seems to baffle the critic. He observes:

> I (the quester) says "returns", but this is different from the forest: in some ways it is a continuation of the original search, only deflected from its human social goal. "I sought then in solitude": the logic of the statement points to the continuity, but in what sense can this be the same search merely redirected? We deduce that the speaker is trying to repeat the "happy mood" which had first prompted the quest.[73]

The quester's return is likely to make sense only when we identify the solitude, to which he returns, with the forest, from which he has initially emerged. When the quester turns from his anti-self to his self perhaps we have no reason to be upset. The return, in other words, is from the field of activity of a practical man to the realm of a Romantic artist. The obscure regions of human consciousness, with which the artist in isolation is primarily concerned, may be symbolized by 'forest' or 'solitude'. Such a view may be largely in consonance with the idea of forest appearing elsewhere in Thomas. In describing the forest of the present poem as 'the forest of prose' Andrew Motion has had to draw a needless distinction

---

72. *ETCP.*, pp. 29-31.
73. *Ariel*, p. 67.

between the earlier and the later poems of Thomas.[74] Michael Kirkham's difficulties seem to spring from his inability to be happy with the implications of the failure of the quest. Perhaps, that is why he feels that the quester's return forms part of another quest. And presumably, it is for the same reason that the sense of harmony purchased at the cost of "obliteration of life"[75] disturbs the critic.

Kirkham's view that the poet's attempt here is to expose "Romantic habits of mind" to "critical analysis"[76] is far from convincing. What is suggested is a tentative exploration of the feasibility of realising the poet's antiself. The exploration leads only to a reassertion of the Romantic instincts of the poet. The quest apparently convinces him that the social being he is after is not of his kind and that he would do well to avoid him.

Edna Longley has drawn attention to Thomas' reference, in prose, to a figure that followed him.[77] The figure called 'The other man' reveals affinities with the poet's real self, unlike 'the other' of the poem. The poet seems to identify himself with 'the other man', when he says:

> ... he could gladly live no longer than a thrush if he could do some one thing as right, as crisp and rich, as the song was ... I mounted. He followed.[78]

Significantly, 'the other man' followed the poet, whereas the quester followed 'the other'. We are reminded of a fervent longing Thomas has recorded elsewhere to be able to pay his son (as rent for the house he hoped to share with the latter in his old age!) "a song/As sweet as a blackbird's and as long".[79] While pointing out that the other man "is slow to open conversation, although not to recognize his replica" (thereby suggesting his affinity with the poet), Andrew Motion seems to equate him with 'the other' of the poem. The image confronted by the quester is thus regarded as the poet's own. The quester's failure to attain "union with his elusive goal" has been traced to the poet's self-consciousness.[80] Though the poet's

74. *PET*., pp. 51 and 133.
75. *Ariel*, p. 69.
76. *Ibid*., p. 71.
77. *PLP*., p.
78. *ALNB*., p. 255.
79. *ETCP*., p. 293.
80. *PET*., pp. 36 & 50.

tormenting self-consciousness is undoubtedly a cause and a symptom of the quest recorded in the poem, the failure of the quest may have to be ascribed to other factors. Presumably, the "moments of everlastingness" that gave him "a solemn quiet mirth" failed to be more than momentary partly because of the impact of self-consciousness. Those ecstatic moments, in fact, mark the rare moments of triumph in an unrelenting war against self-consciousness waged by Thomas. And they constitute his imaginative endeavour to organize innocence in the manner of the great Romantics. If these moments reveal a relative lack of solidity, it may speak of a difference in degree rather than in kind promoted by the intenser self-consciousness of the new context.

What the quest symbolizes would thus seem to be an unavailing attempt on the part of the poet to reconcile himself with his antiself. Perhaps it also represents an earnest bid on his part to come to grips with the realities of life for giving them poetic expression. His ultimate decision to join the army may perhaps be taken as a desperate–and disastrous as it turned out to be – effort on the part of a Romantic artist to realize his antiself, through living the life of a practical man. All the same, he seems to have been aware that his innate gifts lie elsewhere and that his attempts at realizing his antiself are bound to fail both in life and letters. "The Other" seems to embody that self-knowledge. A disturbing aspect of the quest is not so much the quester's ignorance as his incapacity or unwillingness to seek solace elsewhere. The choices available to the quester seem to have been presented in their negative aspects for the same reason. In other words, we may say that the attitude towards realism revealed by the poem is rather negative. Michael Kirkham has rightly drawn attention to the "unavailability" to the poet of all but the shallowest and most transient of social experiences.[81]

The impact of agnostic tendencies on the work of Edward Thomas cannot, after all, be wished away. Indeed, in that respect he was sharing the ethos of the new century. His modern sensibility seems to revel in uncertainties. The modern man lacks faith not only in God and Nature, but also in himself. Neither the past nor the future assures him of anything. He keeps wavering both inwardly and outwardly. Thomas' "Aspens" seeks to give expression to that modern predicament most poignantly:

81. *Ariel*, p. 76.

> Whatever wind blows while they and I have leaves
> We cannot other than aspen be
> That ceaselessly unreasonably grieves
> Or so men think who like a different tree.[82]

Perhaps, the truth is that even those who have much liking for Thomas are apt to feel that his ceaseless grieving is rather unreasonable. We are reminded of Thomas' remark that the sadness in Richard Jefferies came of his appetite for joy.[83] We wonder whether it is the case with Thomas too. In any case, we are not likely to miss the essential distinction between the aspen and the poet. While the shivering of the aspen is more outward than inward, with Thomas it is perhaps the other way round. The tree seems to gain inner stability as it is anchored to the earth. But a similar anchoring to the earth perhaps proves inadequate for the stability of Thomas' mind. It has to be anchored to a faith of some sort or other – religious, social or political. Thomas offers no conclusive proof of an abiding attachment to any faith, whatever the critics may say.

Nevertheless, in enhancing and enlarging our awareness through allowing us insights into his inner life, the outer nature and the life beyond, Thomas has certainly helped make our existence on the face of the earth meaningful. His achievement in this regard amounts to a contribution towards the enrichment of the Romantic tradition in the present century.

82. *ETCP*., p. 233.
83. *ALNB*., p. 179.

CHAPTER III

'FACILE' ROMANTICISM OF WALTER de la MARE

The unobtrusive attempt made by Edward Thomas to evolve an adequate poetic strategy, consistent with the sane values of the tradition he inherited, had gone largely unnoticed for long. And presumably, the over-all poetic situation in the early years of the century was so sickening that the shock-treatment administered by the Modernists appeared very much called for. Yet surely, not all poets writing in English at the time were in need of shock-correctives. There were perhaps quite a few who could take care of themselves. Thomas Hardy, William Butler Yeats, Walter de la Mare, and D.H. Lawrence might have figured prominently among them. The solidity of the convictions of Thomas Hardy, which was more personal than Victorian, must have undermined his capacity for Romantic perceptions. In other words, we may say that the rigidity of the Hardyan character perhaps stifled the Romantic potentialities of his personality. The Romantic leanings of D.H. Lawrence were indeed pronounced. Yet the Romantic strain in him having defied intellectual control, thus denying itself a distinctive aspect of modernity, he too may have to be excluded from the scope of the present work.

The poetry of Walter de la Mare may deserve a special mention in the context, as the intellectual strain therein, particularly in its earlier phase, has perhaps been much too subtle. The attempts of his adult mind to get allied to the spiritual vision of the child have indeed allowed ample scope for misapprehension. But the quality of his imagination was not so angelic as some critics believed. A closer look at it might yield hints of a firm cerebral control. Though the influence of William Blake was writ large on the early poetry of de la Mare in the importance he attached to dreams and childhood visions, the latter's affinity was more to Blake's Songs of Experience than to those of Innocence. In other words, we may observe that he was certainly closer to the fallen state of man.

While Blake found Eternity shadowed in the productions of

time, de la Mare was prone to identify the shadows with the substance. In a sense he eliminated the distinction between the natural and the supernatural. The positivists were naturally sore about this tendency, as it ran counter to their own endeavour to naturalize the supernatural with the help of science. Yet some of us cannot possibly believe that all traces of magic and mystery have been blotted out from the surface of the earth by science. For de la Mare, the world we live in is a world of infinite possibilities. In the words of W.H. Auden, his view is that "our eyes and ears do not lie to us, but do not, perhaps cannot, tell us the whole truth, and those who deny this, end up by actually narrowing their visions."[1] It is as much as to say that de la Mare takes the physical aspect seriously enough, but regards it only as part of a more inclusive reality. The sensory perception, thus, prepares the way for an extrasensory perception of deeper significance, as it does for Wordsworth. Such an attitude, however, betrays a partiality for the latter achievement, as it helps in the apprehension of the uncommon aspects of common objects.

Coleridge's effort to bring about a suspension of disbelief while recording his apprehension of the supernatural exemplified the role of the conscious mind in the process of poetry-making. The moralizing he attempted also constituted a similar effort. The concreteness and precision achieved in his word-pictures (including those of the dream-product, "Kubla Khan") resulted, again, from conscious cerebration.

De la Mare seems to have been inspired in a large measure by Coleridge's examples, though he did not share the latter's moralistic zeal. Coleridge's positing pleasure as the immediate object of a poem was, however, congenial to him. He had, as one of his poems alludes to, two deep clear eyes.[2] A deep and clear physical vision resulted from the efficient functioning of his conscious mind and entailed a bid to achieve a Unified Sensibility in which

Heart bids mind
Wonder:
Mind bids heart
Ponder.[3]

---

1. Auden, W.H. (ed.), *A Choice of de la Mare's Verse* (London: Faber and Faber, 1963), Introduction, p. 21. Henceforth referred to as *A Choice*.
2. *Ibid.*, p. 142.
3. *Ibid.*

Coleridge's attempts at recording his apprehensions of the supernatural suggest that he had taken it in all seriousness. The sublime moralizing function that he assigned to supernatural agencies also implies a faith in their existence probably shared by the poet and his contemporaries.

De la Mare's attitude towards supernatural presences was no less serious, though he could not be sure enough of their divinity. They did not exist to provide metaphors for his poetry, as they perhaps did for Yeats'. He did not have any moralistic ends either for them to serve. Their presence in de la Mare appears to be an end in itself. Its apprehension, however, seems to help in heightening our awareness through sensitizing and refining our sensibility. Maybe, de la Mare's use of the Romantic evil and terror has left much to be desired, as pointed by David Perkins.[4] But we would do well to remember that de la Mare was looking at the supernatural from a child's angle. The great Romantics who made better use of it were living in a different environment. The modern man's extreme self-consciousness, scientific obsessions, and sceptical bent of mind have made it nearly impossible for him to give himself up to a belief in supernatural presences. And, except for his earnest bid to gain the visionary intensity of childhood, de la Mare himself might have failed to give credence to them.

W.H. Auden has pointed out how the gentleness of the English landscape can sometimes tempt those who love it into "writing genteely". According to him, de la Mare was protected from the temptation by a "conviction that what our senses perceive of the world about us is not all there is to know" and, by a "sense of the powers of evil."[5] As a possible third factor, we may mention his acute self-consciousness which apparently evoked in him a sense of isolation and otherness when he found himself among the presences of nature.

The rabbit in his burrow keeps
No guarded watch, in peace he sleeps;
The wolf that howls in challenging night
Cowers to her lair at morning light;
The simplest bird entwines a nest
Where she may lean her lovely breast,

4. *HMP.*, pp. 182-183.
5. *A Choice.*, p. 21.

Couched in the silence of the bough :
But thou, O man, what rest hast thou?[6]

And elsewhere he says:

... every thorn,
And weed, and flower,
And every time-worn stone
A challenge cries on the trespasser:
Beware!
Thou art alone![7]

De la Mare's world has been called 'a world of one', as there are no relationships in it.[8] The modern man's sense of alienation from nature and lack of other abiding attachments might account for the tendency. Possibly, the absence of didactic intentions or moralistic preoccupations on the part of de la Mare also influenced it to some extent.

An overwhelming sense of isolation promoted by a tormenting self-consciousness has often found eloquent expression in de la Mare:

Oh, why make such ado —
This fretful care and trouble?
The sun in noonday's blue
Pours radiance on earth's bubble
What though the heart-strings crack,
And sorrow bid thee languish,
Dew falls; the night comes back;
Sleep, and forget thine anguish.
Oh, why in shadow haunt?
Shines not the evening flower?
Hark, how the sweet birds chaunt,
The lovely light their bower.
Water her music makes,
Lulling even these to slubber;
And only dead of darkness wakes
Stars without number.[9]

De la Mare evidently believed that children were refreshingly

6. *Ibid*., p. 153.
7. *Ibid*., p. 102.
8. Cox, C.B., Dyson, A.E., *Modern Poetry: Studies in Practical Criticism* [London: Edward Arnold (Publishers) Ltd., 1963], p. 42. Henceforth referred to as Cox & Dyson.
9. de la Mare, Walter, *Collected Poems* (London: Faber and Faber, 1942, Eleventh Impression, September 1954), p. 134. Henceforth referred to as *WDCP*.

free from self-consciousness, and were thus capable of maintaining a wholesome link with both natural and supernatural presences. His desire to look at the world from a child's angle represents a typically Romantic yearning to organize innocence. He also believed that children shared that awareness with lesser animals and supernatural presences. Though Wordsworth also credited children with an identical capability, he would not perhaps have approved of the idea of treating man as inferior to nearly all sub-human creatures. Having sought to partake of the visionary intensity of childhood as a possible antidote to his disquieting self-consciousness, de la Mare would seem to have succeeded in his bid to a remarkable extent. If an achievement of this order failed to inspire in him a Wordsworthian faith in himself and human potentialities, his self-conscious mind, again, is largely to blame. The ease and grace with which his perceptions found expression have been undoubtedly admirable. Coleridge's attempts in this regard look rather laboured, in comparison.

The skill with which de la Mare has managed to evoke an awareness of supernatural presences in his celebrated poem, "The Listeners" has won universal acclaim. The imagery of the poem reveals a rare keenness and precision. Of course, it is all meant only as a means to promote an awareness of the supernatural. To convince us of the quality of light by means of a description of darkness is indeed no mean achievement.

The concreteness and precision achieved in the process does not, however, spring from a desire on the part of de la Mare to be faithful to natural phenomena. His descriptions in most cases had other ends to serve. In "The Phantom", for example, he says:

> Wilt thou never come again,
> Beauteous one?
> Yet the woods are green and dim,
> Yet the bird's deluding cry
> Echoes in the hollow sky,
> Yet the falling waters brim
> The clear pool which thou wast fain
> To paint thy lovely cheek upon,
> Beauteous one![10]

The woods, birds, echoes and waters appearing here would hardly have mattered to him, unless they helped in lending credibility

10. *Ibid.*, p. 277.

to the Beauteous one. His Keatsian flair for painting sensuous word-pictures out of the most-unpromising material is revealed by the portraits of idleness[11] and Miss Apathy.[12]

Assuming the intensity of a child in spiritual perceptions is obviously an achievement of the faculty of imagination. The adult intellect of the poet must have remained intact in the process to play its own part in recording such perceptions.

De la Mare's dream-imagery also abounds in concrete particulars. A comparison between his "I Dream of a Place" and W.B. Yeats' "Lake Isle of Innisfree" may be interesting.

"THE LAKE ISLE OF INNISFREE"

I WILL arise and go now, and go to Innisfree,
And a small cabin build there, of clay and wattles made:
Nine bean-rows will I have there, a hive for the
    honey-bee,
And live alone in the bee-loud glade.

And I shall have some peace there, for peace comes
    dropping slow,
Dropping from the veils of the morning to where
    the cricket sings,
There midnight's all a glimmer, and noon a purple glow,
And evening full of the linnet's wings.

I will arise and go now, for always night and day
I hear lake water lapping with low sounds by the shore;
While I stand on the roadway, or on the pavements grey,
I hear it in the deep heart's core.[13]

"I DREAM OF A PLACE"

I dream of a place where I long to live always:
Green hills, shallow sand dunes, and nearing the sea;
The house is of stone; there are twelve lattice windows,
And a door, with a keyhole – though lost is the key.

Thick-thatched is the roof; it has low, white-washed
    chimneys
Where doves preen their wings, and coo, Please, love:
    love me!

There martins are flitting: the sun shines; the moon shines;
Drifts of bright flowers are adrone with the bee;

11. *A Choice.*, pp. 60-61.
12. *Ibid.*, pp. 62-73.
13. Jeffares, A. Norman, *W.B. Yeats: Selected Poetry* (Pan Books in association with Macmillan, London, reprint 1976), p. 16.

And a wonderful music of bird-song at daybreak
Wells up from the bosom of every tree.

A brook of clear water encircles the garden,
With kingcups, and cress, and the white *fleur de lys* –

Moorhens and dabchicks; the wild duck at evening
Wing away to the sun, in the shape of a V;

And the night shows the stars, shining in at the windows,
Brings nearer the far-away sigh of the sea.

Oh, the quiet, the green of the grass, the grey willows,
The light, and the shine, and the air sweet and free!–

That dream of a place where I long to live always:
Low hills, shallow sand dunes – at peace there to be![14]

Each of these poems presents for the poet a land of his heart's desire. But, ironically enough, the 'dream-land' of the latter poem looks more concrete and true than the Lake Isle. We find more of cliches in Yeats' poem. Though it is more picturesque than most other poems of Yeats, the honey-bee, cricket and linnet seem to form a conventional Romantic landscape. And, in spite of the nine bean-rows, the picture looks rather vague, sentimental and undistinguished, unless we tend to read esoteric significances into it. We must, however, concede that the poem has its own appeal.

De la Mare's poem, on the contrary, is replete with sensuous details. Its imagistic precision speaks of the influence of an alert intellect. Of course, we are aware that Yeats' strength lay elsewhere.

In its intensity, the 'dream-experience' of de la Mare seems akin to the experience of an inspired moment, when the unconscious level of the mind becomes active. The product of such a dream may be hardly distinct from that of imagination. We wonder whether 'dream' is a word chosen by the poet to name his experience of imaginative intensity. The presence of a lively consciousness to record the experiences of such exalted dream-like states without losing sight of actualities perhaps renders his 'dream-images' as concrete as any other.

Presumably, de la Mare's endeavour to develop in himself the spiritual vision of a child and his belief in the special awareness shared by children and lesser animals rendered his attitude towards sub-human creatures unusually warm. Yet, his portraits of them,

---

14. *A Choice*, pp. 30-31.

while revealing an imaginative intensity, are too concrete to be sentimental.

"Jenny Wren" may serve as an example:

Of all the birds that rove and sing,
    Near dwellings made for men,
None is so nimble, feat, and trim
    As Jenny Wren.

With pin-point bill, and tail a-cock,
    So wildly shrill she cries,
The echoes on their roof-tree knock
    And fill the skies.

Never was sweeter seraph hid
    Within so small a house –
A tiny, inch-long, eager, ardent,
    feathered mouse.[15]

His poignant awareness of the callous attitude of adult humans towards lesser animals is admirably embodied in "Reserved":

... 'I was thinking, Mother, of that poor old horse
    They killed the other day;
Nannie says it was only a bag of bones,
    But I hated it taken away.'

'Of course, sweet; but now the baker's man
Will soon have a nice new motor van.'

'Yes, Mother. But when on our walk a squirrel
    Crept up to my thumb to be fed,
She shoo'd it away with her gloves-like this!
    They ought to be shot, she said.'
'She may have been reading, darling, that
    Squirrels are only a kind of rat.'

'Goldfinches, Mother, owls and mice,
    Tom-tits and bunnies and jays –
Everything in my picture-books
    Will soon be gone, she says.'

'You see, my precious, so many creatures,
    Though exquisitely made,
Steal, or are dirty and dangerous,
    Or else they are bad for Trade.'[16]

The poem also suggested de la Mare's aversion to scientific education and the achievements of science, though it was not perhaps as overwhelming as that of D.H. Lawrence.

15. *Ibid.*, p. 38.
16. *WDCP.*, p. 50.

The progress of de la Mare's poetry was apparently from the impersonal to the personal, though his earlier poetry was not wholly devoid of the personal element. Having played "Hide and Seek" for quite some time –

Hide and Seek, says the Wind,
In the shade of the woods;

Hide and seek, says the Moon,
To the hazel buds;

Hide and Seek, says the Cloud,
Star on to star;

Hide and Seek, says the Wave
At the harbour bar;

Hide and Seek, say I,
To myself, and step

Out of the dream of Wake
Into the dream of Sleep.[17]

– he seems to have grown weary of the game. "The Veil" expresses his impatience with disguises:

... beneath that veil
A happy mouth no doubt can make
English sound sweeter for its sake.
But then, why muffle in, like this,
What every blossomy wind would kiss?
Why in that little night disguise
A daylight face, those starry eyes?[18]

The questions obviously are directed at the poet's Muse. The poem also appears to testify to the presence of the personal element in the "escapist" poetry of his early years:

The tip of a small nose I see,
And two red lips, set curiously
Like twin-born cherries on one stem,
And yet she has netted even them.[19]

It was indeed quite some time before the veil wholly disappeared. The poetry, then, gained a new look, as the elvish aspects of the earlier work gave way to a new robustness. And it often had a stunning impact:

---

17. de la Mare, Walter, *Collected Rhymes and Verses* (London: Faber and Faber, 1944, reprint 1975), p. 250.
18. *WDCP*., p. 120.
19. *Ibid*., p. 119.

What, do you suppose, we're in this world for,
    sweetheart?
What – in this haunted, crazy, beautiful cage –
Keeps so many, like ourselves, poor pining human
    creatures,
As if from some assured, yet withholden heritage?
Keeps us lamenting beneath all our happy laughter,
Silence, dreams, hope for what may not come after,
While life wastes and withers, as it has for all mortals,
    Age on to age, on to age?[20]

This new poetry brought de la Mare closer to the Modernists. No doubt, even earlier his understanding of the adult-world had been hardly different from theirs. But this approach then had appeared rather feminine, owing largely to a lack of proper appreciation of the latent intellectuality of his work. His sense of isolation and alienation and want of belief in himself and human potentialities were symptomatic of an abiding self-consciousness characteristically modern.[21] The laughter-sense much valued by the Modernists was also well within his range. S.C. Duffin has elaborated it.[22] It was perhaps de la Mare's self-consciousness that gave him the detachment needed to poke fun at his own self as "The Dunce" exemplifies:

Why does he still keep ticking?
    Why does his round white face
Stare at me over the books and ink,
    And mock at my disgrace?
Why does that thrush call, 'Dunce, dunce, dunce!?'
    Why does that bluebottle buzz?
Why does the sun so silent shine? –
    And what do I care if it does?[23]

It is an ability which the earlier Romantics (except perhaps, Keats) badly lacked. Wordsworth, for instance, was inclined to be too sure of himself and the divinity manifested through the presences of nature to entertain such impressions.

In its later phase de la Mare's poetry turned into a vehicle of thought rather than pleasure to suit the taste of the moderns and revelled in stark realism and melancholy.

---

20. *A Choice.*, p. 141.
21. See *HMP.*, p. 185. David Perkins has drawn attention to the modernity of de la Mare's self-consciousness.
22. Duffin, Henry Charles, *Walter de la Mare: A Study of His Poetry* (London: Sidwick and Jackbon Limited, 1949), pp. 143-161.
23. *A Choice.*, p. 60.

A note of melancholy was, in fact, characteristic of de la Mare's poetry, though it became explicit only in his later phase. While commenting on it, Edward Thomas remarked that such a tendency could not surprise any one who realised how few of any man's hours could after all be given to reverie and how difficult and unlovely must appear the broken, scattered, and jangled things outside that province.[24] Thomas' use of the word 'reverie' in the context does not seem altogether happy, particularly when we remember the affinity between de la Mare's dream-experiences and imaginative perceptions. The choice of the word perhaps suggests Thomas' partiality for the earth, his own susceptibility to the skyward urge notwithstanding. In any case, the notion that de la Mare's melancholic tendency was the off-shoot of his reveries may not be sustainable. It was perhaps the other way round.

Edward Thomas, however, described de la Mare's poetry as "the most feather-weight original poetry of our time" and found the best of Coleridge and Poe in it.[25] The compliment seems handsome enough. Perhaps, it also makes amends for his use of the word 'reverie' earlier. De la Mare's contribution towards advancing the Coleridgean strain of Romanticism by way of promoting an awareness of the unknown modes of being has no doubt been significant. The perception of the supernatural recorded in his poetry seems to have a ring of authenticity about it, though skilful design perhaps accounts for a part of that achievement.

If the early work of de la Mare contained too much of poetry as observed by Edward Thomas,[26] the later work perhaps revealed too little of it. His *Winged Chariot,* [27] for instance, tended to be earth-bound, thanks largely to its immense thought-content. It is not, however, to belittle either the significance of the accompanying emotions or the excellence of the native brand of symbolism which got perfected through his deft and delicate handling.

It is perhaps to the credit of Walter de la Mare as a man, that the shattering experiences which cast a dismal shadow on his poetry, did not wholly shake his faith in a spirit that guided him,

24. *ALNB.*, p. 102.
25. *Ibid.*, p. 102.
26. *Ibid.*, p. 102.
27. *A Choice*, pp. 163-217.

though the massive Hopkinsian faith echoed earlier in "The Scribe"[28] eluded him:

> Age shall not daunt me, nor sorrow for youth that is gone
> If thou lead on before me;
> If thy voice in the darkness and bleak of that final night
> Still its enchantment weave o'er me.
> Thou hauntest the stealing shadow of rock and tree;
> Hovering on wings invisible smilest at me;
> Fannest the secret scent of the moth-hung flower;
> Making of musky eve thy slumber-bower.[29]

That strange spirit, to be sure, had an aspect of divinity about it. It must naturally have helped the poet to keep his own spirits afloat, while he was caught in the flood of disgusting and debilitating emotions evidenced in his poetry.

---

28. *WDCP.*, p. 173.
29. *Ibid.*, p. 311.

CHAPTER IV

EARLY POETRY OF W.B. YEATS

William Butler Yeats has a distinct place among the Romantic poets of the twentieth century, as he typifies in himself the transformation in Romanticism witnessed in the modern context. And unlike some of his distinguished contemporaries, he did not fight shy of acknowledging his debt to the Romantic tradition.

There has indeed been universal agreement among critics on the Romantic affinities of Yeats, though many of them have found Romanticism only in his earlier poems. A note of dissent in this regard has, however, been struck by a few. Allen Tate, for example, says:

> While it is true that Yeats, like every poet in English since the end of the eighteenth century, began with a romantic use of language in the early poems, he ended up very differently, and he is no more to be fixed as a romantic than Shakespeare as a Senecan because he wrote passages of Senecan rhetoric. If one of the historic marks of romanticism is the division between sensibility and intellect, Yeats' career may be seen as unromantic (I do not know the opposite term) because he closed the gap. His critics would, then be the romantics ... Yeats had a more inclusive mind than any of his critics has had.[1]

It may not be difficult to appreciate the generous intention that prompted Allen Tate to take such a stand in regard to Yeats' affinities. The tenor of his argument suggests an exalted opinion of Yeats and his attempt perhaps is to place the latter on a par with Shakespeare. And he was apparently irked by the tendency of critics (represented by Edmund Wilson[2] and Louis MacNeice[3]) to brand

---

1. Tate, Allen, "Yeats' Romanticism: Notes and Suggestions", *The Southern Review*, VII, 3 (Winter, 1942), and *On the Limits of Poetry* (The Swallow Press and William Morrow and Company, 1948). Reprinted in *The Permanence of Yeats* (ed.) James Hall and Martin Steinmann, Collier Books, New York, 1961, p. 98. Henceforth referred to as *The Permanence of Yeats*.
2. Wilson, Edmund, "W.B. Yeats", *Axel's Castle* (New York: Charles Scribner's Sons, 1931), pp. 26-64.
3. MacNeice, Louis, *The Poetry of W.B. Yeats* (Oxford University Press, 1941). Henceforth cited as MacNeice, Louis.

Yeats as an escapist. In any case, the vehemence with which Harold Bloom has reacted to Tate's comments appears uncalled for.[4]

Allen Tate's view may have to be seen in the context of the anti-romantic upsurge of the present century. The distortion in the conception of romanticism occasioned by the abuse of romantic modes by the Decadents and the common run of the Georgians may account for it. The gap between sensibility and intellect referred to by Tate was certainly not characteristic of the works of the great Romantics. While Yeats' contribution towards closing that gap has doubtless been commendable, it may not make his career unromantic as maintained by Tate. The aggressive bid made by the Modernists in the same direction was anticipated by Yeats, when he insisted on blood, imagination, and intellect running together.

While Yeats himself has never expressed any doubt regarding his affiliation to the Romantic tradition, it is perhaps odd that his critics should find it a bone of contention. In fact, we have reason to believe that he nearly gloried in the thought of being reckoned as a Romantic:

> We were the last romantics -- chose for theme
> Traditional sanctity and loveliness;
> Whatever's written in what poets name
> The book of the people; whatever most can bless
> The mind of man or elevate a rhyme;
> But all is changed, that high horse riderless,
> Though mounted in that saddle Homer rode
> Where the swan drifts upon a darkening flood.[5]

It was in the mood of depression that prevailed in the last lap of his life that Yeats said this. The lump in his throat was perhaps slightly relieved by the memory of his proud past as a Romantic.

The credit for introducing Yeats to the Romantic tradition should go to his father. He impressed on the poet that 'getting on' in the world should not be the primary concern of a gentleman. The young William was also made to share his father's partiality for the dramatic form, though he found it rather cumbersome for his purposes.

---

4. See Bloom, Harold, "Yeats and the Romantics", *Modern Poetry: Essays in Criticism* (ed.). John Hollander (Oxford University Press, 1968), p. 502.
5. Yeats, W.B., "Coole Park and Ballylee, 1931", *The Collected Poems of W.B. Yeats* (London: Macmillan and Co. Limited, 1952), p. 276. Henceforth cited as *WBYCP*.

Yeats's early dramatic poems, written under the influence of Spenser, Shelley, Rossetti and Morris, reveal great relish for the distant and the dreamy. The fairy-world also enchanted him. Yet, Yeats was too complex a person to find lasting peace in such worlds. His interest in packing the fairy-world of "The Wanderings of Oisin" with secret significances, as he confessed in a letter to Katharine Tynan,[6] provides a hint of that complexity. He was able to cure himself of his escapist tendencies soon enough. His feeling for the past of Ireland, however, remained intact all through his life. The intensity of it perhaps had certain unwholesome implications. The great Romantics were seldom guilty of such infatuations. As pointed out by Graham Hough, they had visited history as spectators, intelligent tourists, and not as exiles from a lost paradise.[7] The obsession is obviously symptomatic of Yeats' lack of humanistic concerns, and want of sympathy with the dominant trends of his times.

Walter Pater had obviously wielded considerable influence on the early Yeats. What J.B. Yeats had told his son on the function of art was largely in consonance with the views of Pater. Of course, as has been pointed out by Frank Kermode, Pater's conception of art was a glaring perversion of the original Romantic view.[8] Surely, the great Romantics had not conceived of a divorce between art and life. Yet, thanks to a misreading of the Keatsian aesthetic, Pater stressed the intensity of emotions and the purity of art. Oscar Wilde and the Decadents drew inspiration from his thesis. Though Yeats was much moved by the plight of the Decadents, judging from his feeling references to them as poets of the Tragic Generation, their influence on his poetry was perhaps only marginal. For he was too hard to indulge himself in a feeling of defeat. He had the inner potential to make a victory of any defeat. As noted by Pinto, their devotion to their art was something that he admired and absorbed in himself.[9] His acquaintance with the French symbolists was

6. Tynan, Katharine, *The Middle Years*, p. 47, quoted in Jeffares, A. Norman, *W.B. Yeats: Man and Poet* (London: Routledge & Kegan Paul Ltd., 1949), p. 46.
7. Hough, Graham, *The Last Romantics* (London: Methuen, New York: Barnes & Noble, 1947), Introduction, pp. XIV-XV. Henceforth cited as *The Last Romantics*.
8. Kermode, Frank, *Romantic Image* (London: Routledge and Kegan Paul, 1957, Paperback 1961), p. 12. Henceforth cited as *Romantic Image*.
9. Pinto, Vivian de Sola, *Crisis in English Poetry, 1880-1940* (London: Hutchinson University Library, 1951. Reprint 1967). p. 89. Henceforth cited as *Pinto*.

helped by the translations of Arthur Symons from French. The French influence apparently intensified his aversion to life. The conception of art as an escape from life, however, did not impress him long. He rose in revolt against that conception and asserted that art was what we tried to escape from. That new thesis must have helped him to rededicate himself to his art without losing sight of the facts of life.

In his early phase Yeats had produced a good number of poems scrupulously adhering to the Romantic modes. But his emphasis on the formal aspects of Romanticism at that stage was to the extent of rendering the Romantic strain in his poetry pitifully thin. Love to him was then a vague, easy and unfelt emotion, yielding little evidence of any cerebral activity. His Rossettian obsession with the theme of love was obviously not backed up by the Rossettian experience as a lover. The note of melancholy in the poems of that phase was very nearly a fashion. The Romantic epithets and situations borrowed from his distinguished predecessors did not mend matters. It was his varied experience as a lover and man of action, as well as his abiding interest in the hitherto unexplored Irish mythology and legends that remedied the situation to a large extent. The former provided him with original feelings and the latter with fresh and lively symbols. His poetry thus gained a new verve. All the same, it also gave scope for a new obscurity, thanks to his deliberate bid to pack multiple significances into his poems. When he addresses the Rose in "To the Rose upon the Rood of Timc"[10] for instance, identifying it with a perplexing variety of things including Ireland, his patriotic readers could hardly have guessed that it had anything to do with their beloved land. The cold realities of the present seem to hold no charms for him. His interest in the poor, foolish things of the present has an air of condescension. His love for them appears to be in proportion to their capacity to manifest Eternal Beauty, as the Rose does.

While tracing the influence of Shelley on the early poetry of Yeats, George Bornstein has pointed out how Yeats' flight from reality in his imitations of Shelley in the eighties matured into a flight from the everyday world toward an ideal one of Intellectual

10. *WBYCP.*, p. 35.

Beauty. Bornstein has maintained that Shelley's poetry, in Yeats interpretation, gave both authority and encouragement to his effort to move "upwards out of life" rather than "downwards upon life."[11]

The mention of the rood in the title of the present poem is apt to arouse the curiosity of Yeats' Christian readers, though they are not likely to be particularly impressed by the contents of the poem. The poetic use Yeats made of religious symbols was obviously of little significance, as he lacked faith in Christianity. Indeed he was too dynamic and sceptical to hold fast to the concepts of a conventional religion. The Rose here may well be identified with Virgin Mary or the Muse, though neither of them apparently mattered much in Yeats' scheme of things.

Yeats' request to the Rose not to come too close to him may yield to varying interpretations.

According to George Bornstein, if Yeats were to be absorbed by the Rose, he could no longer sing of lesser subjects, for "he would then be using a tongue men do not know".[12] The view amounts to crediting Yeats with an abiding concern for the problems of humanity, and may be contrary to facts as we have known them.

Harold Bloom says that the poet here demonstrates the "struggle between his hunger for La Belle Dame's faery food, and a skeptical fear of the natural starvation the hunger brings as it did to Keats' quester." He calls it a characteristic pattern of vacillation. And, according to him, "a little space" is needed "for the natural odour of less occult roses to pervade."[13] Such an interpretation might be unwarranted in the context. The Rose-breath referred to could after all be the breath of the same Rose and not necessarily of lesser ones. Of course, we are aware that Yeats was capable of looking for lesser roses, while professing a single-minded passion for a greater one. But the vacillation in the present case would seem suggestive of a strength rather than a weakness. Perhaps it speaks of the robust commonsense that guarded Yeats against being swept off his feet in all weathers. It is perhaps this strain of toughness that makes him

11. Bornstein, George, *Yeats and Shelley* (Chicago and London: University of Chicago Press, 1970), p. 45. Henceforth cited as *Yeats and Shelley*.

12. *Ibid*., p. 53.

13. Bloom, Harold, *Yeats* (London, Oxford, New York: Oxford University Press, 1970), p. 111. Henceforth cited as *Yeats*.

a Romantic with a difference. A part of his being was capable of looking askance at a thing believed ardently by another part. We may associate this toughness with a scepticism characteristically modern. It is apparently the same strain of toughness that enabled him to be a man of action while being a Romantic at another level. His flair for self-dramatization and wearing masks may also be traced to it. This seeming weakness obviously helped in the invigoration of his poetry, too, through detecting its foibles and devising the means of remedying them without detriment to its essential affiliation to the Romantic tradition.

George Bornstein has pointed out how "To the Rose upon the Rood of Time" falls short of M.H. Abrams' idea of a greater Romantic lyric.[14] He rightly finds it lacking in "mental action". For, while invoking the rose to come near him, he refuses to visualize a union with it and himself stands in the way of the poem's progression towards becoming a greater Romantic lyric with the "out-in-out" pattern referred to by Abrams.[15] If the failure involved could be traced to the early Yeats' lack of proper maturity as a Romantic poet, a wholesome awareness of the depressing realities concerning his relations with Maud Gonne might also have come in the way of a more satisfactory treatment of the theme. The poem also suggests that Yeats was probably aware of the risk of his losing the scent of the Rose and ceasing to be a singer of songs, in the event of Maud Gonne's getting too close to him. Yet he would fain have thrown all caution to the winds and married her at any cost, if only she had nodded in his favour. But it was not to be. Perhaps, we must give Maud Gonne the credit for a true understanding of Yeats' nature as of the importance of his contribution as a poet. A marriage with her might well have proved a calamity, as it was likely to result in the drying up of a perennial source of poetic inspiration.

The modification made by Yeats in the Shelleyan conception of Intellectual Beauty seems significant. The fact that Maud Gonne was left suffering in the midst of others could probably have made him imagine Intellectual Beauty as a thing suffering with other men

14. Bornstein, George, *TR.*, p. 72.

15. Abrams, M.H., "Structure and Style in the Greater Romantic Lyric," *From Sensibility to Romanticism*, (ed.) Frederick W. Hilles and Harold Bloom (New York: Oxford University Press, 1965), p. 528.

and not as something pursued from afar and symbolized by the Shelleyan star. Yeats' choice of the earthly rose in preference to the heavenly star may also be ascribed to the same fact.

Having taken to the lyrical form without heeding the warning of his father, Yeats was hard put to the task of finding some ways of curbing his emotional and egotistical tendencies. He tries to regulate his emotions through singling out certain aspects of his personality and giving them names and tongues. It was thus symbolic figures like Hanrahan, Michael Robartes and Aedh came into being. The way in which Yeats could leave them out later on, proved that they had no life of their own. He also tried certain masks with a similar end in view.

The assumption of poetic masks by Yeats has rendered his sincerity suspect to many, as it gave scope for contradictory assertions. But Yeats, as noted by David Perkins, obviously felt that "the self always involves the anti-self, and thus contradictory assertions may be equally sincere" in such cases.[16] J.B. Beer has assumed, on the authority of Keats' letters, that Keats himself would gradually have come to mask his identity as Yeats did for saving it from submersion. He says:

> The adoption of a 'mask' in such circumstances is not an act of hypocrisy: it is simply the adoption of one interpretation of the universe as a framework for art, the poet accepting the structuring of vision with which for the time being he will look at the world, as continuing to live within these self-imposed limitations, until he finds that he has worked his way beyond them.[17]

It is akin to T.S. Eliot's attempt at depersonalization, as it helps the poet to detach himself from the subject. The Yeatsian talent revealed in the context may differ from Keats' negative capability not so much in kind as in degree.

Yeats had a low opinion of Wordsworth because of the latter's inability to wear a mask and imagine himself as different from what he was. He evidently regarded the wearing of masks as an exercise in self-discipline. Yet surely, not all people could be expected to

---

16. Perkins, David, *Wordsworth and the Poetry of Sincerity* (Cambridge, Massachusetts: The Belknap Press of Harvard University Press, 1964), p. 6. Henceforth cited as *Wordsworth and the Poetry of Sincerity*.
17. Beer, J.B., *Coleridge the Visionary* (London: Chatto & Windus, 1970), p. 24. Henceforth cited as *Coleridge the Visionary*.

have a fancy for it. Moreover, Wordsworth obviously lacked the Yeatsian flair for self-dramatization. He set greater store by sincerity and spontaneity as the terms were understood in the common parlance.[18]

While the impact of the French symbolists promoted purity in Yeats' poetry, the fresh symbols drawn from the Irish folklore, mythology and legends enlivened it. But the zest for the occult lore, that suggested a bid on the part of Yeats to make up what had been missed because of his lack of formal education, has done more harm than good to his poetry.

The influence of Maud Gonne on the poetry of Yeats was perhaps unique in certain respects. For one thing, it was refreshingly free from sensuality. That gap, however, was sought to be filled by Yeats' experiences with Diana Vernon. The credit for bringing the Yeatsian Romanticism down to earth was partly hers, too.

Yeats' romantic thoughts involving Maud Gonne thus revealed a sort of sublimity. The factors that lifted it out of the common plane of vulgarity had obviously rendered his personal life pathetic for long.

Yeats' attitude towards nature also had something unique about it. He did not care for the physical aspects of things even as much as William Blake, not to mention either Wordsworth or Walter de la Mare. The symbolist preoccupation need not, after all, have obscured his physical vision as much as it did. His poor eyesight had perhaps something to do with it.

Yeats' early poems often present a sense of dichotomy between man and nature. David Daiches has commended the manner in which he implicitly criticized the "falsity and sentimentality" of a conventional Romantic attitude towards nature.[19] He cites "The Sad Shepherd"[20] and "The Madness of King Goll"[21] as instances from Yeats' early poetry. But it seems doubtful whether Yeats'

---

18. A recent tendency has been to regard the Wordsworthian sincerity itself as a mask.

19. Daiches, David, "The Earlier Poems: Some Themes and Patterns", *In Excited Reverie : A Centenary Tribute to W.B. Yeats, 1865-1939,* (ed.) A.N. Jeffares and K.G.W. Cross (Macmillan, 1965), p. 55. Henceforth cited as *In Excited Reverie*.

20. *WBYCP*., p. 9.

21. *Ibid*., pp. 17-20.

intention in presenting such a sense of dichotomy could be construed to mean so much. For we also find him using nature for mood-creation in certain other poems of the same period, as noted by Daiches himself.[22] "Ephemera"[23] and "Falling of the Leaves"[24] provide examples. It is likely that Yeats found the sense of dichotomy more fruitful poetically. Yeats, as acknowledged by Daiches again, always evinced a special interest in presenting contraries, partly at least because of the influence of Blake.[25] "The Two Trees"[26], for instance, tells us of the Tree of Life and the Tree of Death, which are largely Blakean in conception, though the impact of the Cabbalistic tree on the imagery cannot also be ruled out.

If Yeats got nearly lost in the superficialities of Romanticism in his early phase, it may be unfair to blame him overmuch for it. It perhaps marks an important stage of a poetic development that helped him to find his anchors. Yeats' endeavour at the stage obviously was not so much to give expression to his genuine feelings as to exercise a proper check on them. The influence of his father on him in this respect was certainly salutary, though it appeared to inhibit him initially. His Romanticism had to gain substance from his experiences. Those experiences also brought a new note of sincerity to his poetry. That note, however, was to remain implicit for some time, thanks largely to the subtlety and complexity of his symbolist method. The delight that he soon found in walking naked did much to impart a new authenticity to his poetry. Though the note of sincerity in Yeats' poetry once again got obscured in his later phase, when he felt constrained to wear a new series of masks, it remained an essential aspect of his poetry all through his life.

While Yeats'achievements as a man of action and his interest in nakedness might create an impression of his having turned a realist, the realities he valued were distinct from those affecting the common run of men and women.

C.H. Sisson probably means as much when he says that "Yeats never entirely moves into a world which is continuous with the

---

22. *In Excited Reverie*, p. 50.
23. *WBYCP*., pp. 16-17.
24. *Ibid*., p. 16.
25. *In Excited Reverie*., p. 50.
26. *Ibid*., p. 55.

world of prose."[27] If Yeats looked for reality, it was "on his own terms", as mentioned by Arthur Mizener, and the main requirement of these terms was intensity of feeling.[28] His early inclination to define truth as "the dramatically appropriate" mentioned by Vivienne Koch remained with him throughout.[29]

F.R. Leavis was one of the earliest critics to point out how Yeats' plays "repudiate the actual world as essentially as his incantatory lyrics and his esoteric prose repudiate it."[30] His political stances were also far from realistic. David Perkins has rightly called his political activity "a kind of wooing".[31] And, when it failed to yield the desired fruit, his pathetic attachment to the past must have got reinforced. The realities he cherished could be perceived only in his moments of heightened awareness. We may call them higher realities. This attitude evidently forms the core of the Yeatsian Romanticism.

If it was Ireland that rescued Yeats from imitative Romanticism, the credit for modernizing his poetic technique should be entirely his own. But his remark that "by 1900 everybody got down off his stilts"[32] hints at a general awakening in the matter. Had it been real, the revolution in poetic technique attempted by the Modernists later on might have become wholly superfluous. We may safely assume that the new awakening was largely Yeats' own. He realized that "we lost in personality, in our delight in the whole man", partly from "lack of that spoken word which knits us to the normal man."[33] Possibly, he also repented having ignored his father's sane counsel that poetry had to be an "idealization of speech".[34] The sentimentality that afflicted his early verse also disturbed him. He knew that it had sprung from lack of thought. His assumption that Donne could be

27. Sisson, C.H., *English Poetry, 1900-1950: An Assessment* (London: Rupert Hart-Davis, 1971), p. 167.

28. Mizener, Arthur, "The Romanticism of W.B. Yeats", *The Southern Review*, VII, 3 (Winter 1942), reprinted in *The Permanence of Yeats*, p. 128.

29. Koch, Vivienne, *W.B. Yeats : The Tragic Phase* (London: Routledge & Kegan Paul Ltd., 1951), Introduction, p. 25. Henceforth cited as *The Tragic Phase*.

30. Leavis, F.R., *New Bearings*, p. 38.

31. Perkins, David, *HMP*., p. 572.

32. Yeats, W.B., *OBMV*., Introduction, p. XI.

33. Quoted in *New Bearings*., p. 47.

34. Perkins, David, *HMP*., p. 568.

devoid of such sentimental sensuality "because he was being permitted to say what he pleased" seems, despite a severe approximation, suggestive of much regarding his own work, both earlier and later.[35] Yet, for the time being, he successfully shook off all constraints on his poetic expression and began to speak with a wholesome integrity like a free, full man.

The conventional Romantic features that Yeats zealously clung to could be safely discarded, when his Romanticism acquired greater substance. What had happened was apparently an assertion of authenticity over strategy. Indeed we are aware how strategy regained an upperhand in Yeats' poetry in the concluding phase of his life. The manner in which the intensity of the emotions expressed in his poems remained intact in spite of it may be a unique aspect of the Yeatsian achievement.

35. Quoted in *The Last Romantics*, p. 208.

CHAPTER V

LATER POETRY OF W.B. YEATS

If the early Yeats committed himself to the Aesthetic conception of art, the later Yeats may be said to have proved that life could be made into art. The manner in which the concrete facts of life provided grist to his Romantic mill may allow scope for such an interpretation. The definition of Romantic poetry as poetry of experience, which offers a contrast to the poetry of meaning, may lend itself to such a view, though the emphasis of the poetry of experience is bound to be on the *inner* experience of the poet.[1] But the way Yeats looked at the realities of life and assimilated them into his poetry adds a new dimension to that definition. It is perhaps his seeming allegiance to the realities of life that made certain distinguished critics misconstrue his poetic affiliation. Yeats conception of reality, as we have noted earlier, had something singular about it. It may account for the static quality found in his poetry by L.C. Knights.[2] Knights has rightly traced it to the adoption of certain fixed attitudes in the face of experience. Having identified the main constituent of Yeats' reality, Arthur Mizener adds how Yeats insisted, in the teeth of evidence, that things are as the mind desires them.[3] The comment implies that the Yeatsian approach to realities was in itself Romantic.

In his earnest bid to bring poetry close to life, Yeats certainly helped bridge the gap between the actual and the ideal. George Bornstein has shown us how the Shelleyan Intellectual Vision of his early phase got replaced by an antinomial Vision of paired opposites.

---

1. *Vide* Langbaum, Robert, *The Poetry of Experience: The Dramatic Monologue in Modern Literary Tradition* (London: Chatto & Windus, 1972), pp. 232-233.
2. Knights, L.C., "Poetry and Social Criticism: The Work of W.B. Yeats (1941), *Explorations* (London: Chatto & Windus, 1951), reprinted in *Critics on Yeats: Readings in Literary Criticism*, ed., Raymond Cowell (London: George Allen and Unwin Ltd., 1971), p. 18. Henceforth cited as *Critics on Yeats*.
3. Mizener, Arthur, *The Parmanence of Yeats*, p. 114.

He says :

> Yeats no longer wanted to ascend to the Intellectual with the skylark, but to immerse himself in just that human world, the lusts of the market-place, which the skylark forsakes.[4]

In other words, the Yeatsian bid was to invigorate poetry by bringing it down to earth. Yet the transformation thus brought about in his poetry, involving the actual and the ideal, was perhaps a little more complex. For the actual in Yeats, as we saw it, had some aspects of the ideal about it. We may observe that the Yeatsian brand of realism was Romanticism in a new garb. Romanticism in his hands may be said to have absorbed certain aspects of realism without yielding up its intrinsic traits. His visionary absorption was perhaps both a cause and a symptom of his weak grasp of realities. He was indeed "a too literal realist of imagination" (as observed by R.P. Blackmur, quoting a remark made by Yeats himself on William Blake), even more than Blake.[5] Blake was certainly not as blind to material aspects. Blake's view that there was no dualism between spirit and nature apparently meant more than what Yeats chose to construe out of it. The hostility between Yeats and the everyday-world is borne out by his tragic view of life. His vision of Evil – "the conception of the world as a continual conflict", as Harold Bloom calls it,[6] must have promoted that hostility.

Arthur Mizener observes how, unlike Yeats, a romantic poet like Shakespeare "could accept completely the life which submits to practical necessity, however intensely conscious he was of life's conflict with the life of the imagination."[7] He appears to blame it on the solipsistic tendencies of Yeats, when he says:

> ...... these early romantics had not yet completely destroyed in them their ability to believe that something beside their own imaginations had made the universe, nor were they so hard-pressed by the complete unwillingness of the scientific thought of their day to lend itself to their purposes. It may, even, indeed be that they were somewhat better advised than Yeats of the difficulties of solipsism....[8]

Arthur Mizener has made this observation while commenting on

4. Bornstein, George, *Yeats and Shelley*, p. 118.
5. Blackmur, R.P., "The Later Poetry of W.B. Yeats", *Language as Gesture : Essays in Poetry* (London : George Allen & Unwin Ltd., 1954), p. 98.
6. Bloom, Harold, *Yeats*, p. 62.
7. Mizener, Arthur, *The Permanence of Yeats*, p. 143.
8. *Ibid.*, p. 135.

Yeats' over-assertive pretensions to mysticism. The bumptiousness in Yeats seems to form part of his wonted poses and gestures. The pride attributed to him by critics like F.R. Leavis[9] and B.L. Reid[10] seems to spring from a similar source. The 'inner coldness' found in Yeats by D.S. Savage may amuse us most.[11] Savage has considered his 'impossible' love and belated marriage to be symptomatic of that coldness. While one could certainly find Yeats guilty of quite a few misjudgments, the critic sounds rather unfair when he suggests that Yeats lacked warmth of feeling. Yeats, as we understand him, was always a warm-blooded person. Stephen Spender rightly calls his humanity "his greatest virtue".[12] Yeats' warm regard for his friends testifies to this. The ecstatic emotions aroused in him by their portraits have found eloquent expression in "The Municipal Gallery Revisited":

> Think where man's glory most begins and ends,
> And say my glory was I had such friends.[13]

Elsewhere we hear him say:

> A brief parting from those dear
> Is the worst man has to fear,[14]

suggesting the poignant feelings of one seeking a sense of fulfilment in human relationships. Such words could hardly have come from an unfeeling heart. Indeed, we are apt to misread him, when he says:

> Cast a cold eye
> On life, on death.
> Horseman, pass by![15]

Hardly any other epitaph would have had so much meaning packed into it. It results from a heightened awareness on the part of the poet. The cold eye in such a context might symbolize art itself, if the tranquillity referred to in Wordsworth's definition of poetry could be identified with a state of coldness. The perplexing variety of masks worn by Yeats could also be regarded as a means of adopting

9. Leavis, F.R. & Leavis, Q.D., *Lectures in America* (London: Chatto & Windus, 1969), p. 71. Henceforth cited as *Lectures in America*.
10. Reid, B.L., *William Butler Yeats : The Lyric of Tragedy* (Norman : University of Oklahoma Press, 1961), p. Henceforth cited as *The Lyric of Tragedy*.
11. Savage, D.S., *The Permanence of Yeats*, pp. 192-93.
12. Spender, Stephen, *Ibid.*, p. 171.
13. *WBYCP*. p. 370.
14. *Ibid.*, p. 398.
15. *Ibid.*, p. 401.

a cold eye. But, as it happens, the person addressed here is a horseman and not an artist. Yeats' partiality for the aristocratic values and mode of life has obviously influenced his choice of the metaphor. Perhaps it also suggests his fancy for 'the high-horse-riding' in the figurative sense of it. In such a context, the cold eye could mean only the coldness deliberately assumed for a heroic defiance of the tragedy of life and death. Yeats' circumstances were propitious enough (he was indeed far from happy with them) for the adoption of a cold eye. But we are left wondering at the naivete that made him expect a young soldier-poet, Wilfred Owen to assume an identical coldness. We cannot afford to forget that Owen's poems were no test-tube babies. Crediting Yeats with the perspective of the aged prophet on the mountain "undisturbed by compassion, unmoved by the prospect of suffering", as Jon Stallworthy has done, can lead us nowhere, unless we are prone to take Yeats' pretensions more seriously than he himself did.[16] His attitude towards Wilfred Owen was perhaps an instance of the curious brand of realism that he was capable of. We are reminded of Arthur Mizener's comment on his way of seeing things. All the same, we may have to concede that in managing matters and men – including, no doubt, women too – he showed much practical wisdom at times.

Perhaps we should thank providence for not allowing Yeats a smooth sailing in his life. Indeed we are aware that Yeats could make memorable poetry out of any kind of experience that was given – or denied – to him. Yet he could hardly have realized his inner potential as well as he did, if he had no quarrel either with himself or with the world. The supreme belief in human potentialities evidenced in the context is the hall-mark of the Yeatsian Romanticism.

The process of stripping English poetry of its "perdamnable rhetoric", was initiated by Yeats in the early years of the twentieth century.[17] While aiming at a classical accuracy, precision, and hardness in his verse, he sought to make it passionate too, going a step ahead of T.E. Hulme. He realized how modern poetical literature had grown "monotonous in its structure and effeminate in its continual insistence on certain moments of strained lyricism."[18]

16. Stallworthy, Jon, "W.B. Yeats and Wilfred Owen", *Critical Quarterly* (Vol. II, No. 3, Autumn, 1969), p. 214.

17. *Vide* Pound, Ezra, *Literary Essays*, ed., T.S. Eliot (London: Faber & Faber Ltd., 1954), p. 11.

18. Quoted in Pinto, p. 90.

He tried to infuse it with the fresh blood of authentic emotions. He meant to make it sound like the utterance of a whole man – "blood, imagination and intellect running together". Moreover, having noticed how Wordsworth's syntax had "lacked momentum" compared with Byron's, and how the former "had sacrificed passion to propriety",[19] he heeded the counsel of J.M. Synge and resolved to make poetry brutal before it could be human. His effort to evolve a passionate syntax while adopting a common idiom meant a march over the great Romantics. But with all his mastery over the poetic technique, passion was not a thing that could be made to order. Indeed his experience – both personal and political – had been exceptionally fruitful that way. But his solipsistic leanings apparently posed him formidable problems in his endeavour to develop a Keatsian capability to harness instant experiences for poetic purposes with an air of detachment. It was quite some time before he could gain the inner stability and calm – 'tranquility', as Wordswoth called it – to give poetic expression to newly acquired emotions. His belated marriage would seem to have gone a long way towards bringing that tranquillity. And it was perhaps natural that the exquisite piece of art that he made a few months before his marriage – "The Wild Swans at Coole" – appeared to be his swan-song. Middleton Murry found it deficient in the "passionate apprehension" of experience.[20]

The poem begins with the description of a placid landscape, perhaps the best of its kind in Yeats' poetry.

> The trees are in their autumn beauty,
> The woodland paths are dry,
> Under the October twilight the water
> Mirrors a still sky;
> Upon the brimming water among the stones
> Are nine-and-fifty swans.

It is autumn and the season seems to symbolize the stage of the poet's own life. Yet the landscape has not been painted arbitrarily. It yields no hint of any attempt at distorting facts to suit the emotional needs of the poet. The atmosphere is serene. But we are aware that the poet was in an extremely depressed state of mind, when the poem was composed. Maud Gonne had once again rejected his proposal. And her adopted daughter Isuelt Gonne had

19. Quoted in Bornstein, George, *TR.*, p. 46.
20. Murry, J. Middleton, *Critics on Yeats*, p. 10.

also turned a cold shoulder on him. He had no ray of hope in sight. He could contrive joy and peace only artistically. What we have here may be proof of a heroic bid in that direction. The swans whose hearts, much like his own, "do not grow old" serve him as an ideal symbol in the context.

The poem is refreshingly free of false sentiments. The accuracy and precision in the description of the landscape perhaps serve to effect a suspension of disbelief. The mention of the exact number of swans reminds us of the nine bean-rows of his Innisfree.[21] The sense of depression implict here is held in leash through an impeccable intellectual control. There is as much ease and grace in the wording of the poem as in the movement of the swans.

Nature appears wholly unconcerned about human predicaments. We find no hint here of the Wordsworthian belief in a special relationship between man and nature. The attitude of the poet towards nature is in tune with the mood of the century. He does not, however, consider nature purposively dangerous as certain later writers of the century have done. Robert Langbaum has called that tendency a pathetic fallacy.[22] It is obviously of a negative type. Langbaum also says:

> .... to feel in nature an unalterably alien, even an unfeeling existence is to carry empathy several steps farther than did the nineteenth century poets....[23]

In the light of this view we may have to credit Yeats with an unusual degree of empathy. But it is doubtful whether Yeats deserves such a compliment. One would think that Yeats' attitude to nature was far from empathic. It was even antipathetic. The Keatsian naturalistic humanism meant little to him. His treatment of swans here may be considered typical. He does not seem to evince any interest in them as living beings. He makes them appear no better than immortal pieces of art like the Grecian Urn. It is interesting to note how Keats' sympathetic imagination breathes life into the lifeless presences on the Urn. But Yeats goes the other way round. His interest in the swans seems to spring primarily from their symbolic value.

---

21. *Ibid*., p. 44.
22. Langbaum, Robert, *The Modern Spirit : Essays on the Continuity of Nineteenth and Twentieth Century Literature* (New York: Oxford University Press, 1970), p. 106. Henceforth cited as *The Modern Spirit.*
23. *Ibid*., p. 104.

It is, however, to the credit of Yeats that the symbolic significance of the poem has not obscured its surface-meaning, as it does elsewhere in his poetry.

It is strange indeed that Yeats should love so much to cling to a world with which he was always at odds. In fact, he needed all his capacity to assume joy in order to keep his spirits intact. Owing to the absence of a stabilizing religious faith, he had to fend for himself in his hours of crises. "Lapis Lazuli" represents a heroic effort in that regard.

It was not old age alone that Yeats had to tackle in his later life. The whole weather in the free Irish Republic had turned foul for him, thanks to his odd preferences in politics. His deep-rooted aversion to the middle-class Philistinism appears to have been generated by the controversies of his early life. His lack of humanistic concern, surely, did not embrace the other segments of society. Lines such as:

> Why should I seek for love or study it?
> It is of God and passes human wit.
> I study hatred with diligence,
> For that's a passion in my own control,[24]

could not have come from a misanthropist. The triumph of the middle-class aroused bitter feelings in him.

Nature might have served Yeats as a source of solace in such contexts, had he cared for it enough. But even as he had trained himself to cast a cold eye on it, Nature responded to him with a matching indifference and allowed him no sense of fulfilment of the Keatsian sort. And he had per force to turn to art. The aimless, senseless joy of a fool was all that he could bargain for. He went all out in pursuit of it. The poems of his last phase contain ample proof of that sad, mad quest. "Lapis Lazuli" is among them.

The opening stanza of the poem gives vent to Yeats' maddening sense of fury and frustration :

> I have heard that hysterical woman say
> They are sick of the palette and fiddle-bow,
> Of poets that are always gay,
> For everybody knows or else should know
> That if nothing drastic is done

---

24. *WBYCP.*, p. 330.

Aeroplane and Zeppelin will come out,
Pitch like King Billy bomb-balls in
Until the town lie beaten flat.[25]

The words here sound sinister. The poet seems to warn the world in a cold, vehement tone that its doom was imminent, if his counsel was not heeded. His remark that those hysterical women who neglect music, painting and poetry for taking to politics will bring about the destruction of everything seems to amount to an open onslaught, strangely enough, on the idol he worshipped for the best part of his life. It may be proof enough of his life-long passions degenerating into a mad fury in the last lap of his life.

The rest of the poem sings the praise of the gay arts which the hysterical women have been scorning. The fury to which Yeats has yielded himself up, seems productive of a tragic joy. He identifies it with the ecstasy felt by the great characters of tragedies. He observes that an artist, if he is worth anything, is gay, even as his entire life's work is reduced to nothing. For he knows that the things destroyed are built again.

After a lengthy preface that contains a lyrical statement of some of his strong private persuasions, Yeats seeks to put them in a dramatic form. The Lapis Lazuli presented to him by someone helps in that effort. It is a carving in stone. It has the figures of two Chinamen, a long-legged bird and a servant carrying a musical instrument. The poet meditates on that scene. "The plum or cherry branch" in the carving attracts his attention. It is amusing to note how little he cared for such things in nature. Their function now is obviously symbolic. The men in the carving are found climbing a hill. Yeats delights himself envisioning their further movements. They seem to be staring at a tragic scene. The poet imagines that one of them is requesting the other to sing sad songs. The poet is able to hear the music produced in response to the request. It brings a visionary moment:

One asks for mournful melodies;
Accomplished figures begin to play
Their eyes mid many wrinkles, their eyes,
Their ancient, glittering eyes, are gay.[26]

The sight of the glittering eyes of the men must have made Yeats'

25. *Ibid.*, p. 338.
26. *Ibid.*, p. 339.

own eyes shine, as he is tempted to believe that they shared his attitude towards tragedy.

Yeats seems to have gone a step ahead of Keats when he imagines the further movement of the men in the carving. It suggests a dynamism, distinct from the static quality of the imagery of the Grecian Urn. Yeats appears to have abandoned the carving in the process "for a world constructed in pure imagination",[27] in a way typical of the Romantics. Yeats concludes the poem without allowing his visionary mood to wither away. Possibly, he is afraid of being thrown back on the rocks of realities. We are reminded of what he said in a letter:

> I thought my problem was to face death with gaiety, now I have learned that it is to face life.[28]

Perhaps we get a clue here to the working of his mind in the last phase of his life. The poet's keenly-felt desire to share his tragic joy with the men on the carving seems to have prompted him to identify himself with them. We have the Yeatsian brand of empathy here. To be sure, he would have had nothing to do with the Chinamen of the carving, had he felt that they were not capable of tragic gaiety. The Lawrencian gift of empathy with modes of life for which one felt little sympathy, referred to by D.J. Enright, was not his.[29]

John Bayley has pointed out that a Mask of Violence was worn by Yeats in the present case, and it helped him to forget the tameness of the modern times.[30] The extreme views packed into the poem and their exasperating expression are thus attributed to the mask. Yet in the mad fury of his last phase, probably, Yeats would not have bothered to dissociate himself from the mask.

Yeats' attitude towards the athletic joy found in the supreme

---

27. Unterecker, John, *A Reader's Guide to William Butler Yeats* (Thames and Hudson, 1959, Third impression, 1965), p. 260. Henceforth cited as *A Reader's Guide to W.B. Yeats*.

28. Yeats, W.B., quoted by Jeffares, A. Norman, "The General and Particular Meaning of 'Lapis Lazuli' ", *Yeats — Last Poems*, ed. Jon Stallworthy (Macmillan, 1968, A Casebook), p. 163.

29. Enright, D.J., *Conspirators and Poets* (London: Chatto & Windus, 1966), p. 99. Henceforth cited as *Conspirators and Poets*.

30. Bayley, John, *RS*., p. 96.

moments of tragedy illustrated by "Lapis Lazuli" is considered part and parcel of his romanticism."[31]

The function of the mask in the poetry of Yeats has been widely discussed. As mentioned by George Bornstein, he felt that the man bent on regaining a Unity of Being must imagine an ideal self opposite to his normal identity, an antiself, as "the complexities of the twentieth century made the conscious personality fragmented and incomplete."[32] The utility of masks as depersonalizing devices has been beyond doubt. A tormenting awareness of his inner inadequacies could also have prompted him to take to masks. His lack of imaginative sympathy, for instance, is perhaps sought to be compensated for that way. His desire to understand mankind "in every possible circumstance and every conceivable situation" may have to be seen as a part of that bid. Thus he tried to put himself "in all the possible situations of life, from the most miserable to those that are so lofty."[33] His belief in the educative value of the assumption of masks was much profound. He says :

> Do you suppose for one moment that Shakespeare educated Hamlet and King Lear by telling them what he thought and believed? As I see it, Hamlet and Lear educated Shakespeare ..... A dramatist can help his characters to educate him by thinking and studying everything that gives them the language they are groping for through his hands and eyes, but the control must be theirs, and that is why the ancient philosophers thought a poet or dramatist Daimon-possessed.[34]

The reasoning that enabled Yeats to associate such a conscious effort on the part of a poet or dramatist with the Daimon has not been altogether convincing. In any case, he could hardly have trusted such a method for gaining "entire wisdom". To most of us, such a wisdom, commendable as it is, would seem to be a poor substitute to what comes out of a genuine compassion. Richard Ellmann has, however, given him superlative praise for the "nobility

---

31. Jeffares, A. Norman, *The Circus Animals : Essays on W.B. Yeats* (Macmillan, 1970), p.
32. Bornstein, George, *Yeats & Shelley*, p. 133.
33. *Vide* Ellmann, Richard, *The Identity of Yeats* (London : Macmillan & Co. Ltd., 1954), p. 245.
34. Yeats, W.B., Letter quoted in Brooks, Cleanth, "Implications of an Organic Theory of Poetry", *Literature and Belief : English Institute Essays, 1957*, ed. M.H. Abrams (New York : Columbia University Press, 1958), p. 67. Henceforth cited as *Literature and Belief*.

and largeness of mind" suggested by the bid and traced it to his "affirmative capability". The talent revealed, we may assume, is a negative capability distinctively Yeatsian.

Ellmann considers the Keatsian capability a lesser talent, as it seems to free the poet "from responsibility of intellectual search or understanding of experience".[35] But the Keatsian ability is backed up by a sympathetic imagination, while the affirmative capability results from a hard-headed effort to cover up the vacuum created by the absence of it. The effort, doubtless, reveals the tremendous inner resources Yeats had at his command.

Yeats' extreme self-consciousness and sceptical cast of mind, which were perhaps more than Keatsian, along with his solipsistic leanings and lack of imaginative sympathy, must have undermined his capacity to identify himself with the objects of nature.

Presumably, an emotional self-fulfilment was an important purpose served by the Yeatsian masks. We have been told what a timid and diffident thing Yeats was, in his early years.[36] A look of toughness afforded by masks must naturally have impressed him. And possibly, the problems and challenges of his early life made him tough enough to think in terms of taking to masks. The failure of his fond hope of marrying Maud Gonne and her hard decision to favour a "vainglorious lout,"[37] who had nothing but a tough exterior to recommend him must have had a positive impact on Yeats. The masks might have made him feel happier through enabling him to see himself in an appropriate light, as indicated by L.C. Knights.[38] They might also have provided a means of escaping "from the hot-faced bargainers and money-chargers".[39] Above all, masks meant to Yeats "playing a game like that of a child, where one loses the infinite pain of self-realization".[40]

Yeats' curious attempts at assuming masks have obscured his personality from the view of certain critics. D.S. Savage, for instance,

---

35. *The Identity of Yeats*, p. 244.
36. *Vide* Perkins David, *HNP*., p. 582 and Bayley, John, *RS*., p. 97.
37. *WBYCP*., p. 203.
38. *Critics on Yeats*., p. 18.
39. Yeats, W.B., Quoted in Knights, L.C., *Critics on Yeats*, p. 18.
40. Yeats, W.B., *vide* Bayley, John, *RS*., p. 94.

calls it a "mask".[41] His subsequent assumption that Yeats' poetic development was essentially a betrayal of the personality-principle has drawn a caustic comment from Balachandra Rajan.[42] It is surprising how he could turn a blind eye on the flood of disconcerting personal emotions, which, in their volcanic thrust, pierced through all masks in the concluding phase of Yeats' life.

What we witness in the poetry of Yeats is perhaps the progressive assertion of his personality over the tendency of his masks to obscure it. G.S. Fraser seems to mean as much when he says :

> As Yeats' poetry matures, one of the things that happens is not so much that it becomes more 'personal', less of a 'mask' as that he gets more of his personality into it.[43]

And it may well be that Yeats himself realised that "his dramatizations had been so often, in essence, self-dramatizations motivated with less dignity than he had supposed," as suggested by Chirstopher Gillie.[44]

After all, Yeats himself could not have been unaware that there was something childish about his fancy for masks. The "phantasmagoria"[45] he deliberately adopted was certainly unworthy of a great poet. For the greatest kind of art, as observed by A.G. Stock, "a man's whole self must be thrown recklessly into the theme with all his powers focused."[46] Yeats would fain have done as much towards the end of his life at least, had he felt free enough to do so. But, as it happened, he was labouring under various constraints. They seem to have thrown him into a fit of fury that defied rational expression. He had neither time nor patience for recollecting that

---

41. Savage, D.S., *The Permanence of Yeats*, p. 193.
42. Rajan, Balachandra, *W.B. Yeats: A Criticial Introduction* (London: Hutchinson University Library, 1965. Reprint 1972), p. 18. Henceforth cited as *A Critical Introduction*.
43. Fraser, G.S., *Vision and Rhetoric: Studies in Modern Poetry* (London: Faber & Faber, 1959), p. 59. Henceforth cited as *Vision and Rhetoric*.
44. Gillie, Christopher, *Movements in English Literature, 1900-1940* (Cambridge University Press, 1975), p. 156. Henceforth cited as *Movements in English Literature*.
45. Yeats, W.B. *Essays and Introductions* (London: Macmillan, 1961), p. 509. Henceforth cited as *Essays and Introductions*.
46. Stock, A.G., *W.B. Yeats: His Poetry and Thought* (Cambridge: University Press, 1964), p. 53. Henceforth cited as *Stock, A.G.*

emotion in tranquillity. It had to be expressed in all its heat. His masks nearly dissolved in that heat. Yet, in a sense, they also helped him simultaneously to conceal and reveal the agitated state of his mind. Borrowing a metaphor from D.H. Lawrence, we may say that Yeats did indeed appear to put his hand on the mouth of the demon in him, but he certainly let the demon say his say.

Critics have been dumbfounded by the sexuality and linguistic violence of the poems of Yeats' last phase. Some of them have perhaps been shocked into silence. Vivienne Koch, however, does not appreciate their sense of delicacy and embarrassment. The comments she has made on Norman Jeffares, for instance, have been astonishing in their lack of perspective.[47] They suggest no awareness of the pioneering contribution towards an understanding of Yeats made by Jeffares. Critics like F.R. Leavis find the poems of Yeats' last phase much too plain.[48] But Vivienne Koch has expatiated on them with a rare relish. Assuming the air of one making a blinding revelation, she says that "sexual energy was the source, subject and theme" of Yeats' major poems of the last decade. She finds it easy enough to trace the upsurge in the sexuality of those poems to the Steinach operation underwent by Yeats.[49] She does not realize that a fall in sexual vitality could also result in such poems: the weaker the flesh, the louder the song. David Perkins seems to mean as much when he says that Yeats "celebrated physical and sexual vitality, life in all its coarseness," against the failing body and the "approaching night".[50] But F.R. Leavis appears to see deeper when he observes that "the ugliest and most disturbing expressions of inner discord and rebellion or despair" to be found in Yeats' *oeuvre* mark his final phase.[51] Graham Hough regards the harshness and violence of the Yeatsian language as the most disturbing feature of that phase.[52] But Vivienne Koch has been significantly silent on that aspect. Presumably, she has not been

---

47. *The Tragic Phase*, p. 17.
48. Leavis, F.R., *Lectures in America*, p. 79.
49. *The Tragic Phase*, pp. 20-21.
50. Perkins, David, *HMP.*, p. 598.
51. Leavis, F.R., *Lectures in America*, p. 79.
52. Hough, Graham, *W.B. Yeats: A Study in Poetic Integration*, *Selected Essays* (Cambridge University Press, 1978), p. 168.

able to grapple with it. Margaret Rudd has aptly called the poems of the phase 'shock-tactic-poems' and has considered their defiant manner more significant than their subject-matter.[53] It would seem likely that Yeats, in his endeavour to give expression to his maddening sense of despair, fury and frustration, found in sexual themes and a shocking vocabulary, a striking, if inadequate, objective correlative. The hysterical quality and linguistic violence of the poems perhaps contribute to their look of authenticity. Yet surely, sexuality in itself does not warrant such a vehemence in linguistic expression.

Such violent expressions are apt to impress us as full-blooded utterances of a man. Yet, as observed by Margaret Rudd, Yeats' poems here are too extrovertly sexual to have much psychological significance.[54] Yeats' achievement in the case may, however, amount to a modulation towards a poetry of open process, as indicated by M.L. Rosenthal, albeit in a clumsy fashion.[55]

The artistic achievement of the Unity of Being proves a formidable task, as it demands a rare degree of co-ordination between the poet's inventive skill and imagination. In other words, it involves the attainment of an intellectual and emotional poise that is hard to come by.

The Byzantium poems would seem to represent a deliberate effort on the part of the poet to achieve such a Unity through evolving a unifying symbol. The urge to make such an attempt was apparently intensified by the problems he confronted in his later life.

The first draft of "Sailing to Byzantium" laments :

> All that men know or think they know, being young, Cry that my tale is told, my story sung.[56]

Possibly, the allusion here is to men like Middleton Murry. They seem to have done him a good turn, as he roused himself with a vengeance to prove them wrong.

---

53. Rudd, Margaret, *Divided Image* : *A Study of William Blake and W.B. Yeats* (London : Routledge & Kegan Paul Ltd., 1953), Chapter VI, p. 181. Henceforth cited as *Divided Image*.
54. *Ibid*., p. 185.
55. Rosenthal, M.L., *Sailing into the Unknown* (New York : Oxford University Press, 1978), p. 205.
56. Quoted in Jeffares, A. Norman, *W.B. Yeats* : *Man and Poet* (London : Routledge & Kegan Paul Ltd., 1949), p. 236.

Yeats' longing to seek shelter in a world of art evidenced in "Sailing to Byzantium" has not involved the suppression of his instinctive feeling for the other world. It is refreshing to hear him speak in his own voice, setting aside all masks. In fact, we are told that the poet had not originally meant to speak in his own person. He had toyed with the idea of putting his words into the mouth of a medieval Irish poet. Such a move might well have appeared dishonest to many. But Yeats was prone to take his flair for wearing masks as a skill which had nothing to do with honesty or sincerity. Insincerity carried no pejorative overtone to him as indicated by John Bayley.[57]

"Sailing to Byzantium" is said to suggest a nostalgia for the world of art. But its imagery betrays an irresistible feeling for the world which he seeks to leave behind, as observed by Norman Jeffares, among others. We are told that an old man in this world is no better than a tattered coat upon a stick, unless the spirit asserts itself in him. Having aligned himself with the body as long as he could, the poet now throws amorous glances at the spirit in a vain bid to compensate for the weakness of the flesh. The Neoplatonist belief that matter occupied only the lowest rung of the ladder was certainly not his.

The song, we are told, has to be louder when the flesh grows weaker. What is heard in the last years of Yeats' life is such a loud singing, though not of the kind conceived of here. It is a case of inner instincts asserting themselves over the cold manoeuvring of the intellect. Evidently, the momentary longing projected here was soon subdued.

The addressing of the sages apparently suggests a moment of awareness:

> O sages standing in God's holy fire
> As in the gold mosaic of a wall,
> Come from the holy fire, perne in a gyre,
> And be the singing-masters of my soul
> Consume my heart away; sick with desire
> And fastened to a dying animal
> It knows not what it is; and gather me
> Into the artifice of eternity.[58]

---

57. Bayley, John, *RS*., p. 96.
58. *WBYCP*., pp. 217-18.

The mention of God in the context is perhaps significant. It might give credence to the view that Byzantium represented Yeats' idea of heaven. Yeats, however, has not thought it fit to count on God's help in his less intense moments. From that fact we may assume that his inability to attach himself to a formal religion was a problem of the conscious mind and his inward urges were pulling him towards an allegiance. In other words, we may observe that his inner personality craved for an abiding faith, while his character wilfully brushed aside that craving and engaged itself in inventing substitutes for a religious faith. When we take such a view, the absence of any reference to God in Yeats' later "Byzantium", may suggest the dominance of the conscious mind in its making.

The artifice of eternity sounds like a novel definition of art, as art is both artificial and eternal. The reference to the "perne in a gyre" relates the poem to Yeats' System. But it does not distract our attention seriously. Nor does it disturb the general significance of the poem. Even after gaining the shape of a golden bird and a place on a golden bough, the poet says that he will continue to sing of "what is past, or passing, or to come." It is odd indeed that he finds nothing better to sing about. The poet's interest is only in getting rid of the fleshly form, obviously because it has grown weak. No wonder that Sturge Moore found nothing superior in the golden bird. And the bird, we are told, is to sing only to the Emperor, lords and ladies, and not to the lesser beings. The peasantry, for whom Yeats always had a soft corner, has deserved no consideration here.

It should be hard indeed to accept the view that the poem is an affirmation of the spirit over the life of the body. At best we may concede that it was perhaps meant to be so. But there is a yawning gap between intention and achievement here. Yet, we must value what is achieved in the context, as a faithful recording of the conflicting passions of the poet. The poem impresses us as an embodiment of Blake's proposition that eternity is in love with the productions of time, as remarked by Balachandra Rajan.[59] The later "Byzantium"[60] constitutes a painstaking effort on the part of the poet to correct that impression.

Harold Bloom finds the poem rather static.[61] If he has meant by

59. *A Critical Introduction*, p. 125.

60. *WBYCP*., pp. 280-81.

61. *Yeats*, p. 347.

the comment that the poet's attitude revealed here suggests no progress, we are one with him. Yeats presumably was not capable of much progression in the direction signalled by the poem. The golden bird's lack of any convincing superiority is a sure symptom of that incapacity. As it is, the journey depicted in the poem seems to end where it began.

The deliberate bid on the part of Yeats to correct the impression created by "Sailing to Byzantium" has not helped to mend matters enough. The new poem bears the stamp of cold deliberation. The Yeatsian flair to make his poems appear products of a moment's thought (which approximated to the Keatsian talent in that regard), alluded to in "Adam's Curse",[62] seems to have failed him in this instance. The laboured construction suggested here yields no trace of emotional spontaneity or artistic inevitability.

The air of depression that precipitated the poem would appear to have been far more suffocating than what the poet confronted while giving shape to the earlier poem. There has apparently been a further stiffening in the poet's posture. The movement, ironically enough, was not in the direction indicated by the affirmations of the poem. Yet it is likely that the poet's desire expressed here to attach himself to the spirit-world was sincere enough at the moment. But he was apparently handicapped in the effort by the pull of his innate instincts in the opposite direction. The vehemence and persistence with which he has sought to repudiate that pull through denigrating the fury and "the mire of human veins" stanza after stanza perhaps betray his awareness of the futility of the effort. The flesh-and-blood-world appears to shadow him wherever he is. Thus, "the view of the initiate" (as John Unterecker calls it) fails to be essentially different from that of "the uninitiated outsider."[63] As observed by T.R. Henn, the complexities appear to run through the fabric of the poem like a thread.[64] The attempt at resolving them made towards the end of the poem looks pitifully feeble in the face of the overwhelming influx of fleshly images:

> Astraddle on the dolphin's mire and blood,
> Spirit after spirit! The smithies break the flood,

---

62. *WBYCP.*, pp. 88-90.
63. *A Reader's Guide to W.B. Yeats*, p. 217.
64. Henn, T.R., *The Lonely Tower: Studies in the Poetry of W.B. Yeats* (London: Methuen & Co. Ltd., 1950, reprint, 1965), p. 221. Henceforth cited as *The Lonely Tower*.

The golden smithies of the Emperor!
Marbles of the dancing floor
Break bitter furies of complexity,
Those images that yet
Fresh images beget,
That dolphin-torn, that gong-tormented sea.[65]

There is a touch of irony in the reference made to the attempt of the smithies to break a flood. The starlit or moonlit dome, the embittered moon, the flames, the dancer and other images of that sort seem to acquire significance only in the light of "A Vision". Attempts at reading esoteric or Neoplatonist significances into the poem are unlikely to enhance its validity as a work of art. The world of Byzantium is apparently free of all religious significance. God, who had a place in the earlier Byzantium has, curiously enough, vanished out of the new city.

If we are to take the absence of God here as an indication of the dominance of the conscious mind in the making of the poem, the validity of the visionary moment recorded therein is bound to be suspect. But the Romantic strain of the realistic perceptions of the poet we have noted earlier is likely to lend some credibility to the moment still. When George Bornstein regards "the summoning of images" as a Yeatsian mode of envisioning, he suggests an awareness of this fact.[66]

T.R. Henn's view that the Yeatsian achievement here is more than the arrested beauty of the Keatsian Urn sounds far from convincing.[67] Maybe, Yeats' poem is the embodiment of a long striving after mathematical perfection. But such an achievement in itself can hardly sustain its pretensions to superiority as a work of art. Keats' picture, in fact, reveals a cogency, vitality and compassion which the world of Byzantium sadly lacks.

We are not also convinced that the later poem on Byzantium is the better of the two. Its system of tensions is certainly more complex and its overtones more significant, as pointed out by Henn.[68] But its overloaded imagery imparts it an air of artificiality which is in sharp contrast to the impression of authenticity conveyed

---

65. *WBYCP*., p. 281.
66. Bornstein, George, *TR*., p. 57.
67. *The Lonely Tower*, p. 215.
68. *Ibid*., p. 215.

by the earlier poem. The genuine emotions of the poet are sought to be regulated – shall we say regimented? – rather arbitrarily. If the experience described is of a mystical order, the poet has taken a bad risk in trying to communicate it. Indeed we are aware that the problem concerns all visionary Romantics. The poem, as a whole, has to be taken as an elaborate record of a visionary moment. The impression of artificiality in its expression may have to be blamed entirely on the conscious intellect.

A concerted bid on Yeats' part to evolve a unifying symbol to reconcile the flesh with the spirit, the living with the dead, the being with the becoming and time with eternity seems to have helped him to arrive at Byzantium. But while packing the images of the poem with multiple significances through a self-conscious effort, he fails to make them look less than artificial. The air of the city tends to be heavy and suffocating, as it were. The apparent lack of a meaningful relation among the images of the poem perhaps accounts for its lack of spontaneity and vitality. Of course, the absence of imagistic coherence and cogency in the poem is apt to disappear, if we are inclined to relate the imagery to the Yeatsian System. It seems easy enough to agree with Harold Bloom as he remarks that "Byzantium" must stand or fall with "A Vision".[69]

All the same, we should not lose sight of the validity of the city envisioned here to Yeats himself. A part of his being, to be sure, craved for a life in Byzantium, as he confessed in "A Vision". The thought of its being beyond his reach must have greatly depressed him.

And what the poet has sought to concretize in the poem is an awareness of great intensity, even if we are prone to take it for the vain longing of the fly, caught in the marmalade, to rise in the sky. Possibly, the city also symbolizes for Yeats an Ireland of his dreams, as suggested by Henn.

Yeats' failure to find a unifying symbol in Byzantium, as also to achieve Unity of Being in the artistic efforts involving it, would seem hardly surprising. We have had hints of his true affinities much earlier. The trend appears to have been set irrevocably as early as 1927. "A Dialogue of Self and Soul" written that year proclaims his partiality for the fleshly world in unambiguous terms :

---

69. *Yeats*, p. 393.

I am content to live it all again
And yet again, if it be life to pitch
Into the frog-spawn of a blind man's ditch,
A blind man battering blind men;
Or into that most fecund ditch of all,
A folly that man does
Or must suffer if he woos
A proud woman not kindred of his soul

I am content to follow to its source
Every event in action or in thought;
Measure the lot; forgive myself the lot!
When such as I cast out remorse
So great a sweetness flows into the breast
We must laugh and we must sing,
We are blest by everything,
Everything we look upon is blest.[70]

Of course, this assertion formed part of a conflict that was still unresolved. Presumably, it was only around 1930 that the die was cast. His long vacillation, thus, comes to an end. The new alignment is indicated with an impressive flourish:

Homer is my example and his unchristened heart.
The lion and the honeycomb, what has Scripture said?
So get you gone, Von Hugel, though with blessings on your head.[71]

The concluding lines of his "Two Songs from a Play" added in the early 1930s may also bear testimony to it:

Whatever flames upon the night
Man's own resinous heart has fed.[72]

The earlier lines of the poem are said to have been written in 1926. Their imagery depends on the Symbolist mode of suggestion and perhaps suffered for want of a statement. The words which embodied that statement have a ring of sincerity about them. It is amusing to note that such an affirmation synchronized with a seeming triumph of the Yeatsian intellect in its quest for a spirit-world.

The laughing and singing referred to in the concluding part of the "Dialogue" grow hysterical thereafter, gaining extra depth and poignancy in a hostile environment. Apparently, the poet, in his old age, is forced to the conclusion that only a 'frenzy' could meet his ends in the conditions that prevailed, as

Neither loose imagination

70. *WBYCP*., p. 267.

71. *Ibid*., p. 286.

72. *Ibid*., p. 240.

Nor the mill of the mind
Consuming its rag and bone,
Can make the truth known.[73]

C.H. Sisson has observed that "'Sailing to Byzantium' is the most consistent attempt on the part of Yeats to give himself over to the intellect, as 'Words for Music Perhaps' is his most consistent attempt to give himself over to the body."[74] But it is doubtful whether Yeats really needed a deliberate bid to give himself over to the body. What was needed for the purpose was perhaps only a slackening of the resolve that made him count on intellectually contrived solutions in his earlier life. The "aesthetic escape-routes"[75] he tried had obviously failed to impress him.

F.R. Leavis' comments on the Byzantium poems do not sound too harsh, though we may find him labouring under positivist obsessions elsewhere. He says:

> "Sailing to Byzantium" doesn't come out of any wholeness of being or mastery of experience, its poetic or quasi-musical satisfyingness as a totality is not an index of any permanant stability achieved by the poet in life ..... [76]

What is implied by the Byzantium escapade is the loss of the inner stability Yeats had earlier found in his life. It obviously meant a desire, momentary though, to run away from the complexities of life, abandoning all attempts to come to grips with them.

Yeats probably meant to protray in the Byzantium poems the life after death, as he conceived of it. But he has acatually done much more. Attempts at explaining them in eschatological terms made by critics like F.A.C. Wilson are, therefore, bound to yield distorted pictures.

When D.S. Savage observes that the development revealed in Yeats' work was a "development in a vacuum,"[77] what he hints at seems to be the absence of a unifying moral subject in his poetry. Stephen Spender has drawn attention to it.[78] Yeats was, in fact,

73. *Ibid.*, p. 346.
74. Sisson, C.H., *English Poetry, 1900-1950: An Assessment* (London : Rupert Hart - Davis, 1971), p. 169.
75. Cowell, Raymond, *W.B. Yeats* (London : Evan Brothers Ltd., 1969), p.
76. *Lectures in America*, p. 75.
77. Savage, D.S., *The Permanence of Yeats*, p. 194.
78. Spender, Stephen, *The Destructive Element* (London : Jonathan Cape Ltd., 1935), p. 130. Reprinted in *The Permanence of Yeats*, p. 169.

refreshingly free of all moral or religious preoccupations. His concern was primarily aesthetic. Spender has also referred to the lack of a philosophy in Yeats. One wonders whether it really matters in Yeats, any more than it does in Shakespeare. Yet a mature attitude towards life and its problems is perhaps something we might bargain for in him. If his tragic view of life, his attempts at self-dramatization, the Romantic strain of his realism, and his desperate decision to fall back on his emotions make severe demands on the impression of maturity that he presents, his exquisite sensibility and integrity may compensate for it all in ample measure.

In his later life Yeats could probably draw assurance from the superficial similarity between his neglect of physical nature and the low opinion of the Neoplatonists about material life. And F.A.C. Wilson, for one, has emphasized the affinity between Yeats and the Neoplatonists.[79] While one would certainly appreciate Wilson's well-meaning endeavour to attach Yeats to an accepted faith, one cannot easily imagine that Yeats could ever have surrendered himself to the Ultimate Reality, as the Neoplatonists did, more than momentarily. Moreover, they could not also have shared with Yeats the Blakean belief that eternity is in love with the productions of time. They would have found his obsession with "fish, flesh or fowl" rather nauseating. One who is so much in love with the wheel of becoming could hardly be expected to climb up the Neoplatonist ladder without a heavy heart.

Yeats' conception of the Unity of Being implied a desire to create in the work of art what he despaired of in life. He was soon to abandon his concern for it. The inner poise and equanimity needed for an achievement of that order were not, however, beyond Yeats. He could find them well before he slipped into the 'tragic phase' of his life. Apparently, they had nothing to do with the maturity that came with age. The poem that marked the zenith of the Yeatsian achievement in this direction is perhaps "Among school children".[80] It was written in 1926. The tranquillity suggested by the poem seems to have been helped largely by the peace that prevailed on his home-front and the world-wide renown that he could gain on his being awarded the Nobel Prize for literature. It

79. Wilson, F.A.C., *W.B. Yeats and Tradition* (London : Gollancz, 1958), pp. 16-19.
80. *WBYCP*., pp. 242-45.

was enhanced too by the first flush of the freedom Ireland had just won. He had also become a Senator in the Free Irish Republic.

As a distinguished senator, Yeats visits a convent school and jots down in his diary a topic for a poem "School chidren and the thought that life will waste them". He also wants to bring in the old thought that life prepared us for what never happens. We are reminded of the remark made by Margaret Rudd on how Yeats spent most of his life in the perfection of a technique "to express a vision that never came."[81] In a letter to Olivia Shakespeare, Yeats calls the poem a curse upon old age. All that certainly looks unpromising material to make an impressive poem. Nevertheless, the product that came out of it bears testimony to a perfect co-ordination between the faculty of imagination and the inventive genius characteristic of Yeats. It is pleasant to see Yeats begin a poem in such a direct, lucid and unassuming manner. Even his smile looks natural and relaxed. He is obviously free of all tensions at the moment.

While watching the lovely forms of young children, the poet's thought flies to a distant past, when a person with a Ledaean body told him a tale. It is easy enough to identify the person alluded to. She was Yeats' Helen. According to the poet, they enjoyed each other's sympathy and confidence then. It was as though their two natures had formed one whole, just as the two hemispheres formed a sphere. Modifying one of Plato's parables he says that they were like the yolk and white of an egg. Plato's parable refers to the suggestion that man was originally double, with two faces, four hands and so on. On being divided into two halves, they strive towards each other in love.[82]

The picture of the relationship between Maud Gonne and Yeats looks slightly exaggerated. Possibly, the attempt at idealizing a hapless thing brought some consolation to the old man.

With the image of Maud Gonne at the back of his mind, Yeats looks at the children in front of him. He wonders whether Maud too had looked like one of them in her childhood. Even Helen-like

---

81. *Divided Image*, p. 187.

82. *Vide* Kermode, Frank & Hollander, John (ed.) "Modern British Literature", *The Oxford Anthology of English Literature, 1800 to the Present*, Vol. II (New York, London, Toronto: Oxford University Press, 1973), p. 1706.

beauties, he thinks, may, after all, have something in common with the lesser ones. When Yeats tries to imagine whether Maud too had her hair and cheek as colourful, his heart grows wild with an ineffable feeling and the image of Maud Gonne as a child comes alive before his mind's eye bringing a moment of intensity.

The poem contains instances of the Yeatsian manner in which ideas drawn from Plato and Aristotle are put to use. It suggests no blind admiration. We have seen how Yeats modified one of Plato's parables for idealizing his relationship with Maud Gonne. Later he refers to Plato's belief that the world we see is only a covering over the real structure of things. The notion must have pleased him as it seemingly justified his neglect of physical nature. But the affinity suggested could hardly be proof of a Neoplatonist leaning, as we have observed elsewhere. Aristotle is said to have whipped Alexander as he was the latter's tutor. And Pythagoras, whose biographer credited him with golden thighs, suggesting immense sexual potency perhaps, discovered the music of the spheres. But all of them were no better than scarecrows in their old age.

The mention of the golden thighs along with the music of the spheres and the reference to whipping by a philosopher may amaze us. But it seems part of Yeats' celebrated bid to achieve Unity of Being – ensuring a harmonious blending of thought, imagination and emotion.

The presence of nuns beside him seems to bring back the poet's thoughts to the present. Now, he thinks of the contrast between the kinds of images dear to nuns and mothers. Inanimate images do not disappoint a nun in the way they disappoint a mother. The nun's love is of a different kind. But it also brings about a fusion of memory, emotion and imagination, as the other kinds of love. He brackets them all together: lover's passion, nun's piety and mother's affection. The images of bronze and marble, lifeless as they are, arouse emotions as well as the living images worshipped by lovers and mothers. The manner in which the poet addresses them is significant.

...... O Presences
That passion piety and affection knows,
And that all heavenly glory symbolise –
O self-born mockers of man's enterprise;[83]

---

83. *WBYCP*., p. 244.

The contrast implied does not seem to concern the different types of images valued by the nuns and the others. For the poet here seems to be in favour of assigning a high pedestal to the bronze and marble statuettes on a par with their counterparts that arouse passion and affection. His concern seems to concentrate on the lifeless images made by enterprising men like himself. The reference might not be to poetic images alone. We are aware how Yeats struggled to construct a religion. The images that he invented for his own worship have obviously failed to deliver the goods. In such a context the traditional images worshipped by those who attached themselves to formal religions must have appeared to him more satisfying and life-like. Hence his craving for an inclusive artistic image on the one hand and for a consoling religious one on the other.

The poem now moves on to its vital conclusion. It presents a moment of heightened awareness. He says that neither body nor spirit is complete in itself. In his view, it is therefore wrong to injure the body for the well-being of the spirit. Both physical beauty and spiritual wisdom have to grow together. The thought appears to have evoked an intensity in the poet. It brings a glorious image before his mind's eye :

> O chestnut-tree, great-rooted blossomer,
> Are you the leaf, blossom or the bole?
> O body swayed to music, O brightening glance,
> How can I know the dancer from the dance? [84]

The Dancer, as noted by Frank Kermode, is one of Yeats' great reconciling images, containing life in death, death in life, movement and stillness, action and contemplation, body and soul.[85] Kermode has observed that the tree, too, provides a traditional analogy in support of the Image's independent life. The way in which these two emblems have been fused into a splendid image is indeed admirable.

The depressing thoughts and emotions expressed in the poem have not resulted in a distressing conclusion. Despair gets indistinguishably dissolved, as it were, in the instinctive joy of life symbolized by the Dancer and the chestnut tree. It is a triumph of the Romantic imagination.

---

84. *Ibid.*, p. 245.
85. *Romantic Image*, p. 48.

John Unterecker has pointed out that the poem is organized around a series of parallel trinities.[86] What is more deliberately planned is perhaps a faithful-looking recording of thoughts and feelings and the drawing of a consoling conclusion by means of a conciliatory image. No doubt, the conclusion has the air of a dramatic revelation owing largely to the visionary moment recorded in it. The imagery, however, has a look of inevitability about it.

Thomas Whitaker's view that the speaker here (as also in "Sailing to Byzantium") is a new species of man who is Yeats' contrary[87] implies that the ecstatic mood of the concluding lines of the poem is beyond the reach of Yeats. To suggest that Yeats was not capable of a momentary ecstasy that makes a dismal life bearable, is to deny him his legitimate pretensions to Romanticism. In the case of "Sailing to Byzantium" we may have to concede that the speaker was, in a sense, the poet's contrary, as the pursuit of spirituality suggested by the poem ran counter to his innate inclinations.

George Bornstein has noted how the poem typifies the genre of romantic poetry defined as the poetry of experience, as it presents not just the Romantic Image but the poet's struggle to create it.[88] It may also be a splendid instance of the Wordsworthian self-confrontation attempted by Yeats.

The poem perhaps gives scope for a solipsistic inference that heavenly glory is a product of human intellect and imagination and it is the mind that makes both hell and heaven. Such a perspective naturally brings him close to the Coleridgean view of man and nature expressed in his "Dejection An Ode". The Colderidgean Theory of Romanticism – called a 'monistic trancendentalism' – was evidently after Yeats' heart as hinted at by G.S. Fraser.[89] When Northrop Frye says :

> Romanticism, on Yeats' theory, would arise as a mask or counter vision, an imaginative protest against the industrial revolution, and end by being a form in which the culture of the industrial revolution expresses itself.[90]

86. *A Reader's Guide to W.B. Yeats*, p. 191.
87. Whitaker, Thomas, *Swan and Shadow : Yeats' Dialogue with History* (Chapel Hill: University of Carolina Press, 1964), p. 274.
88. Bornstein, George, *TR.*, pp. 24-25.
89. *Vision and Rhetoric*, pp. 27-28.
90. Frye, Northrop, *Fables of Identity: Studies in Poetic Mythology* (New York, Burlingame: Harcourt Brace & World Inc., 1963), p. 235.

he seems to refer to the cause and effect of the transcendental vision.

Symbolist poetry had, in fact, embodied the protest against the industrial revolution much earlier. But thanks to the anti-intentionalist stance of the Symbolists, their poetry tended to enforce a divorce between life and art. The Yeatsian contribution was primarily in bringing it back to earth. Denis Donoghue, however, tends to dispute his claims to Symbolism on that score, when he says:

> Yeats was not after all a thorough-going Symbolist. Even in the elegy on Robert Gregory he allowed his system to be bewildered, brought to silence by brute fact, by "the abrupt indiscretion of events", as Symons said ..... Yeats' sense of fact and his sense of justice admit the rival terminology, however rude. The admission undermines his security as Symbolist, but it gives with one hand what it took away with the other; it allows him, by entertaining conflict, to find a more inclusive and a greater art .... In his mature poems Yeats does not allow his sense of life to be overwhelmed by the charm of a system, even one of his own devising: he became a major poet when he determined to live by that creed.[91]

If Yeats could grow into a major poet by attaching himself to life, we may safely assert that Symbolism itself matured into a major force because of his influence. And in-so-far as the Symbolist symbol was regarded as "a self-sufficient vehicle pointing to an unnamed tenor",[92] there was need for "intellectual armature"[93] to make such symbols intelligible. Yeats, for one, tried to tackle the problem in his own way. John Bayley has shown us how Yeats made use of "conversational armature" between self-contained symbols in poems like "Sailing to Byzantium".[94] "Leda and the Swan"[95] and "The Second Coming"[96] may also exemplify a manner in which he came to grips with the problem. The merging of the two distinctive genres of Romantic poetry, identified as the Symbolist poetry and the poetry of experience, achieved by Yeats implied a masterly bid

---

91. Donoghue, Denis, *Yeats* (Fontana: Collins, 1971), p. 80. Henceforth cited as *Donoghue on Yeats*.
92. Rayan, Krishna, *Suggestion and Statement in Poetry* (London : University of London, The Athone Press, 1972), p. 88. Henceforth cited as *Suggestion and Statement*.
93. Bayley, John, *RS*., p. 124.
94. *WBYCP*., pp. 217-218.
95. *Ibid*., p. 241.
96. *Ibid*., pp. 210-211.

to tackle the same problem. While the Symbolist method derived largely from William Blake and S.T. Coleridge has found favour with Frank Kermode (who was rather disenchanted with Symbolism as an exclusive poetic creed) and the New Critics (who, amusingly enough, showed little awareness of their Romantic legacy), the poetry of experience favoured by Wordsworth, Shelley and Keats has found wider acceptance in our times, owing largely to its clarity and allegiance to experience. Indeed the difference between the two genres has often been a matter of emphasis. While excessive insistence on non-propositional imagery was the bane of the Symbolist mode, the poetry of experience, in its Wordworthian lucidity and emphasis on the mental action leading to the moment of epiphany, ran the risk of getting diluted into plain, prosaic statement.

Denis Donoghue has observed how Ezra Pound, an admirer of Yeats as he was, rebuked Yeats for his excessive leaning towards Symbolism.[97] Pound insisted that "the given world, such as it is to common imagination, was more durable than the bronzes of Symbolism." The later poetry of Yeats yields conclusive evidence of the manner in which he responded to the advice of this younger friend. It may be a measure of the Yeatsian humility though critics have often tended to lose sight of it.

The Symbolist movement in the direction of an autonomous art severed from life and experience had, in fact, amounted to deviation from the ways of the great Romantics from whom the Symbolists had inherited their technique. The Yeatsian endeavour was largely to correct that deviation. Yeats' indifferent attitude towards nature, and his weak grasp of realities, which we have mentioned earlier, might have come in the way of his effort in that regard. While he could see the world as "a symbolic dramatization of eternity",[98] he showed no interest in physical nature on that score. The sense of otherness that he felt shut out a splendid treasure-house of symbols from him. Yet, his archetypal images and the 'self-begotten' ones of his later poetry brought a good amount of respectability to his Symbolist poetry. We have already seen how it was initially helped by the fresh and lively symbols drawn from the Irish Mythology and legend. The concreteness and precision consciously promoted by the later Yeats also meant a signal service to Symbolism.

97. *Vide* Donoghue on Yeats, pp. 80-81.

98. Pinto, p. 106.

The impression of concreteness in the later poetry of Yeats resulted partly from its stark diction. It is in fact reckoned as an aspect of modernity. The manner favoured by the later Yeats was indeed classical. But his adoption of such a new garb constituted an attempt to bring Romantic poetry abreast of the times. It has helped a good deal in the revival of the Romantic tradition in the modern context.

The later Yeats was so much entangled in the revelations recorded in "a Vision" that he found it nearly impossible to keep them out of his poetry. And they naturally brought much obscurity to some of his poems. But in his best poetry he was able to keep his pet theories well under control. "Leda and the Swan", and "The Second Coming" may serve as instances. "The Double Vision of Michael Robartes" is a poem marred by the intrusion of his theories. "Among School Children", as we have seen, is refreshingly free of its influence. The seeming lack of coherence and cogeny in the imagery of "Byzantium" seems to spring largely from its relationship to "A Vision". Its failure is perhaps the failure of the pure symbolist method shorn of all statement. Yeats' decision to confine himself to the "foul rag-and-bone shop of the heart" in his last phase involved the abandonment of his "Visionary" obsessions for good.

"Leda and the Swan"[99] has perhaps been the most celebrated sonnet of our century. Its appeal has indeed been universal. Yeats himself, we are told, was proud of it.

Having meant to make it a political poem Yeats has told us how the bird and lady took "such possession of the scene that all politics was out of it."

The poem seeks to present a moment that resulted in the birth of the Greek civilization. A more dramatic opening for a poem can seldom be thought of:

> A sudden blow : the great wings beating still
> Above the staggering girl, here thighs caressed
> By the dark webs, her nape caught in his bill,
> He holds her helpless breast upon his breast.

A dazzling image is thus presented. An attempt at expounding its symbolic significance through the insertion of a prosaic statement

99. *WBYCP.*, p. 241.

in the poem was bound to dilute the efficacy of the symbol. The questions that follow presumably represent a Yeatsian bid to get over that problem rhetorically:

> How can those terrified vague fingers push
> The feathered glory from her loosening thighs?
> And how can body laid in that white rush,
> But feel the strange heart beating where it lies?

The lines make his meaning explicit. The poet, then, seeks to tighten up the poem soon enough, through reverting to the Symbolist method:

> A shudder in the loins engenders there
> The broken wall, the burning roof and tower
> And Agamemnon dead.

The lines constitute the visionary moment of the poem, along with the lines of the opening section. The rhetorical question that follows marks the end of the vision:

> Being so caught up,
> So mastered by the brute blood of the air,
> Did she put on his knowledge with his power
> Before the indifferent beak could let her drop?

The enlargement of the 'subject' here is apparently aimed at throwing light on the symbol. The rhetorical questions reveal that the intellectual faculty of the poet had not been wholly submerged in the flood of emotions aroused by the portrait. The impact of the bird and the lady on Yeats may be identified with the influence of the visionary moment on the Romantic poet. It was only momentary. The poet has thus succeeded in mingling blood, imagination and intellect in his poetic effort. The questions resorted to may also suggest a wholesome awareness of the need of curbing the Symbolist tendency (shared by the Imagists) to smoke out discursive element from poetry at the cost of obscurity. They may also be proof of a Keatsian scepticism that helped Yeats to hold his visionary inclinations in leash.

A picture from Michaelangelo is said to have inspired Yeats to write the poem. But then, he has not been faithful to it. Critics like T.R. Henn and John Unterecker have tried to search out the other sources that might have prompted Yeats to alter the details of the portrait. It seems odd that they should expect Yeats to care for minute details, while the bird and the lady took possession of the scene – including perhaps the poet's own inner landscape. Even otherwise, Yeats lacked patience for such details. He was very much an impressionist and cared mainly for the impact. The tendency, in its aggravated form, perhaps accounts, partly at least, for the unnatural appearance of the natural landscapes of his later poetry. What we have in "Leda and the Swan" is an imaginative reproduction of the picture from Michaelangelo.

A distinguished friend of Yeats', George Russell (known as 'A.E.') is said to have refused to publish the poem, as he felt that it would not be understood. A.G. Stock says that the real obstacle was that it could not be misunderstood.[100] To be fair to Yeats, we have to observe that the difficulty with the poem is of seeing it in perspective, without being carried away in the violent sweep of the orgasmic moment portrayed in it.

Harold Bloom desires the reader to ask himself: "What is there of value in the poem?"[101] Presumably, the critic believes that it has nothing valuable about it. The irreligious tendencies suggested by the poem seem to have irked him. But are we to expect a salutary lesson, consistent with accepted moral codes, from every work of art? Are we to attach no value at all to the sheer excellence of workmanship? Can it be that aesthetic pleasure means nothing to the critic? It is true that the poem presents only a single moment, as pinpointed by Bloom. But what is done is done with incredible skill and dramatic force. Bloom, surely, is not unaware of it. But then, he says that clarity and fulness are sacrificed for the sake of dramatic shock. We cannot possibly believe that Bloom would really have liked the moment portrayed here to be more elaborately detailed and 'full'.

We must, however, concede that the pleasure afforded by the poem is not of the highest kind and could not possibly secure the poet's claims to greatness. For a very good poet, as T.S. Eliot puts it, has something to give us besides pleasure. "Leda and the Swan" may well be the nearest equivalent to "pure" poetry that the modern world is capable of.

Harold Bloom has also expressed a wish that the sonnet had a touch of the Shelleyan scepticism about divine power and know-

100. Stock, A.G., p. 209.

101. *Yeats*, p. 365.

ledge.[102] As we know, Yeats was sceptical about things almost to a fault. We are aware how he failed to give complete credence to his own vaunted System. His inability to attach himself to a traditional religion may also have to be traced to the same predicament. To suggest that such a man trusted the Greek legends completely may be scandalous, to say the least. Yvor Winters also seems to labour under an identical misconception, when he questions the authenticity of the legend used here.[103] It is incredible that these learned men should have so much difficulty in appreciating the positive aspects of the Yeatsian achievement here. It is odd too that they should pick up such a flimsy stick to hit him with, after so much has been said of the relationship between poetry and belief in our century.

Another poem noted for its distracting imagery is "The Second Coming".[104] It is known for its prophetic significance too.

While "Leda and the Swan" deals with the starting of a cycle, "The Second Coming" envisions the genesis of the next one, marking the end of the Christian era.

The birth of the antithetical spirit represented by the Sphinx is the subject of "The Second Coming". The images of the poem are drawn from what Yeats calls *Spiritus Mundi*, which is virtually a storehouse of archetypal images.

The existing state of the world is picturesquely portrayed in the opening lines of the poem. The falconer is said to have lost control over the falcon. Critics, by and large, have been identifying the falconer with Jesus Christ. Harold Bloom, however, sounds a note of discord when he takes the falconer for man and the falcon for nature.[105] He certainly reveals much ingenuity in arguing that the falconer's control of the falcon could symbolize man's mastery over nature. But it is not clear how the momentous achievements of science witnessed in our times could be deemed proof of man's loss of hold over nature.

A state of anarchy is said to prevail everywhere, the blood-dimmed tide having drowned the ceremony of innocence. "The ceremony of innocence" has deep significance in the Yeatsian

---

102. *Ibid.*, pp. 364-65.
103. Winters, Yvor, *The Poetry of W.B. Yeats* (Denver : Allan Swallow, 1960), p. 7.
104. *WBYCP*, pp. 210-11.
105. *Yeats*, p. 321.

terminology. The poet associated it with the horn of plenty and the laurel tree that symbolized peace and harmony. They are, in fact, the two major symbols in his poem "A Prayer for My Daughter". In Yeats' view, the absence of ceremony resulted in the flood of hatred and arrogance that we witness in the present-day-society. For him the drowning of the ceremony of innocence coincided with the rising of the middle-class Philistinism. His statement that

> The best lack all conviction, while the worst
> Are full of passionate intensity.

may not, however, amount to an attempt at identifying the best with the members of aristocracy. Maybe, he subscribed to a feeling that his own sceptical leanings suggested a superior mind. If his tone here sounds rather too assertive to suggest a sceptical bent of mind, his mood of frenzy may have to be blamed for it.

In that mood Yeats is sure of the possibility of a revelation that ends the present plight of the world. He calls it the Second Coming, allowing the poem a Christian denotation. Even as he prophesies the Second Coming, the vast image of a rough beast is said to have troubled his sight. It is a macabre thing, in its outward features:

> A shape with lion body and the head of a man,
> A gaze blank and pitiless as the sun,
> Is moving its slow thighs, while all about it
> Real shadows of the indignant desert birds.

The appearance of the beast marks the visionary moment of the poem. The beast keeps moving in a clumsy manner. Its look is blank and pitiless. The "reeling shadows of the indignant desert-birds" enhance our sense of horror. They seem to represent nature's fury.

The vision comes to an abrupt end. Then, curiously enough, the poet himself explains its significance, in a seeming bid to make up for the inadequacy of the Symbolist method. He says that it will bring to an end the twenty centuries of stony sleep. The air of certainty in the statement is the contribution of the Yeatsian System. The end of the stony sleep is expected to stem the blood-dimmed tide let loose on the world.

Does the poet feel a certain relish, as he mentions 'the blood-dimmed tide'? Louis MacNeice, for one, believes that he does.[106] He ascribes it to Yeats' fascist tendencies. Graham Hough also

---

106. MacNeice, Louis, pp. 119-20.

inclines towards such a view.[107] To George Bornstein, however, the phrase 'rough beast' suggests horror rather than delight. He does not believe that the speaker rejoices.[108] Denis Donoghue also thinks on the same lines.[109] It is certainly possible that the speaker is both horrified and delighted at the same time. While the sense of delight may well be attributed to his fascist trends, his feeling nature may account for the sense of horror. Louis MacNeice has suggested that the poet felt happy about the prospect of the worst assuming powers.[110] We have no reason to believe that the passionate intensity of the worst had great fascination for him. If it had, he would not probably have envisioned the Second Coming.

Significantly, the poet has not chosen to stick to the mood of frenzy. He sounds fully alive to the gravity of the situation. A conscious bid to exercise a cerebral control over it is apparent. That is why the darkness is allowed to drop again, bringing about the pattern of the greater Romantic lyric.

Yeats, here, appears to have held in check his tendency to assume tragic gaiety in difficult situations. A sober awareness of the disquieting implications of his prophecy may partly account for that restraint. The sceptical cast of his mind would, no doubt, have saved him from giving full credence to it, as remarked by Frank Kermode.

Yeats' nature was delicate and sensitive. Yet it was complex and nearly intractable. Apparently it hankered after a prop of some sort or other to keep its poise. His intense hatred of scientific rationalism and objectivity coupled with his inability to seek solace in a conventional religion must have rendered the problem extremely acute for him. He was thus left struggling to construct a religion on his own. He was prone to believe in the mystery of the world. As observed by John Unterecker, he felt that there was incontrovertible evidence everywhere of an invisible, but eminently active, spirit-world.[111] David Holbrook says:

> It is possible to be "religious" without having a specific belief. That is, it is possible to allow the mystery of the world... to share a degree of the "spiritual dimension" with those who have faith.[112]

---

107. *The Last Romantics*, p. 249.
108. Bornstein, George, *TR.*, p. 63.
109. Donoghue on Yeats, p.
110. MacNeice, Louis, p. 120.
111. *A Reader's Guide to W.B. Yeats*, p. 19.
112. Holbrook, David, *Lost Bearings in English Poetry* (London : Vision Press Limited, 1977), p. 44. Henceforth cited as *Lost Bearings*.

In such a broad sense, Yeats may be found to be religious. His comment on T.S. Eliot in his introduction to the Oxford Book of Modern Verse suggests an intimate understanding of the ethos of a religious person. He says:

> (Eliot's) religion, compared to that of John Gray, Francis Thomson, Lionel Johnson in "The Dark Angel" lacks all strong emotion; a New England Protestant by descent, there is little self-surrender in his personal relation to God and the soul....[113]

Presumably it was a comparable inability on the part of Yeats to surrender himself entirely to God that prompted him to keep a safe distance from all formal religions. And probably he was amused to find a similar inability in one who chose a path that was different from his. We may assume that it was the element of scepticism that promoted such an inability in these poets. Eliot, however, seems to have managed to suspend his disbelief to the extent of being able to believe in a formal religion in order to "set my lands in order."[114] Yeats might well have considered such a move dishonest. Apparently, he hated to wear a mask in matters concerning religion. His effort to remake himself did not affect his attitude towards established religions. He had to count on his own inner resources for creating joy and self-assurance. Indeed his attempts in this regard may appear rather ridiculous to those who look up to conventional religions for meeting such needs. Yet, we cannot help admiring the honesty of his intentions. Even the challenge of his old age did not make him turn to dishonest solutions. An absolute faith of the conventional type perhaps demanded a certain simplicity of mind. It was beyond Yeats. His failure to thrash out an intellectual solution to his problems made him fall back on his emotions. He concludes that

> ... being but a broken man
> I must be satisfied with my heart....[115]

And he tended to believe that "Eternity is passion." Indeed the belief smacks of an attempt to make a virtue of necessity. Yet he imagines himself as "a passion-driven exultant man". He began to sing out "sentences he has never thought".[116] The subordination of

---

113. Yeats, W.B., *OBMV.*, Introduction, p. XXII.

114. Eliot, T.S., *The Complete Poems and Plays of T.S. Eliot* (London : Faber & Faber, 1969), p. 74.

115. *WBYCP*, p. 391.

116. *Ibid.*, p. 332.

the thought-content to the emotions of the heart was not a matter of regret for Yeats, if we are to judge him by the tone of his assertions. It was perhaps a fitting finale to the life of a "supreme poet" of passions[117] that he was. In the Wordsworthian terminology we may say that the poems of the phase embodied a spontaneous overflow of powerful feelings in spite of the masks assumed.

Yeats' equation of passion with eternity may lend a new dimension to these poems. In fact, Edith Sitwell has gone to the extent of describing the "Words for Music" as "undoubtedly the greatest lyrics of the last hundred years, because of their intense fusion of spirit and matter, because of their overwhelming fire and their strange world-old wisdom".[118] Elizabeth Drew observes that the Crazy Jane poems have combined "universal, mystical wisdom with racy sensual and primitive elements".[119]

Passions, vulgar and sublime, assumed and authentic, found adequate expression in Yeats' poems. His vast and varied experience as a lover must have helped him to present the theme of sexual love in all its complexity.

To those who miss the spiritual aspect of the poems of Yeats' last phase, they may appear to be overy emotional stuff. T.S. Eliot, for one, could not possibly have acknowledged their spiritual import. He has made no secret of his disenchantment with the Yeatsian ideas of the supernatural.[120] He believed that Yeats' supernatural world was of the wrong kind. Yet he valued the last poems of Yeats for the forthright and uninhibited quality of the emotions expressed in them.[121] They made him revise his idea of impersonality and even recant his opinion on Yeats. He was convinced that the impersonality found in the later Yeats was deeper and more substantial, compared with what could be contrived by a skilful craftsman. He had to concede that it was the latter sort that he had advocated in his early criticism. His later poetry testifies to his change of heart in this regard. J.B. Beer has observed how Keats maintained that a poet should seek for a knowledge which is at the

117. *A Critical Introduction*, p. 192.

118. Sitwell, Edith, *Aspects of Modern Poetry* (London : Duckworth, 1934), p. 89.

119. Drew, Elizabeth, *Poetry* (Dell Publishing Co., 1959), p. 210.

120. Eliot, T.S., *After Strange Gods : A Primer of Modern Heresy* (Faber & Faber Ltd., 1934), p. 46.

121. Eliot, T.S., "Yeats", *OPP.*, pp. 257-58.

same time universal and spontaneous within his own mind.[122] The Odes are found to enshrine Keats' success in the search. The Yeatsian achievement acknowledged by Eliot may be an identical one. When Vivienne Koch remarks that in Yeats' last poems the man who suffered and the man who wrote were, in the most creative sense of suffering, one, she is only reiterating what Eliot made explicit years ago.[123]

Finding such an inclusive voice that was both personal and universal does not, however, amount to the achievement of Unity of Being. The emotional side of the Yeatsian personality which found abundant expression in the last phase of his life is obviously only a part of the whole. The Unity of Being implied an inclusive view embracing all aspects of the human personality for giving them harmonious expression. It had to be an intellectual, imaginative and emotional effort at the same time.

It is amusing to note how Yeats managed to suspend his disbelief – his sceptical bent of mind – to the extent of being able to believe in the adequacy of emotions in the context, even as Eliot opted for a faith of a higher order to grapple with his problems. The Yeatsian belief in the blood – in the basic instincts of man – evidenced here has a Lawrencian tint. But while Lawrence held fast to such a belief throughout his life without allowing the meddling intellect to dilute it, the Yeatsian intellect made its presence felt in the invention of masks. In fact, it also tried to assert itself over his emotions as instanced by the Byzantium poems. The Keatsian faith in the truth of emotions had not allowed him to surrender himself to them more than momentarily. While Yeats revealed an affinity with Keats in his sceptical tendencies, the concluding phase seems to have brought him closer to the Lawrencian mode of thinking "with the blood". His tendency to identify the sensual with the mystical was also Lawrencian. His sceptical approach, however, would seem to have saved him from the Lawrencian lack of humour. It may, however, be fallacious to assume that Yeats modelled himself on Lawrence. His reliance on passions must have been inspired largely by the Blakean belief in their holiness and in their adequacy as a means to eternity, as noted by Elizabeth Drew.[124]

122. Beer, J.B., *Coleridge the Visionary*, p. 18.

123. *Vide*, The Tragic Phase, p. 26.

124. *Poetry*, p. 118.

Yeats' achievement in his last phase included the narrowing of the gap between the lyrical and the dramatic – the personal and the impersonal – in art. The poet's much-lamented decision to hand himself over to Crazy Jane and Jack the Journeyman helped in that effort. It was, in fact, anticipated by the unavailing attempt of his earlier phase to escape from the complexity of the flesh-and-blood-world into a world of art. The invasion of his inner scene by emotions was the inevitable consequence of the inability of his intellect to assert itself.

The means resorted to by Yeats for filling the void created by his want of faith in a formal religion should not have made a matter for ridiculing him. Critics like D.S. Savage, however, have shown no inclination to appreciate the magnitude of the problem confronted by him. The hollowness at the centre of his work mentioned by Savage[125] in a seeming bid to disparage him, perhaps alludes to that void. Paul Tillich has presented the facts concerning the typically modern malady suggested by that void:

> The decisive event which underlies the search for meaning and the despair of it in the twentieth century is the loss of God in the nineteenth century .... This is felt both as a loss and as a liberation. It drives one either to nihilism or to the courage which takes non-being into itself .... On this basis Existentialism, that is, the great art, literature, and philosophy of the twentieth century, reveals the courage to face things as they are and to express the anxiety of meaninglessness.[126]

Yeats, for one, has revealed that "courage to face things as they are and to express the anxiety of meaninglessness." What B.L. Reid takes for spiritual arrogance in Yeats may well be reckoned courage. He observes how, in Yeats' world, "man stands naked before tragic fact, his destiny being his own to make. While Reid has given due credit to Yeats for his absolute integrity by calling him "that uncommon thing, a completely honest poet",[127] he does not seem to realize that an honesty of such a class should naturally involve the courage of conviction.

Yeats' case was in a sense rather peculiar, as he developed his hostility towards science after allowing it to nullify his faith. His

125. Savage, D.S., *The Permanence of Yeats*, p. 192.

126. Tillich, Paul, "The Concept to Be", 1952, quoted in Spears, Monroe K., *Dionysus and the City : Modernism in Twentieth Century Poetry* (New York : Oxford University Press), 1970), pp. 54-55.

127. *The Lyric of Tragedy*, p.

sceptical cast of mind must have affected his attitude to science, too. He was thus saved from the modern "obsession with the mechanical truths of empirical science". As observed by Anne Smith, this obsession has led poets into the blind alley of nihilism and away from "the realities of art which help to lift life out of its mediocrity".[128] The notion that nihilism is a possible romantic consequence which modern poets must work through *en route* to a new poetry of reality,[129] neglects the extent to which that working through is the chief ingredient in romanticism itself, as pointed out by George Bornstein.[130]

Thanks to its capacity to look beyond the material aspects of the objects of nature, the Romantic imagination has helped promote faith in the mystery of the world. Thus, it has been able to provide a viable substitue for religious faith that helps fill the void caused by the loss of God referred to by Paul Tillich. David Holbrook has noted that nihilism and cultural sensationalism often result from a failure of confidence in the powers of mind.[131]

Yeats, with a creative imagination backed up by an amazing inventive skill revealed in his attitudinizing and wearing of masks, was able to hold out against all sorts of challenges.

The hysterical quality revealed in the concluding phase of Yeats' life might be taken for a failure of his imagination. But the failure involved was presumably of his nerves. It results in the slackening of his resolve to pursue Unity of Being. The failure does not affect his inventive genius either, if his persistent wearing of masks even in his 'tragic phase' is any indication. F.R. Leavis rightly calls it the abandonment of all concern for the resolution, or paradoxically creative management of the complexity of life.[132]

Donald Davie has said that poetry to be great "must reek of the human, as Wordsworth's poetry does".[133] Judged by that criterion, Yeats' claims to greatness are beyond dispute. But the visionary intensity evidenced in his poetry may be equally relevant. It is a

128. *Vide*, *Lost Bearings*, Editional Note by Anne Smith.

1_9. Miller, J. Hillis, *Poets of Reality : Six Twentieth Century Writers* (Cambridge, Massachusetts : The Belknap Press of Harvard University Press, 1966), p. 1.

130. Bornstein, George, *TR.*, p. 19.

131. *Lost Bearings*. It is the crux of David Holbrook's argument in the book.

132. *Lectures in America*, p. 75.

133. Davie, Donald, *AE.*, p. 165.

Romantic legacy that he inherited through a heroic effort. In its absence his poetry might have had nothing but "passive suffering" for its theme. The Yeatsian contribution to the Romantic tradition seems to lie in the manner in which he endowed his visionary efforts with an aspect of heroism, and used it for salving, if not healing, the sores of life.

CHAPTER VI

CONTRIBUTION OF T.S. ELIOT TO THE ROMANTIC TRADITION

In the English literary arena of the first half of the twentieth century, the most influential and assertive voice has perhaps been that of T.S. Eliot. Yet, paradoxically enough, it has also been one of the suavest and most tentative of voices. The manner in which Eliot has combined in himself such contrasting traits may account, partly at least, for his reputation.

Eliot's kinship with the Romantic tradition has already been under a flood of light, thanks to a galaxy of critics including Yvor Winters, Stephen Spender, Herbert Read, Graham Hough, Frank Kermode, G.S. Fraser, M.H. Abrams, Eliseo Vivas, Murry Krieger, Richard Foster, C.K. Stead, Robert Langbaum, George Bornstein, Bernard Bergonzi and Balachandra Rajan among others.

When D.H. Lawrence remarked, with a characteristic vehemence, that Eliot's "classiocity is bunkum",[1] he was seeing through the latter's strategy. Only the mould of Eliot's poetry belongs to the classicist in him. His devotion to 'tradition' (in its distinct sense) makes him conscious of his place in history, and prompts him to make a serious endeavour towards curing English poetry, as he found it, of its ills. "The sense of tradition", in the words of Bernard Bergonzi, "is a life line that keeps the poet in touch with order and reality, while he is submerged in the dark waters of the creative imagination".[2] The good health of the embryo that develops into a poem demands "the saturation of the poet's sensibility in the vats of tradition and orthodoxy".[3] If Eliot appeared to suffer from a certain impatience and irritation in the context, judging from his inability to take an objective view of the Romantic achievements of the past, it may suggest, more than anything else, his involvement in the problems of the day.

---

1. Quoted in *Lecture in America*, p. 31.
2. Bergonzi, Bernard, *T.S. Eliot*, Masters of World Literature Series (New York : Macmillan, 1972), p. 72. Henceforth cited as Bergonzi, Bernard, *T.S. Eliot*.
3. Stead, C.K., *NP*., p. 137.

In recent years we have been witnessing an ever-increasing trend to emphasize the personal element in the poetry of Eliot. It is exemplified by the works of James E. Miller, Jr., and Lyndall Gordon.[4] The new trend has come partly as a reaction against the tendency of earlier critics to over-stress the apparently impersonal aspect of poems like "The Waste Land". Lyndall Gordon, for instance, holds Eliot guilty of suppressing personal expereince.[5] Critics like her tend to lose sight of the general import of the curbing of excessive emotions attempted by Eliot. A sobering of the personal element in the poetry of the early twentieth century through a conscious intellectual effort was perhaps a historical necessity. Eliot was responding to that need in a distinctive fashion, when he sought to curb his own sentimental leanings. The fact that "The Waste Land" meant only "a rhythmical grumbling"[6] to him does not preclude the possibility of its having a wider significance. For, Eliot himself has said elsewhere:

> The tension within the society may become also a tension within the mind of the more conscious individual...[7]

The comment may throw light on the manner in which the waste land he portrayed became a symbol of his own inner chaos. The restoration of the outer waste land to fertility involves his own personal redemption: the setting of "my lands in order".[8] Eliot makes a serious effort in that direction in his later life.

When we remember that "The Waste Land" was written in "a state of emotional derangement",[9] we may note a striking similarity

4. Miller, Jr., James E., *T.S. Eliot's Personal Waste Land* (Pennsylvania State University Press, 1977). Miller argues that *The Waste Land* is Eliot's *In Memoriam* for a French medical student, who was killed in the first World War; Gordon, Lyndall, *Eliot's Early Years* (New York: Oxford University Press, 1977).
5. Gordon, Lyndall, Remarks quoted in Draper, R.P., "Recent Approaches to Eliot", Review in *Critical Quarterly* (Vol. 20, No. 1, Spring, 1978), p. 78.
6. Eliot, T.S., quoted in Hough, Graham, "Vision and Doctrine in *Four Quartets*", *Critical Quarterly* (Vol. 15, No. 2, Summer 1973), p. 122. Henceforth cited as "Vision and Doctrine".
7. Eliot, T.S., *Notes towards the Definition of Culture* (London : Faber and Faber Limited, 1948), p. 25. Henceforth cited as *Notes towards the Definition of Culture*.
8. Eliot, T.S., *The Complete Poems and Plays of T.S. Eliot* (London: Faber & Faber, 1969), p. 74. Henceforth cited as *TSECPP*.
9. Bornstein, George, *TR.*, p. 148. Seel also Gardner, Helen "The Waste Land, Paris, 1922", *Eliot in His Time : Essays on the Occasion of the Fifth Anniversary of the Waste Land*, ed., Walton Litz (Princeton University Press, 1972), p. 73. Henceforth cited as *Eliot in His Time*.

between the innate propensities of A.E. Housman[10] and Eliot. The depersonalizing devices that he evolved, however, seem to have rescued him from the Housmanian sentimentality. If he had meekly yielded up to his Romantic instincts and given them unrestrained expression, the flood of mawkish sentiments that invaded the literary arena, when he launched himself into it, would have gone largely unchecked. Indeed this is not to belittle the contributions of poets like Thomas Hardy, Edward Thomas and W.B. Yeats. As hinted at earlier, their efforts failed to make adequate impact on the poetry of the time, owing largely to a lack of aggressiveness. It is amusing to note how aggressive tactics yielded quick results even in the field of letters. Of course, an achievement of that kind is apt to bring in its train a fresh crop of problems, entailing a search for new remedies. But it may not detract from the importance of the achievement at the moment.

The problems tackled by Eliot are virtually the problems of the critic in him. And they concerned only the conscious level of his mind. The inconsistencies in the critical utterances of Eliot had to be tackled at that level. In his innate instincts he remained wedded to the Romantic tradition. Such a view may imply that Eliot was anti-romantic without being unromantic. But a close look at his critical utterances suggests that they are heavily slanted in favour of Romanticism even in his early phase. His comments on the Wordsworthian definition of poetry, for instance, yields clear enough hints of his deep affinity to the Romantic tradition. His preference for the term 'concentration' to the Wordsworthian 'recollection' accentuates the unconscious activity involved in poetry-making.[11] His insistence that the conscious level of the mind is entirely at the mercy of the unconscious in the process suggests the violent nature of the Romantic instincts in him. His anti-romantic stance perhaps betrays his dread of them. And presumably, his conscious effort to escape the influence of Shelley and Milton referred to by S.Viswanathan in his sketch of the shifts in the attitude of Eliot towards Shelley is but a symptom of it.[12] George Bornstein has drawn attention to the crux of the problem when he says :

10. See Housman, A.E., "Name and Nature of Poetry", *A.E. Housman – Poetry and Prose: A Selection*, ed. F.C. Horwook (London : Hutchinson Educational, 1971, reprint, 1972), pp. 243-248.
11. Eliot, T.S., *SW*., p. 58.
12. Viswanathan, S., "Eliot and Shelley: A Sketch of Shifts in Attitude", *Ariel* (Volume II, No. 1, January, 1971), p. 60.

> (Eliot) recognizes imagination as a violence from within, but not as a rage for order. He, therefore, relies on external authority to contain the irrationality of composition: first literary tradition and later religious orthodoxy. These he continually berates the romantics for lacking.[13]

Eliot's persistent awareness of the problem is suggested by the deliberate quality of his art. "There is a great deal in the writing of poetry", says he, "which must be conscious and deliberate".[14] The great Romantics have evidently not chosen to stress that aspect of the poetry-making effort. But when Coleridge assigns the transcendental function to the highest form of self-consciousness, he does not deny the lower forms their due place. Wordsworth, apart from describing imagination as "Reason in her most exalted mood,"[15] also insists that "our continued influxes of feeling are modified and directed by our thoughts."[16] The insistence on the need of "prehending" emotion "intellectually and emotionally at once",[17] inspired by Eliot perhaps suggests a slight misreading of the Wordsworthian thesis. Obviously, neither Coleridge nor Wordsworth finds any conflict or contradiction in assigning such a dual role to the mind. But, whereas they emphasize the function of the transcendental faculty, Eliot stresses the role of the conscious mind. Their differing traditions may account for the variance in their attitudes. But the great Romantics were perhaps at an advantage, as their environment apparently allowed them to respond to their inward urges in a relatively uninhibited fashion. The situation that confronted Eliot was distinct from theirs. He had to assume the strident voice of a classicist for correcting the sensibility of his time. Sensibility, he knew, was apt to degenerate into sentimentality,[18] in the absence of a cerebral check. He had also to subject his Romantic urges to classicist procedures. They were tasks only for the self-conscious level of his mind. Eliot's awareness of the fact is suggested when he says :

---

13. Bornstein, George, *TR.*, p. 112.
14. Eliot, T.S., *SW.*, p. 58.
15. Wordsworth, William, *The Prelude*, quoted in Abrams, M.H., *The Mirror and the Lamp* (Oxford University Press, 1953, reprint, 1974), p. 314.
16. Wordsworth, William, Preface to *Lyrical Ballads*, ed. R.L. Brett and A.R. Jones (London : Methuen & Co. Limited, 1963, reprint 1968), p. 246.
17. Introduction to *Oxford Poetry*, 1927, quoted in Spender, Stephen, "Remembering Eliot", *T.S. Eliot : The Man and His Work*, ed. Allen Tate (London : Chatto & Windus, 1967), p. 45. Henceforth cited as *The Man and His Work*.
18. See Read, Herbert, *Phases of English Poetry* (London : Leonard & Virginia Woolf at the Hoggarth Press, 1928), p. 144.

> Impressions and experiences which are important for the man may take no place in the poetry and those which become important in the poetry may play quite a negligible part in the man, the personality.[19]

The association here of 'personality' with 'man' and not with 'poetry' seems significant, as it happens in the earliest of his major critical essays. The idea implied may link 'personality' with 'persona' rather than with 'person' and bring it close to Herbert Read's conception of "character". We are also reminded of Simone Weil's statement that "our personality is the part of us which belongs to error and sin".[20] Perfection, on the other hand, is considered impersonal. Eliot's conception of impersonality suggests a correlation with Simone Weil's ideas. While Wordsworth and Coleridge attribute the achievement of impersonality to the imaginative faculty of the mind, Eliot shuns, perhaps deliberately, the use of the word 'imagination' in the context. George Bornstein has observed how "Eliot's aesthetic lacks the key-stone of romantic theory – imagination as stabilizing and synthesizing force".[21] Surely, Eliot's affinity to the Romantic tradition cannot be denied on that score. If anything, the difference only bears out the relative violence of Romantic instincts in Eliot and his awareness of the need of holding them in leash.

Eliot's insistence on escaping from personal emotions is believed to form the core of his anti-romantic stance. But, the use of the word 'escape' in the context is perhaps less than apt, as what is implied thereby is only the curbing of emotions.[22] We have already noted how Eliot's formulation of the 'objective correlative' lends substance to such a view, as it testifies to his belief in the emotive origin of poetry as conceived by the great Romantics. The conscious intellect can have only a subordinate role in such a scheme of things.

The critical utterances of Eliot's later life, however, make his affiliation to the essential aspects of Romanticism explicit. Interestingly enough, they come in the wake of the famous declaration of his triple allegiances in 1927. In "The Social Function of Poetry" (1945), for instance, he maintains that "poetry has primarily to do

---

19. Eliot, T.S., *SW.*, p. 56.
20. Weil, Simone, remark quoted in "Poetry and 'Impersonality': Some Discriminations", *Critical Quarterly* (Vol. XXX, No. 1, January, 1980), p. 53. Henceforth cited as *Poetry and Impersonality*.
21. Bornstein, George, *TR.*, p. 112.
22. Eliot, T.S., *SW.*, p. 58.

with the expression of feeling and emotion and that feeling and emotion are particular whereas thought is general".[23] In his essay on Rudyard Kipling (1941) he says that the conscious mind is concerned only with the craftsman's problems.[24] The profounder meaning, according to him, has to emerge from a deeper level. Such a view involves the denial of the name of "poetry" to the "verse" made in the conscious mind, including Kipling's. What is implied here is the Arnoldian belief that genuine poetry is conceived and composed in the soul, though Eliot would have denied it at that point of time.

His later essay "The Three Voices of Poetry" (1953) confirms his allegiance to the Romantic tradition. He sounds particularly soft towards the first voice. It has found favour with him. While identifying himself with the views expressed by a German poet Gottfried Benn in a lecture, he adds that the expression of the obscure impulse referred to by the latter may be the sole concern of a poet. "The Poet", he says,

> "is oppressed by a burden which he must bring to birth in order to obtain relief. Or, to change the figure of speech, he is haunted by a demon, a demon against which he feels powerless, because in its first manifestation it has no face, no name, nothing; and the words, the poem he makes, are a kind of form of exorcism of this demon. In other words again, he is going to all that trouble, not in order to communicate with anyone, but to gain relief from acute discomfort..."[25]

The confession highlights the Dionysian aspect of Eliot. Of course, the Apollonian traits of his personality manifest themselves in his classical concerns.

While the poetry of the second voice may be exemplified by the rhetorical verse of the pre-modernist era such as Kipling's, Eliot's own early depersonalized work and later plays may illustrate the poetry of the third voice. The involvement of the inventive genius in the making of such poetry may mean an important role for the conscious mind. But unlike the poetry of the second voice, it does not involve the befogging of the unconscious. A proper coordination between the two levels may be important in its making. Indeed the conscious level would seem to have an upper hand in that process.

In "The Love Song of J. Alfred Prufrock", for example, the poet

---

23. Eliot, T.S., *OPP.*, p. 19.
24. *Ibid.*, p. 238.
25. *Ibid.*, p. 98.

seems to have invented a persona wholly unlike himself in outward looks mainly to guard himself against being identified with it. But then he allows himself a free hand to use the persona for illustrating the impact of extreme self-consciousness on a modern mind, much like his own. In the dramatic account of the poem we find matter enough to be convinced of the manner in which the conscious level of the mind seeks to distract Romantic instincts controlled by the unconscious. The Romantic leanings of the protagonist are echoed when he says:

> We have lingered in the chambers of the sea
> By sea-girls wreathed with seaweed red and brown
> Till human voices wake us and we drown.[26]

The human voices here are to be identified with the voice of the intellect. The drowning alluded to is virtually of the imaginative faculty. Indeed it is only a momentary feeling accurately portrayed. Yet we are moved when Prufrock says:

> I should have been a pair of ragged claws
> Scuttling across the floors of silent seas.[27]

As remarked by Elizabeth Drew, what is suggested here is a "compulsive infantile and primitive craving" "for uncomplicated animal existence", which may make "a safe haven where his inner universe is no longer disturbed by any tormenting human problems".[28] The consciousness of the impossibility of such a regress may not nullify the significance of the longing. Similarly, when we hear a persona confess –

> I keep my countenance,
> I remain self-possessed
> Except when a street-piano, mechanical and tired
> Reiterates some worn-out common song
> With the smell of hyacinths across the garden
> Recalling things that other people have desired
> Are these ideas right or wrong?[29]

what is apparent is an attempt of the self-conscious mind to stifle a romantic longing. The author seems to have put an intimate thought of his own into the mouth of a persona when the latter says :

---

26. *TSECPP.*, p. 17.
27. *Ibid.*, p. 15.
28. Drew, Elizabeth, *T.S. Eliot: The Design of His Poetry* (New York : Charles Scribner's Sons, 1949), p. 36. Henceforth cited as *The Design of His Poetry*.
29. *TSECPP.*, p. 20.

And I must borrow every changing shape
To find expression ... dance, dance
Like a dancing bear,
Cry like a parrot, chatter like an ape.[30]

We are aware how long the poet persisted with the self-dramatization alluded to here. It forms part of his depersonalizing effort for meeting a need that was both personal and general. The general need was of purging the Romantic poetry of his time of its emotional excesses. The fact that he could drown the distinction between the personal and the general so early in his life may redound to his credit, though he spells out the possibility of such an achievement only much later:

> The second impersonality is that of the poet, who, out of intense and personal experience, is able to express a general truth; retaining all the particularity of his experience, to make of it a general symbol.[31]

The statement forms part of a handsome encomium paid to Yeats. The achievement of such an impersonality was apparently one of his objectives as an artist. Indeed it is also a measure of his social consciousness. It accounts for the miracle of a poem which meant to its maker "the relief of a personal and wholly insignificant grouse against life"[32] becoming a criticism of the contemporary life.

In its formal and technical aspects *The Waste Land* appears rather disturbingly loyal to the Imagist ideals. The "rhythmical grumbling" attempted in the poem perhaps demands a rigorous cerebral control. When T.E. Hulme ridiculed the tendency promoted by the Romantics to think that "verse means little more than the expression of unsatisfied emotion",[33] he did not possibly realize that unsatisfied emotion could consort with "hard, dry and classical" verse, without a word of direct, plain statement as it does in *The Waste Land*. The poem, however, turns out to be virtually a string of images, with no apparent structure. But the mythical method adopted from James Joyce gave it a shaping principle. It represents a bid on Eliot's part to tackle the problems of rhetorical discontinuity promoted by the Imagists under the influence of the French Symbolists. Krishna Rayan says :

30. *Ibid*., p. 21.
31. Eliot, T.S., *OPP*., p. 255.
32. Eliot, T.S., Remarks quoted in Ellmann, Richard, "The First Waste Land," *Eliot in His Time*, p. 52.
33. Hulme, T.E., *TCC*., p. 99.

> A problem of contemporary poetry and poetics is that of how a long poem in the strict Symbolist manner, composed exclusively of non-propositional imagery, can exist as a whole poem and not as a mere string of symbols. But the solution was presented when the problem itself was first presented in *The Waste Land*.[34]

The use of the mythical method, "manipulating a continuous parallel between contemporaneity and antiquity",[35] instead of the traditional mode of narration implies the adoption of the Spatial form (as Joseph Frank calls it)[36] with its emphasis on non-naturalistic style. Natural landscapes thus give way to townscapes. Eliot has been called "the great master of the city-theme"[37] among modern poets. In that respect Eliot was apparently inspired by the example of Baudelaire. Eliot was also largely responsible for exposing English poetry to new areas of experience in the modern context.[38] David Perkins has pointed out how *The Waste Land* broke "the fixed association between verse and the agreeable, the beautiful or the ideal."[39] The outer landscapes served as objectives-correlative for projecting the emotions of the poet as they did for the earlier Romantics. What we have in *The Waste Land* is thus righly called "a pioneering inward voyage".[40] The modernist experiment proves that "no object is inherently unpoetical; whether a poet can create an image from any given object depends first upon the imaginative intensity of his own response to it, and secondly upon the extent to which this object has been assimilated by the general consciousness".[41] In the history of Romantic poetry, it means a progress from innocence to experience.

C.K. Stead has said that in composing *The Waste Land* Eliot "has created a mock-heroic surface and then broke it plunging beneath to sources of feeling which lay deeper". In this process

---

34. *Suggestion and Statement in Poetry*, p. 50.
35. Eliot, T.S., "Ulysses, Order and Myth" in *The Modern Tradition*, ed., Richard Ellmann and Charles Feidelson, Jr. (New York : Oxford University Press, 1965), p. 681.
36. Frank, Joseph, remarks quoted in Spears, Monroe, K., *DC*., pp. 64-66.
37. Spears, Monroe K., *DC*., p. 76.
38. Alvarez, A., "English Poetry Today", reprinted in *On Contemporary Literature : An Anthology of Critical Essays*, ed. Richard Kostelanetz (New York: Avon Books, 1964), p. 83. Henceforth cited as "*English Poetry Today*".
39. Perkins, David, *HMP*., p. 501.
40. Rosenthal, M.L., *Sailing into the Unkncwn* (New York : Oxford University Press, 1978), p. 178. Henceforth cited as *Sailing into the Unknown*.
41. Lewis, C. Day, *The Poetic Image*, p. 90.

Eliot is said to have lived out his "neo-Romantic revolt against his own neo-classicism".[42] The idea sought to be conveyed by Stead seems substantially true, though the manner of its expression has perhaps been rather insinuating. The classicism in Eliot, as we understand it, is largely a matter of surface; the inner core belongs to Romanticism.

It may be worth pondering whether the mythical method adopted by Eliot has amounted to the expression of a nostalgia. One may be tempted to think that it has, particularly in view of the Romantic tendencies of Eliot. But Eliot's modern sensibility, with its tormenting self-consciousness and sceptical leanings could hardly have allowed scope for such a simple feeling, as testified to by "The Love Song of J. Alfred Prufrock". Derek Traversi has rightly said that "the past offers Eliot no ready way of escape from the 'immense panorama of futility and anarchy' which is contemporary history". Eliot's social awareness and involvement in the problems of the day might also have undermined his nostalgic feeling. "The contrary intimations of living significance" were perhaps another potent factor that helped to sustain his spirits in the face of 'futility and anarchy', as hinted at by Traversi.[43]

After presenting a depressing picture of the human society "rotten at heart and crumbling, where pleasure is corrupt and the spirit is dead"[44] Eliot seeks to arrive at a consoling conclusion in the last section of *The Waste Land*. But Elizabeth Drew, for one, finds it ineffective, as its atmosphere, in her view, "is coloured far more strongly by the image of destruction". The words repeated in the context, according to her, remain "in foreign tongues, not translated into his own inner experience".[45] Edith Sitwell, on the contrary, is nearly overwhelmed by the same words. She says:

> "Da Datta Dayadhvam Damyatha" the sounds have the actual reverberations of the sound of the thunder echoing over mountains, and the Voice of God is embodied in form.[46]

---

42. Stead, C.K., "Eliot, Arnold and the English Poetic Tradition" *The Literary Criticism of T.S. Eliot*, ed. David Newton-de Molina (University of London, The Athlone Press, 1977), p. 203.
43. Traversi, Derek, *T.S. Eliot : The Longer Poems* (London, Sydney, Toronto : The Bodley Head, 1976), pp. 19-20.
44. Nicholson, Norman, "T.S. Eliot", *Writers of Today* (London : Sidwick and Jackson, 1946), p. 140. Henceforth cited as *Writers of Today*.
45. *The Design of His Poetry*, p. 90.
46. Sitwell, Edith, *Aspects of Modern Poetry* (London : Duckworth, 1934), p. 137.

Such reverberating sounds are, in fact, characteristic of Sanskrit. It is likely that Eliot's choice of the words was influenced by that fact.

"The Hollow Men" has been found to present the poet's sense of depression in its extreme form. Allen Tate considers the poem the last example of Eliot's pure poetry.[47] But it carries hints of the probability of Grace coming to the rescue of the poet. Nevertheless, the poem remains an expression of unrelieved despair. It is hardly surprising that Eliot in his later life should have refused to read it in public. We are told that "he had come to doubt the right of an artist to give voice to such despair".[48] We may note a significant coincidence between the attitudes of Yeats and Eliot in the matter. Yeats, like Matthew Arnold earlier,[49] insisted that passive suffering was not a theme for poetry. In spite of the contrasting approaches of Eliot and Yeats towards conventional religions, there is something in common between them in their belief in the visionary intensity afforded by the Romantic imagination. What "The Hollow Men" lacks is perhaps the impact of that intensity. Yeats' refusal to attach himself to an established religion does not seem to have affected the visionary intensity of his poetry by any means.

Elizabeth Drew has described "The Hollow Men" as "the Yeatsian emblem of the scarecrow, the empty man without heart". But for Eliot, she says, "they are the men whose ideals have not grown from the centre of regeneration".[50] Eliot has resort to religious Grace to make up for that disability, which appeared as much his own as that of his persona. His failure to believe in human creativity referred to by F.R. Leavis may be attributed to it. David Holbrook has drawn attention to the presence, in Eliot's work, of "images of love which has failed – failed in encounter, and failed in meaning". In his view, Eliot's central theme is the "sterility of his own relationship with the other and the world". Eliot is said to have "translated this into a criticism of our civilization and its spiritual and cultural emptiness

47. Tate, Allen, *The Man and His Work*, p. 34.

48. Gillie, Christopher, *Movements in English Literature*, p. 151.

49. See Arnold, Matthew, *The Essential Arnold*, ed. Lionel Trilling (Chatto & Windus, 1949), p. 187. The subsequent modification in Arnold's stand referred to by Jon Stallworthy (*vide* "W.B. Yeats and Wilfred Owen" *Critical Quarterly*, Vol. II, No. 3, Autumn, 1969, p. 207) does not seem to have altered the position substantially.

50. Drew, Elizabeth, *Poetry*, p. 158.

and fragmentation".[51] Eliot's achievement has certainly meant more, as we have noted already.

We have evidence of Eliot's creative quest to "set my lands in order" from the Ariel poems onwards. It came close on the heels of his acceptance of Anglo-Catholicism. Hugh Kenner has mentioned how *Poems 1909-1925* "seemed likely to slip ineluctably into the past as the complete poetical works of T.S. Eliot."[52] A renewed religious feeling apparently helped him to realize that "man's vision can redeem his world, filling it with mystery, meaning and human gratitude for existence".[53] But the early Ariel poems do not suggest that awakening. What they project is only a sense of weariness and impatience. The protagonist of the "Journey of the Magi", for instance, speaks for the poet when he says:

> ... no longer at ease here, in the old dispensation,
> With an alien people clutching their gods.
> I would be glad of another death.[54]

The adoption of a new faith was initially only a source of 'hard and bitter agony' for the poet, as the new birth was for the Magus. Kathleen Raine has maintained that Eliot, in his statement of the worst, "has always implied the whole extent of the reality of which the worst is only a part".[55] Although we may be inclined to agree with such a view, the early Ariel poems are likely to prove exceptions to it. For what they suggest seems to be the Dark Night of the Soul, a necessary stage in the progress of the soul towards a dawn of new light. The death mentioned in the context is apparently a prelude to that new birth. When Helen Gardner says that the Ariel poems "treat the exhaustion of spirit in isolation," she seems to hint at their lack of a balanced view.[56]

The imagery of the poem, particularly in its opening section, reveals an arresting concreteness and precision. It seems to present

51. Holbrook, David, *Lost Bearings in English Poetry*, pp. 91 and 93.
52. Kenner, Hugh, *The Invisible Poet : T.S. Eliot* (London: Methuen & Co. Ltd., 1960, University Paperback, 1965), p. 208.
53. Holbrook, David, *Lost Bearings*, p. 88.
54. *TSECPP*., p. 104.
55. Raine, Kathleen, "The Poets of our Time", *T.S. Eliot : A Symposium for his Sixtieth Birthday*, ed. Richard March and M.J. Tambimuttu (Chicago : Henry Regnery Co., 1949), p. 79.
56. Gardner, Helen, *The Art of T.S. Eliot* (London : Faber & Faber Limited, 1949), p. 125.

a commonplace perspective. Presumably, Eliot's imagery grows subtle and imprecise when a higher reality is apprehended. The sense of despair and regret expressed in the poem may suggest that the Magi are no better than the Hollow Men. The physical hardships suffered by the Magi assume symbolic significance when we realize that Eliot himself has much in common with them. The Magi, like him, had to tackle the revolt of the conscience too. It is suggested by "the voices singing in our ears".[57]

The temperate valley presents lively images. "The running stream" and "the water-mill beating the darkness" have obvious signifiance. But the reference to the three trees, alluding to crucifixion, chills us. The appearance of the white horse relieves our sense of horror a little, because of its association with Christ. The tavern and vine leaves symbolize life. Then comes the image of the six hands dicing for pieces of silver to drown us in depression once again. The manner in which an image drawn from private experience could gain significance for Eliot is exemplified here.[58] But, ironically enough, all such significances mean little to the Magi. They "had the experience but missed the meaning", as Audrey F. Cahill puts it.[59] At last, we are told, they reached their destination, and presumably had a look of the Christ-child too. Still, the Magus says that it was just 'satisfactory'.

According to George Williamson, the tone of the poem is that of understatement and the use of 'satisfactory' in the context is proof of it.[60] But instead, the word seems to suggest mainly the absence of a real satisfaction. And perhaps an ambivalence too.

In fact, the next stanza proves beyond doubt that the tone of the poem is not of understatement. The Magus does not mince words. He asks, with an astonishing vehemence, whether they were led all the way for birth or death. He asserts that "this Birth was hard and bitter agony for us, like Death our Death".

57. *TSECPP.*, p. 103.

58. Eliot, T.S., *The Use of Poetry and the Use of Criticism* (London: Faber and Faber Ltd., 1933), p. 148. Henceforth cited as *The Use of Poetry and the Use of Criticism*.

59. Cahill, Audrey F., *T.S. Eliot and the Human Predicament* (Laurence Verry Incorporated, Mystic, Connecticut and University of Natel Press, 1967), p. Henceforth cited as *T.S. Eliot and the Human Predicament*.

60. Williamson, George, *A Reader's Guide to T.S. Eliot : A Poem-by-Poem Analysis* (London : Thames and Hudson, 1955, reprint 1976), p. 165. Henceforth cited as *A Reader's Guide to T.S. Eliot*.

The Magi find no peace even in their own kingdoms. Both the people and their idols seem alien to them. And they keep longing for another death. They do not seem to grasp the cause, significance or impact of the new birth. They do not possess either hindsight or insight or foresight. Their faith, abiding as it is, seems to lead them nowhere. What they reveal is apt to be taken for a spiritual incapacity.[61] But what is implied may be a dying to this world which has to precede the birth into another world, symbolized by the appearance of Marina.

As a visionary attempt to project the intimate consciousness of an individual in all its intensity by means of religious symbols, the poem reveals a Romantic trait.

Like 'Journey of the Magi' the second Ariel poem, 'A Song for Simeon' is also based on a biblical story.

Simeon, according to the Bible, had the good fortune of seeing the infant Jesus. And he is said to have sung the song of praise. Eliot's poem, however, contains no clear enough hint of it. There is no sense of triumph here. A premonition of the evil that is in store provides the burden of the 'Song'.

The poem is addressed to the Lord. Yet, at the very outset some secular images are presented. The Roman hyacinths are said to bloom in bowels. B.C. Southam points out that the Roman variety of hyacinths is suitable only for indoor cultivation.[62] But here they seem to represent a "fertility" that has to be "protected from the rigors of the season".[63] And the image acquires a new significance in the context of the new birth, as adverse surroundings are bound to pose problems to the new-born. The winter-sun is said to "creep by the snow-hill" in a sinister fashion. The season is called stubborn and does not seem likely to allow new growth to flourish.

In such a depressing set-up Simeon says that his light life, much like a feather, is waiting to be blown away by the death-wind. The

---

61. Smith, Grover, *T.S. Eliot's Poetry & Plays : A Study in Sources and Meaning* (Chicago and London : The University of Chicago Press, 1950, Eighth Impression, 1967), p. 127. Henceforth cited as *Grover Smith*.
62. Southam, B.C., *A Student's Guide to the Selected Poems of T.S. Eliot* (London: Faber and Faber Ltd., 1974).
63. Cahill, Audrey F., *T.S. Eliot and the Human Predicament*, p.

wind will also blow away the dust in sunlight that disturbs his vision and the memory in the corners of his mind that sustains his spirits.

Simeon requests the Lord to grant him peace. He says that he has lived a long life of faith and fast and has helped the poor. He has also exchanged honours and pleasures with others. None has gone from his door disappointed. Yet, the good things he has done, he fears, may not help his progeny in their hours of distress. He believes that they are doomed to suffer. He feels that only the lesser animals are likely to be helpful to them, when they are driven away by aliens.

Simeon prays to the Lord to grant him peace before the advent of those difficult days. He is already eighty and has nothing to look forward to.

A pious life, according to Simeon, brings in its train only sufferings. The glory achieved in the process is accompanied by derision. Simeon does not desire anything except a peaceful death. He knows that his flesh has grown weak. He has no wish to climb the stair of a saint. A martyr's death is also not for him. Nor is he capable of either the ecstasy of thought and prayer or the ultimate vision. His awareness of such possibilities may be a measure of his superiority to the Magus.

Simeon is able to see in a vision the sufferings Christ and others will be undergoing in future. He experiences those sufferings vicariously. He knows for certain that the new dispensation will work havoc with the old one. His flesh, he feels, is too weak to witness it all.

The imagery of the poem effects a blending of the religious and the secular.

There is obviously a good deal in common between "Journey of the Magi" and "A Song for Simeon". But while the Magus reveals a sad inability to grasp the significance of the new birth, Simeon shows a disturbing awareness of its grave implications. Simeon's incapacity seems to be largely physical and the Magus' spiritual. Simeon's prescience, in fact, seems rather incredible, while what surprises us in the Magus is his ignorance. The poem throws clear enough hints of the spiritual progress achieved by Eliot, though it lacks biblical authority. The negative stance of the Magus has been left behind.

Interestingly enough, Eliot's Simeon sounds more faithful to the poet than to his original. The skill with which Eliot has used his persona to project a shade of difference in his mood is perhaps something unsurpassed. To be able to think of abandoning the old 'unworthy ship' in favour of a new one, he has indeed to go farther ahead.

The sense of weariness projected in the earlier Ariel poems might well have given room for a temptation in the poet to beat a retreat. "Ash Wednesday" provides conclusive proof of his having resisted that temptation manfully. It has been called "a poetic document of rebirth".[64] It is essentially a reaffirmation of the poet's new-found faith, in spite of the penitential demands it has made on him. The religious import of the series seems to have rendered the abandonment of all distancing devices imperative for Eliot, as he finds "a pious insincerity" the bane of "most religious verse".[65] Yet if the distinction between the speaker and poet has not been wholly eliminated here, his preoccupation with the problem of finding a voice, that is both personal and universal at once, may be responsible for it.

Surely, the speaker does not pretend to have glossed over all sorts of problems. His acceptance of a new faith was "no easy leap from skepticism to assurance", as Elizabeth Drew puts it.[66] His sense of depression persists still. A lack of zest for life seems to be at the root of his problems. An abiding awareness of the commonsense-world seems to oppress him. His attitude to the realities of life is not 'Romantic' like Yeats'. He accepts things as they are. Yet he is now bent on constructing "something upon which to rejoice".[67] We are reminded of the Yeatsian attempt in the same direction, without surrendering to the codes of an established religion. After making a vain intellectual bid to attach himself to a spiritual world, Yeats retreats into the cosiness of his heart, as it were. But such a choice could not impress Eliot. He trusted to the efficacy of a traditional belief for sorting out his problems. A retreat for him was unthinkable. He knew that his heart, unlike Yeats', could not be equal to the

64. Gillie, Christopher, *Movements in English Literature*, p. 151.
65. Eliot, T.S., *After Strange Gods : A Primer of Modern Heresy* (Faber and Faber Limited, 1934), p. 28.
66. Drew, Elizabeth, *Poetry*, p. 237.
67. *TSECPP.*, p. 89.

challenge. The solution could only be intellectual. He makes no effort to hide his sense of regret for all that he has to miss when he submits himself to a religious discipline:

> Because I cannot drink
> There, where trees, flowers and springs flow, ... [68]

The confession is a measure of his sincerity. And he has humility enough to brand himself as a sinner.[69]

Even while climbing up the Neo-Platonist stair, the speaker's mind remains much distracted. He is tempted to throw backward glances at "carnal loveliness".[70]

> Blown hair is sweet, brown hair over the mouth blown,
> Lilac and brown hair;
> Distraction, music of the flute, stops and steps
> of the mind over the third stair,
> Fading, fading; strength beyond hope and despair
> climbing the third stair.[71]

His repeated words "Lord, I am not worthy" have a ring of sincerity about them. Perhaps it is more authentic than the notes we have heard in the earlier poets with the possible exception of G.M. Hopkins. We have been told how sincerity itself constituted a mask at times. Robert Langbaum, for example, says :

> Turning Yeats' concept of the mask upon the poetry of the Romanticists, we now see that Wordsworth, Shelley and Keats who appeared in their poems were themselves personae, and the autobiographical connection was itself an artistic strategy. It is difficult to know to what extent the so-called real poet is not himself an artistic construction which he himself took over from his poems...[72]

According to Sean Lucy, "the poses of romantic emotions had been vaild..., personae, truly significant masks through which the poet could speak with real effect".[73] But in the case of the later Eliot, we felt that he cares more for fidelity to truth than for "effect".

In such a context, the glimpse of a vision recorded in the concluding section of "Ash Wednesday" may have to be taken

68. *Ibid*., p. 89.
69. *Ibid*., p. 90.
70. Bergonzi, Bernard, *T.S. Eliot*, p. 138.
71. *TSECPP*., p. 93.
72. Langbaum, Robert, *The Modern Spirit*, p. 169.
73. Lucy, Sean, *T.S. Eliot and the Idea of Tradition* (London: Cohen & West, 1960), p. 150.

seriously. It has certainly been helped by the spiritual leanings promoted by his new faith. But its poetic expression constitutes an achievement of the Romantic tradition:

> Who walked between the violet and the violet
> Who walked between
> The various ranks of varied green
> Going in white and blue, in Mary's colour,
> Talking of trivial things
> In ignorance and in knowledge of eternal colour
> Who moved among the others as they walked,
> Who then made strong the fountains and made fresh the
> springs
> Made cool the dry rock and made firm the sand
> In blue of larkspur, blue of Mary's colour,
> Sovegna vos.[74]

The vision seems to make Eliot's first step towards redeeming the time.

The last poem in the Arieal series – "Marina"[75] – records a more assuring visionary moment without the help of religious symbols. The poem has its source in Shakespeare's *Pericles, the Prince of Tyre*. According to the play, Marina, the daughter of Pericles, was born at sea and was lost to her father even as a baby. The father believed that she had been murdered by the men who were meant to take care of her. The imagery of the poem may gain extra significance when we identify Marina with Eliot's innate Romantic instincts and the men left in charge of her with the intellectual framework – the classical mould – he insisted on. We are told that Marina was restored to her father after several years. The "ultradramatic" quality of the scene (an Eliot calls it) [76] in which the father's ecstatic feelings at the moment of restoration find expression, had a tremendous fascination for Eliot. The scene came in handy when he sought to project his own sense of ecstacy at a crucial point of his life.

The epigraph to the poem is a quotation from Seneca's *Hercules Furens*. Hercules in the play is said to have uttered these words when he returns to sanity after killing his own wife and children in a fit of madness. Eliot has said that the epigraph is meant for "a

74. *TSECPP*., p. 94.
75. *Ibid*., pp. 109-110.
76. Eliot, T.S., remarks quoted in Drew, Elizabeth, *The Design of His Poetry*, p. 102.

criss-cross effect."[77] But he has not chosen to be explicit. The "criss-cross effect" may not be a matter of simple contrast as maintained by Audrey F. Cahill.[78] Grover Smith's comments suggest the complex nature of the contrast. He says:

> The total situation,, antithetical to that in *Pericles*, disclosed in contrast with the discovery of Marina in Eliot's poem not only the horror of death but the horror of personal defeat suffered by Hercules. With such a career of arrogant boastfulness, leading to deprivation and ruin, Eliot contrasted the gracious experience of Pericles by a somewhat oversubtle mingling....The underlying parallel to the Hercules recognition serves to qualify for the reader the flash of pure delight felt by Pericles .... [79]

As remarked by George Williamson, the horror of Seneca and the vision of Marina may be said to "complement one another" in a sense.[80] The poet is not quite sure that he can regain the lost innocence represented by Marina. In such a situation the contrasting reference to the plight of Hercules is bound to project a subtle awareness of the protagonist and thus contribute to the authenticity of the emotions expressed. The probability of an allusion here to Eliot's own past which might perhaps have appeared, by his own exacting standards, rather unsatisfactory need not also be ruled out.

The imagery of the poem reveals a progression away from the concreteness and precision of Eliot's early poetry. According to Stephen Spender, it has resulted in a loss of sensuous quality.[81] But the loss perhaps has its compensation. The movement in Eliot is apparently from the earthy toward the ethereal. In "Marina" a series of disturbingly sharp images, suggesting bellicosity, pride, sloth, and lust, is said to have become insubstantial because of 'Grace'. It may account for the loss referred to by Spender.

Incidentally the first of the images ("Those who sharpen the tooth of the dog") is often taken for an allusion to gluttony, as if the dog's sharp teeth were used only for eating.[82] Of course, we are

---

77. Eliot, T.S., mentioned in a letter to Sir Michael Sadler, in May, 1930, See Grover Smith, p. 131.
78. Cahill, Audrey F., *T.S. Eliot and the Human Predicament*, p.
79. Grover Smith, p. 133.
80. Williamson, George, *A Reader's Guide to T.S. Eliot*, p. 185.
81. Spender, Stephen, *Sensuousness in Modern Poetry* (London: Penguin New Writing, No. 16), p. 124, mentioned in Maxwell, D.E.S., *The Poetry of T.S. Eliot* (London : Routledge & Kegan Paul, 1952), p. 150.
82. See Williamson, George, *A Reader's Guide to T.S. Eliot*, p. 186.

aware that gluttony is regarded as a deadly sin. But in the modern context, bellicosity might seem more menacing and relevant than gluttony.

The lack of precision in the imagery of the later part of the poem may have to be traced to the elusive nature of the reality perceived. The qeustion "given or lent?" reveals a sense of uncertainty that seldom arises while dealing with earthly images. Presumably Eliot's absorption with deeper realities entails the blurring of his physical vision.

A Wordsworthian 'spot of time' is then presented in a manner typically Eliotian:

> Whispers and small laughter between leaves and hurrying
> Under sleep, where all the waters meet.[83]

The poem refers to the "unworthiness" of the ship by which the speaker has hitherto travelled. The new light gained perhaps involves the abandonment of the old ship in favour of new ones. The speaker has high hopes of finding them when he listens to the voice of the woodthrush coming through the fog. The fog seems to symbolize the commonplace perception, regarded by Eliot mainly as a hindrance. His transcendentalism has nothing to do with the Wordsworthian "sensationalism".[84]

> ... let me
> Resign my life for this life, my speech for that unspoken.
> The awakened, lips parted, the hope, the new ships.[85]

The longing projected here may lend extra substance to Eliot's allegiance to the Romantic tradition. Dying into a new life is of course a basic religious conception, as observed by Donald Gutierrez. But he adds that the Romantics are also endlessly concerned with it, as it means to them the "lapsing of consciousness which is yet the discovery of a deeper consciousness, the dissolution of the hard in-tact, ready-made ego".[86]

83. *TSECPP.*, p. 109.
84. Garrod, H.W., *Wordsworth: Lectures and Essays* (London : at the Clarendon Press, Oxford, 1923, reprint, 1958), p. 105.
85. *TSECPP.*, p. 110.
86. Gutierrez, Donald, "Lapsing Out : Ideas of Mortality and Immortality in Lawrence", *Twentieth Century Literature* : *A Scholarly and Critical Journal* (Vol. 24, No. 2, Summer 1978), p. 169.

The "tentatively defining exploration that takes the place of a positive affirmation or statement" in "Marina" referred to by F.R. Leavis is perhaps the hallmark of an exquisite modern sensibility.[87]

Helen Gardner's painstaking study of the composition of *Four Quartets* helps us to illustrate the manner in which Eliot read new significances into his everyday experiences. Commenting on section III of "Burnt Norton" which contains among other things an elaboration of the negative way, she says:

> Eliot travelled daily from Gloucester Road Station, whose two means of descent, by the stairs or by the lift, suggested to him the movement down and 'the abstention from movement', while being carried down...[88]

The analogy bears eloquent testimony to the inventive genius Eliot had at the service of his imagination.

It has been observed that "the greatness of Eliot's religious poetry derives from the its scrupulously honest depiction of his own states of mind, its precise analysis of his indecisive religious apprehensions and the completely honest recording of his uncertainties."[89] *Four Quartets* may illustrate it all.

The flashes of light projected in Quartets owe their vitality to the inner stability and assurance gained by Eliot on his conversion. They have given the series its superb passages of poetry and saved it from being reckoned as an abstract philosophical treatise. As it is, *Four Quartets* may be regraded as a meditation on the timeless moments "in and out of time".[90] But, while such momentary flashes seek to redeem the dreary stretches of time, the poetry produced at those points of intensity, "when the force of emotions fuses the utterance to a glowing heat",[91] has to lend vitality to the dry stretches of discursive passages in the Quartets. In fact, the *locus standi* of the Quartets to pass for poetry has come to be challenged on that score. The unkind conclusion of John W. Aldridge that Eliot "gave up being a poet in order to become secure in the universe"

87. Leavis, F.R. *Lectures in America*, p. 91.
88. Gardner, Helen, *The Composition of Four Quartets* (London and Boston : Faber and Faber, 1978), p. 86. Henceforth cited as *The Composition of Four Quartets*.
89. Cox, C.B. and Dyson, A.E., *Modern Poetry : Studies in Practical Criticism* [London : Edward Arnold (Publishers) Ltd., 1963], p. 74.
90. *TSECPP.*, p. 190.
91. Read, Herbert, *TVF.*, p. 146.

may serve as an example.[92] It amounts to an attempt to attribute to him only the second voice – the voice of the propagandist. But even perceptive critics like C.K. Stead have expressed uneasiness about the alliance of discourse and image in the Quartets. Stead refers to "large portions of abstraction" untransmuted into "the living matter of poetry".[93] Graham Hough also inclines towards such a view when he says that "the timeless moments are rare and fleeting, and seem to do nothing to redeem the long stretches of insignificance in-between.[94] Perhaps we have no reason to be unduly perturbed by those discursive passages, as Eliot himself has had no illusions about them. He says:

> ... if our verse is to have a wide range that it can say anything that has to be said, it follows that it will not be 'poetry' all the time. It will only be 'poetry' when the dramatic situation has reached such a point of intensity that poetry becomes that natural utterance, because then it is the only language in which the emotions can be expressed at all. [95]

Evidently it is his desire to ensure 'a wide range' that prompts him to suffer the abstract stretches of the Quartets. The meditations on "sad time/stretching before and after"[96] his visionary moments, have been dull and dry perhaps appropriately. When Keith Alldritt observes that the method of the Quartets allows for weariness, uncertainty, inaccuracy and flaccidity, he is perhaps driving at such a view.[97]

It is amusing to note how certain critics have found sheer poetry in the abstract passages of the Quartets. F.R. Leavis himself had apparently fallen prey to such a tendency in his *Scrutiny* years.[98] Of course, he was able to see it all in perspective soon enough.

As pointed out by R.P. Bilan, it was Eliot's attitude towards D.H.

---

92. Aldridge, John W., remarks quoted in Rajan, Balachandra "The Detail and the Pattern", *The Overwhelming Question : A Study of the Poetry of T.S. Eliot* (Toronto and Buffalo : University of Toronto Press, 1976), p. 131.
93. Stead, C.K., *NP*., p. 179.
94. Hough, Graham, *Vision and Doctrine*, p. 114.
95. Eliot, T.S., *OPP*., p. 74.
96. *TSECPP*., p. 176.
97. Alldritt, Keith, quoted by W.W. Robson, "T.S. Eliot, the Noise of Life, And the Harmony of Poetry" Review in *Sewanee Review* (Winter, 1980), p. 99.
98. See Leavis, F.R., "T.S. Eliot's Later Poetry" (1943), reprinted in *Education and the University : A Sketch for an English School* (London : Chatto & Windus, 1965), pp. 88 and 94.

Lawrence that inspired a new awareness in Leavis in the matter.[99] Having used his powerful guns for defending Eliot earlier, he now trained them for offence. The highlighting of the negative aspects of Eliot's contribution by one who had eulogized him for providing "New Bearings" to English poetry must have shocked a few. P.H. Butter, for one, has tried to plead Eliot's case.[100] But Leavis' findings on the life-denying quality of the quartets would seem nearly irrefutable. In fact, Leavis' view in this regard has been backed up by other prestigious voices like those of D.W. Harding[101] and Helen Gardner.[102] Eliot's attempts at redeeming time through trapping, as it were, its timeless moments do not seem effective enough. They benefit only certain secluded spots of time. And the impact of it is but momentary. The "celebration of the wedding of the eternal and temporal orders" towards the close of the Quartets referred to by R.P. Bilan is more symbolic than real.[103] In any case, sublimity can hardly be a substitute for vitality or humanity. P.H. Butter also argues that the timeless moments are evoked by the mention of familiar things.[104] What he tends to forget is that those familiar things do not deserve Eliot's love by themselves. Graham Hough has rightly commented that "Eliot's is not the poetry that can accept and love the manifest surface of the natural world".[105] While quoting some agreeable passages from Hough, Butter does not take cognizance of what the former has said on "the steady depreciation of the natural life" in the Quarterts.[106] Yet he has conceded that there is at least "a hint of a recoil" in Eliot's reference to 'Dung and Death'.[107] It is indeed true that "for most of

99. Bilan, R.P., "F.R. Leavis' Revaluation of T.S. Eliot", *University of Toronto Quarterly* (Winter, 1977-78), p. 151. Henceforth cited as "F.R. Leavis' Revaluation of T.S. Eliot."

100. Butter, P.H., "*Four Quartets* : Some yes-buts to Dr. Leavis," *Critical Quarterly* (Vol. 18, No. 1, Spring, 1976). Henceforth cited as *Four Quartets*: Some yes-buts to Dr. Leavis.

101. Harding, D.W., remarks quoted by F.R. Leavis in *English Literature in our Time and the University* (London : Chatto & Windus, Paperback, 1969), pp. 145-146.

102. Gardner, Helen, *Eliot in His Time*, p. 76.

103. Bilan, R.P., "F.R. Leavis' Revaluation of T.S. Eliot," p. 154.

104. Butter, P.H., "*Four Quartets* : Some yes-buts to Dr. Leavis", p. 34.

105. Hough, Graham, "Vision and Doctrine", p. 127.

106. *Ibid.*, p. 127.

107. Butter, P.H., "*Four Quartets* : Some yes-buts to Dr. Leavis", p. 35.

us most of the time, the hills are the hills".[108] But for Eliot the hills are less than hills, unless they serve him as symbols. George Bornstein's view that he "rejects nature because he fears that it will reawaken his interior powers",[109] is not altogether convincing. The dominant impression is of a relative incapacity for a full-blooded sensory perception. We cannot afford to forget how even a common man often finds a sense of fulfilment and joy in his bare existence on the face of the earth. The feeling that Eliot "retreats from the complexity of human love into an attenuated and disembodied idea of religious love" mentioned by Martin Scofield, is nearly irresistible.[110] That is where Yeats shines by contrast. A crucial distinction between the approaches of Yeats and Eliot in this regard has been highlighted by Richard Ellmann, when he says:

> ... Eliot puts his faith in spiritual perfection, the ultimate conversion of sense into spirit. Yeats, on the other hand, stands with Michaelangelo for 'profane perfection of mankind' in which sense and spirit are fully and harmoniously exploited, and 'body is not bruised to pleasure soul.' So strongly does he hold this view that he projects sensuality into heaven to keep heaven from being ethereal and abstract. He presents this faith with such power and richness that Eliot's religion, in spite of its honesty and loftiness, is pale and infantile in comparison ....[111]

In their distinct ways both Yeats and Eliot 'cast a cold eye' on the external nature. But while the assumption of a cold eye by Yeats apparently demands a deliberate bid on his part, it seems to come quite effortlessly to Eliot. The implications of that difference, rather disparaging as they are to Eliot, cannot be wished away. Yeats, unlike Eliot, cares an immense deal for human nature. Meanwhile, the humans engaged in sexual relations in Eliot's world are hardly superior to the lesser animals. F.R. Leavis deserves to be complimented on insisting, without mincing matters, that Eliot's poetry is "centrally flawed", because of his inability to contemplate the relations between men and women without revulsion or disgust.[112] Stephen Spender has significantly commented that a return to

108. *Ibid*., p. 38.

109. Bornstein, George, *TR*., p. 151.

110. Scofield, Martin, "A Gesture and a Pose : T.S. Eliot's Images of Love", *Critical Quarterly* (Vol. 18, No. 3, Autumn, 1976), p. 5.

111. Ellmann, Richard, *The Identity of Yeats* (London: Macmillan & Co. Ltd., 1954), p. 246.

112. See *Lectures in America*, pp. 30-53. *English Literature in Our Time and the University* (London : Chatto & Windus Paperback, 1969), pp. 136-157.

human affection, acceptance of sensual experience and perhaps even a less catastrophic attitude towards society would have made a fitting finale to Eliot's work.[113]

Eliot's view that "our lives are mostly a continual evasion of ourselves, and an evasion of the visible and sensible world"[114] suggests a refreshing self-awareness. Harold Bloom's term "anti-nature poetry", referred to earlier, would seem apt when we apply it to the poetry of Yeats or Eliot. Stephen Spender has said:

> Eliot is the very opposite of everything that is meant by a "nature poet". He is never like Lawrence, describing nature with the mind fixed on some object described, making the reader re-experience all the sensations aroused by the object. His mind is always on the poem, on what is created by the mind, and he picks out the phenomena observed by the mind to suit the poem.

Spender has also noted the tendency revealed in Eliot's later poetry to appeal "to a world of belief that is external to the individual mind."[115]

Eliot's anti-nature stance perhaps explains the difference between his moments of epiphany and the Wordsworthian 'spots of time'. While Wordsworth uses external nature as a 'runway' in his flights into the transcendental, Eliot soars into visionary heights more in the fashion of a helicopter, starting off, so to speak, at "The point of intersection of the timeless/With time".[116] Indeed he was able to see the world of time in a new light, when he looked at it from those heights. Wordsworth "relates his moments of illumination to the whole experience of a long ordered lifetime" as pointed out by Graham Hough. The Eliotian moments, on the other hand, reveal no such relationship. They are "unassisted by their place in a total structure" and "must work by their own immediate impact".[117] Apart from Eliot's lack of zest for life, the influence of the Imagists (to whom "presentational accuracy"[118] meant much) on him may account for this curious aspect. The long stretches of discursive

---

113. Spender, Stephen, "Remembering Eliot", *The Man and His Work*, p. 60.

114. Eliot, T.S., *The Use of Poetry and the Use of Criticism*, p. 155.

115. Spender, Stephen, *The Destructive Element* (London : Jonathan Cape Toronto, 1935, reprint, 1938), p. 144.

116. *TSECPP*., pp. 189-190.

117. Hough, Graham, "Vision and Doctrine", p. 115.

118. Hough, Graham, *Image and Experience : Studies in a Literary Revolution* (London : Gerald Duckworth & Co. Ltd., 1960), p. 13.

verse do little to help the poetic passages of the Quartets, though they seem to tighten up the Symbolist mode adopted by Eliot through the "inter-leaving of suggestion with statement".[119] Their help in creating an impression of sincerity in the work has, however, been valuable. Eliot must have realised how the lack of it promoted aesthetic discontinuity in the Symbolist and the Imagist poetry of the earlier years. His achievement in this regard amounts to a contribution to the Romantic tradition in its Symbolist manifestation and distinguishes his work from the genre of Romantic poetry, which emphasizes the presentation of the mental action, known as the poetry of experience.

When George Orwell comments that Eliot's "faith does not in itself give him any fresh literary impulse", he stresses an aspect likely to be lost sight of.[120] The literary impulse evidently belongs to a deeper level of the poet's consciousness and has nothing to do with the intellectual activity affecting religious preferences. But the inner stability and assurance needed for promoting the proper function of the unconscious could be provided by a religious faith, as in Eliot's case.

Presumably, T.E. Hulme's tirade against the Romantics has been largely responsible for the notion that Romantic instincts invariably negate belief in God. For he says:

> You don't believe in God, so you begin to believe that man is a god. You don't believe in Heaven, so you begin to believe in a heaven on earth. In other words, you get romanticism.... Romanticism, then, and this is the best definition I can give it, is spilt religion.[121]

I.A. Richards' contention that poetry will retain its saving power only if severed from belief, from the 'Magical View' of the world,[122] perhaps gave a further impetus to that notion. Indeed the basic requirement of a traditional religion is belief in God. Romanticism with its faith in the power of imagination may appear to run counter to the religious view. But the tendency to believe in one's imagination

---

119. Rayan, Krishna, *Suggestion and Statement in Poetry*, p. 93.

120. Orwell, George, review in *Poetry London*, 1942, reprinted in *T.S. Eliot : Four Quartets*, A case book, ed. Bernard Bergonzi (London: Macmillan, 1969, reprint, 1975), p. 86. Henceforth cited as A case book.

121. Hulme, T.E., *TCC.*, p. 95.

122. See Bush, Douglas, *Science and English Poetry : A Historical Sketch, 1590-1950*, (New York: Oxford University Press, 1950), p. 164. Henceforth cited as *Science and English Poetry*.

need not necessarily be in conflict with one's faith in God. Eliot, for one, has proved beyond doubt how belief in God could not only co-exist with a faith in one's own self, but could even give a fillip to it. If Eliot's religious poetry suggests a lack of faith "in the present goodness and progressive perfectibility of man" as observed by F.O. Matthiessen,[123] his belief in the potency of human imagination remains largely undiminished in spite of it.

We are aware that "a good deal of modern poetry has done more to heighten and propagate despair than to provide spiritual leadership".[124] Eliot's poetry has been a happy exception. Of course, his religious poetry suffers from a severe limitation because of his tendency to see divinity only in favoured spots and moments. The Hopkinsian ability to see God in every living thing and feel for the whole range of God's creation is not his. Graham Hough tries to account for that inability, when he says:

> His method springs from a post-Christian world, from a world that has lost a whole faith and can only live by gleaned and assembled fragments.[125]

Hough's comment implies that modern scepticism is the villain of the piece. But Eliot's problems appear to spring primarily from his own lack of zest for life. The impact of scepticism on his mind has not perhaps been as disastrous as it is often made out to be.

Leonard Unger has elaborated on the preoccupation of the later Eliot with the imagery of the Rose Garden.[126] Eliot's desire to provide an adequate structure to his visionary glimpses is borne out by his play *The Family Reunion*. In that effort a secular framework was apparently found more congenial than the religious setting of *Murder in the Cathedral*. The Rose Garden symbolizes for Eliot the moment in and out of time. Harry Blamires says:

> The rose-garden is the might-have-been dream-world we never quite got inside. It is also our 'first world' the lost world of childhood innocence, and the lost paradisal Eden of humanity's unfallen condition.[127]

123. Matthiessen, F.O., *The Achievement of T.S. Eliot : An Essay on the Nature of Poetry* (New York: Oxford University Press, 1935, A Galaxy Book, 1958), p. 123.
124. Bush, Douglas, *Science and English Poetry*, p. 150.
125. Hough, Graham, "Vision and Doctrine", p. 127.
126. Unger, Leonard, *T.S. Eliot : Moments and Patterns* (Minneapolis : University of Minnesota Press, 1956, reprint, 1966), pp. 69-91. Henceforth cited as *Moments and Patterns*.
127. Blamires, Harry, *Word Unheard: A Guide through Eliot's Four Quartets* (London: Methuen & Co. Ltd., 1969), p. 8.

It is in fact the symbolic equivalent of the still point of the turning world, which has found repeated mention in Eliot's later work, as noted by critics like Norman Nicholson[128] and Louis L. Martz.[129]

Graham Hough has observed that Eliot's secular epiphanies are "revelations of 'what we call spirit', but they have no manifest or necessary connection with divinity in its Christian meaning". He approvingly quotes Lionel Trilling's view that they are "appropriate to the idea of divinity."[130] If their secular quality perhaps diminishes their value for the denominational religion, their significance for the Romantic tradition remains beyond all doubt.

R.N. Higinbotham expresses dissatisfaction with the images chosen by Eliot for symbolizing the timeless moment. He feels that "they are not existent enough," being "too uniform." He calls them "a poeticising device, a private code, whose ciphers are often determined by the obsolete emotional associations attached to certain words in poetic convention."[131] The failing pinpointed here resulted possibly from a conscious concern for clarity and an obsessive regard for the content of the vision rather than the technique of its expression. In any case, what is suggested is a craftsman's problem. And it may be unfair to blame it on the Romantic imagination.

Eliot's attempt to temper the negative way with his visionary leanings has naturally disturbed orthodox minds. Having chosen the negative way, he was probably expected to restrain his visionary impulse and restrict it to accepted religious channels. Obviously, Eliot was too much of an individual to stick to beaten tracks. He meant to be true as much to himself as to the church. The affirmative way did not suit him as he lacked a zest for life. Yet he was not for suppressing his innate instincts. It was thus a conscious choice that made him blend the negative way with his visionary impulses. When Fr. Lynch calls his imagination 'heretical' he is perhaps barking up

128. Nicholson, Norman, *Writers of Today*, pp. 141-142.

129. Martz, Louis L., "T.S. Eliot : The Wheel and the Point", *The Poem of the Mind : Essays on Poetry, English and American* (Oxford University Press, 1966, A Galaxy Book), pp. 107-109.

130. Hough, Graham, "Vision and Doctrine", p. 113.

131. Higinbotham, R.N., "Objections to a Review of 'Little Gidding' ", *Scrutiny* (Vol. XI, No. 4, Summer, 1943), p. 260.

the wrong tree.[132] And presumably, it was a choice inspired by a desire to harmonize religion and art. His partiality for secular imagery in poems of religious import can be appreciated only if we are in sympathy with that ideal. Maybe, it also forms part of his endeavour to universalize his experience through making them valid for his non-Christian readers too. He seems to have sought to secularize certain passages of *Four Quartets* with that end in view. In "Little Gidding", for instance, he cut out some lines of explicitly Christian significance such as

> Soul of Christ, sanctify them,
> Body of Christ, let their bodies be good earth,
> Water from the side of Christ, wash them,
> Fire from the heart of Christ incinerate them.[133]

Of course, it is also likely that Eliot tended to distrust the pious rhetoric of these lines.

Leonard Unger has said that it is the 'voice' that makes Eliot's poetry "so tremendously" popular. It has been widely acknowledged as the true voice of feeling characteristic of Romantic poetry. It is also the intimate voice of an exquisite "modern sensibility", presenting the "steps and stops of the mind", as mentioned by Unger.[134] In the Eliotian sense, we must call it an impersonal voice, as it includes and transcends personality. Calling it a personal voice, as John N. Serio, for instance, has done, may amount to limiting its significance.[135]

Eliot's desire to harmonize art and religion may remind us of Matthew Arnold's postulation of poetry as a substitute for religion. In Eliot's view, the artistic sensibility is impoverished by its divorce from the religious sensibility and the religious, by its separation from the artistic.[136] He says:

> Aesthetic sensibility must be extended into spiritual perception, and spiritual perception must be extended into aesthetic sensibility and disciplined taste before we are qualified to pass judgment upon decadence or diabolism or nihilism in art. To judge a work of art by artistic or religious standards, to judge a religion by religious or artistic

---

132. Lynch, William F., *Christ and Apollo* (New York: Sheed & Ward, 1960), reprinted in A Casebook, pp. 249-250.
133. Gardner, Helen, *The Composition of Four Quartets*, p. 230.
134. Unger Leonard, *Moments and Patterns,* pp. 157, 159 & 160.
135. Serio, John N. "Landscape and Voice in T.S. Eliot's Poetry", *The Centennial Review* (Vol. XXVI, No. 1, Winter, 1982), pp. 33-50.
136. Eliot, T.S., *Notes towards the Definition of Culture*, p. 26.

> standards should come in the end to the same thing: though it is an end at which no individual can arrive.[137]

The concluding clause suggests the extreme self-consciousness characteristic of Eliot. That self-consciousness apparently brought him under the shadow of the "gray rock" and made him "a dancer before God."[138]

The views expressed here represent the lofty concerns of a modern mind and should not be brushed aside as impractical. The harmonizing of the temporal life with the spiritual seems to be Eliot's prescription for the maladies of the modern world, such as diabolism, decadence and nihilism.[139] The attitude revealed here suggests a lofty humanistic concern. Along with his supreme regard for integrity, it perhaps makes amends for his relative lack of humanity and vitality.

The "utter and relentless fidelity to the event" referred to by Balachandra Rajan is the distinctive quality of Eliot's poetry.[140] The thinness of his visionary moments has perhaps something to do with it. In fact, that thinness suggests an exquisite quality which makes the Wordsworthian solidity appear rather archaic. Maybe, the Eliotian moments do not strengthen us for our existence in time like the Wordsworthian 'spots', as implied by George Bornstein.[141] Yet they certainly help in relieving the boredom of our everyday existence. Even the hostile critics of Eliot cannot possibly deny that in his poetry "there is always the communication of some new experience or some fresh understanding of the familiar or the expression of something we have experienced but have no words for, which enlarges our consciousness and refines our sensibility".[142] His raids "on the inarticulate"[143] testify to it. Their unmistakable affinity to the Romantic endeavour to express the inexpressible is bound to win him a place of honour in the company of the great Romantics.

---

137. *Ibid.*, p. 30.
138. *TSECPP,* p. 605.
139. Eliot, T.S., *Idea of a Christian Society* (London: Faber and Faber Limited, 1939), p. 54.
140. Rajan, Balachandra, "The Unity of the Quartets", *T.S. Eliot : A Study of His Writings by Several Hands*, ed. Balachandra Rajan (London: Dennis Dobson Ltd., 1948, reprint, 1971), p. 95.
141. Bornstein, George, *TR.*, p. 154.
142. Eliot, T.S., *OPP.*, p. 18.
143. *TSECPP.*, p. 182.

CHAPTER VII

POST-MODERNIST TRENDS AFFECTING PROSPECTS OF ROMANTIC TRADITION

The background of the twentieth century poet, as observed by Kathleen E. Morgan, "often resembles the bleak landscape and 'the growing gloom' depicted by Hardy in 'The Darkling Thrush'. "[1] And in the depressing situation emerging out of it, "anti-traditional, destructive, nihilistic forces"[2] have been abroad, like prowling beasts of prey. The major poets of the first half of the century have struggled hard to hold out against them. The Romantic disposition "to seek within and beyond the actual, for the ideal world that will soften the asperities of the actual, or better-interpret them in such a way as to suit the needs of the heart" has been of immense help in the context.[3] In the previous chapter, we saw how a religious sensibility, far from impeding such a Romantic effort, could contribute positively to it. The later poetry of W.H. Auden illustrates how a religious feeling, with its distinct inwardness, could be more conducive to the upsurge of Romantic instincts than an atheistic creed.

The inner potentialities of Eliot and Auden were indeed different. The early phase of Auden proves the infinite harm a self conscious mind, backed up as it was, by constricting political passions and a scientific bent, could do to the deeper instincts of man – both religious and Romantic. Even as Eliot sought to "cure Romanticism through analyzing it", Auden could blot out all traces of it from his mind by means of a clinical and analytical approach. The depersonalizing effort on the part of Auden was apparently more effective than Eliot's. Auden's early work, however, carries

---

1. Morgan, Kathleen E., *Christian Themes in Contemporary Poets: A Study of English Poetry of the Twentieth Century* (London: SCM Press Ltd., 1965), p. 15. Henceforth cited as *Christian Themes in Contemporary Poets*.
2. Spears, Monroe K., *DC*., p. 230.
3. Beach, Joseph Warren, "English Literature of the Nineteenth and the Early Twentieth Centuries – 1798 to the First World War", Vol. IV of *A History of English Literature* (Oxford University Press, 1950, New York : Collier Books; London : Collier-Macmillan Ltd., 1962), p. 20.

unmistakable hints of an emotional immaturity – "a flaw of feeling", as Stephen Spender calls it[4] – coinciding with an intellectual virtuosity. It must naturally have rendered his depersonalizing effort relatively easy. We seldom feel the presence of a strong personality behind the experiences presented in his poems. The personal voice in Eliot, on the other hand, proves too strident to be suppressed by depersonalizing efforts. Auden's technical habits have indeed been "clever-clever"[5] to a disturbing degree.

While commenting on the "enormous self-consciousness" Eliot and Auden have in common, John Bayley has highlighted a crucial distinction between them. He says that in Eliot self-consciousness "takes the form of a deprecation, an honest enquiry, an implied refusal to posture before the reader and dazzle him with a display of poetical virtuosity"[6]. He also illustrates how Eliot seeks to create "an atmosphere of sincerity". Auden, on the contrary, is said to make no attempt "to disguise the fact that he is a virtuoso, whose job it is to give a good performance". Bayley also points out that for Eliot poetry is "part of a general ethos which is of very great importance", and "for Auden it is not".[7] The view amounts to denying Auden the seriousness usually associated with the idealism of the Romantic artist. John R. Boly has observed how Auden "rejected romanticism's naive faith that the god of unleashed desire could build a New Jerusalem", though he moved in the contrary direction in his later phase.[8] Boly has also suggested that Auden's conversion to Christianity "arose from his determination to regain contact with the strength of romantic origins".[9] That determination must have been energized by Auden's disenchantment with the existentialist fancies of his early life. His attempt at "a deconstruction

4. Spender, Stephen, "W.H. Auden and His Poetry", reprinted in Spears, Monroe K., (Ed.), *Auden: A Collection of Critical Essays* -- Twentieth Century Views Series (New Jersey, Prentice Hall, 1964), p. 30. Henceforth cited as *Twentieth Century Views*.
5. Hoggart, "Introduction to Auden's Poetry", reprinted in *Twentieth Century Views*, p. 116.
6. Bayley, John, "W.H. Auden", reprinted in *Twentieth Century Views*, p. 72.
7. *Ibid.*, p. 73.
8. Boly, John R., "Auden and the Romantic Tradition in The Age of Anxiety," *Daedalus: Journal of the American Academy of Arts and Sciences*, Summer, 1982, p. 150.
9. *Ibid.*, p. 151.

of romantic humanism"[10] through the "adventurous misreading of Freud" mentioned by Boly seems to form part of a self-conscious strategy. And we cannot quite believe that it has appreciably affected the fortunes of the Romantic tradition in the century. The feeling of sacred awe – "a sense of the power and meaning that permeates experience"[11] referred to in his later essays certainly suggests a shift in his attitude in favour of Romanticism. His belief that "poetry is rooted in imaginative awe" expressed in his inaugural lecture as Professor of Poetry at Oxford in 1956 may confirm that view.[12] In his "New Year Letter" Auden has shown how "any of us can unexpectedly have a moment of vision, which is given, not achieved by an effort of will", as observed by Kathleen E. Morgan.[13] The moulding of his Byronic temperament to such a shape is evidently an achievement of his new-found religious faith.

Hillis Miller's view that "nihilism is one of the possible consequences of romanticism" seems to fly in the face of this evidence.[14] Geoffrey H. Hartman has maintained that Romantic art has a function analogous to that of religion, inasmuch as the traditional scheme of Eden, fall, and redemption merges with the new triad of nature, self-consciousness and imagination.[15] Viewed thus, art and religion seem to provide alternative – and not contrary – modes of belief. The lofty ideal of Eliot to harmonize art and religion implies a belief in their complementary traits.

Nihilism may well be called a bye-product of the enormous development achieved in the fields of science and technology in modern times. The change from the religious view (or "magical view", as I.A. Richards calls it) to the scientific view in modern consciousness, marking man's increasing mastery over nature, has involved a progressive loss of hold on the spiritual aspects of man's inner and outer universe. The resulting situation is expertly symbolized by Yeats when he says :

10. *Ibid.*, p. 152.
11. See Ohmann, Richard M., "Auden's Sacred Awe", reprinted in *Twentieth Century Views*, p. 178.
12. Spears, Monroe K., "Auden in the Fifties : Rites of Homage", *The Sewanee Review*, Summer, 1961, p. 375.
13. *Christian Themes in Contemporary Poets*, pp. 31-32.
14. Miller, J. Hillis, *Poets of Reality* : *Six Twentieth Century Writers* (Cambridge, Massachusetts: The Belknap Press of Harvard University Press, 1966), p. 1.
15. Hartman, Geoffrey H., "Romanticism and Anti-self-consciousness" reprinted in *RC.*, p. 54.

> The falcon cannot hear the falconer;
> Things fall apart; the centre cannot hold;[16]

A welcome awareness of this menacing trend is suggested by the words of Marjorie Grene:

> ... In the bare mathematical bones of Nature, there is truth; all else is illusion: yet that "all else" includes the very roots of our being, and we forget them at our peril.[17]

David Holbrook tells us how "Darwin used to blush whenever he saw a peacock's tail as he could not explain this in terms of his Evolutionary theory."[18] An ability to see into and beyond the physical realities of life provided by Romanticism may come as a saving grace in the context.

Hillis Miller has drawn attention to the progress made by Eliot and Yeats, among others, from nihilism towards "reality".[19] Although he has used the term "reality" in the context in a limited sense, it may be stretched to mean the transcendental reality pursued by the Romantic artist. For, even as Yeats' preoccupation with what Miller calls "the infinite plenitude of the instant of intense experience" coincided with a belief in moments of heightened awareness, Eliot owed his interest in "here and now and always" to the still points of the turning world.[20]

These twin concerns of Eliot and Yeats suggest "a fruitful tension" in their poetry. What we miss in the poetry of the post-modernist Movement is that tension, as pointed out by Monroe K. Spears.[21] The wayward trends of the earlier decade perhaps demand an extreme reaction from the poets of the Movement. The self-indulgent Romanticism of Dylan Thomas and his tribe cast reflections on the Romantic tradition. While a good part of their poetry was marred by extreme cerebration, an obsessive fancy to explore the obscure regions of human consciousness afflicted another part. C.D. Lewis says:

> ... if we send images as scouts far into the unknown, there is always the

---

16. *WBYCP.*, pp. 210-211.
17. Grene, Marjorie, *Approaches to a Philosophical Biology*, p. 51, reprinted in *Lost Bearings*, p. 19.
18. *Lost Bearings*, p. 23.
19. *Poets of Reality*, pp. 11-12.
20. *Ibid.*, p. 189.
21. Spears, Monroe K., *DC.*, p. 230.

> danger that they will lose contact both with the main body and with each other.[22]

The prose poems of Dylan Thomas and most of the work of the New Apocalypse group may illustrate Lewis' statement. The poets of the latter group apparently believed in the capacity of the poetic imagination to function without the help of the rationalizing intellect. Poetry thus got approximated to automatic writing. Perhaps it marked the extreme limit to which the Symbolist aesthetic, subscribed to by the Imagists and their modernist followers, could take English poetry. But, as observed earlier, the major poets of the modernist phase like Eliot and Yeats, tried to invigorate the Symbolist technique in various ways. The modernist experiment did not involve a belittling of the role of the intellect in the process of poetry-making. The "peripheral revolution" they attempted did not damage the essential aspects of the Romantic tradition. Yet for quite some time in the past, a tendency to blame the leading lights of the modernist revolution for the unwholesome developments of the 1940s was nearly fashionable. The "stroke of luck" suffered by English poetry because of Ezra Pound and Eliot was certainly not so "atrocious" as maintained by Philip Hobsbaum.[23] Indeed we are aware that the post-modernist trend to trace the ills of the immediate past back to a previous generation had a mighty precedent earlier.

In the recent past we have been witnessing a welcome effort to see the contribution of the modernists in a better perspective. Donald Davie, who spearheaded the post-modernist revolt earlier against "American" innovators, has thoughtfully conceded that American poetry has influenced our poetry "very properly".[24]

If the reversal of the poetic strategy in 1955 has been rather abrupt, it has, ironically enough, been followed up by yet another reversal. The attitude of the poets of the Group may testify to it. Moreover, the Movement proves "too constricting for its more talented members".[25] The frequency of such reversals in the twentieth

22. *The Poetic Image*, pp. 59-60.
23. Hobsbaum, Philip, *Tradition and Experiment in English Poetry* (Macmillan, 1979), p. 304. Henceforth cited as *Tradition and Experiment*.
24. Davie, Donald, "Personification", F.W. Bateson Memorial Lecture, *Essays in Criticism*, Vol. XXXI, No. 2, April 1981), p. 104. Henceforth cited as "Personification". Davie has perhaps been a little too conscious of the nationalities of writers.
25. *Tradition and Experiment*, p. 298.

century may have to be traced to the acute self-consciousness characteristic of the times. Davie again seems to have taken the lead when he says that Romanticism is no longer regarded as an "aberration in our cultural past which we have the ability and the duty to expunge from our consciousness".[26] We may be pleasantly surprised by his conciliatory tone, when we remember how he cried halt to the tendency, which he attributed to the Romantics, "to minimize the responsibilities of poetry" towards sense.[27] As a sensitive poet-critic, he must have been alive to the general softening of attitudes towards Romanticism. Modifying a phrase used by Alfred Alvarez (while maintaining that English poetry up to the Movement had seemingly "been controlled by a series of negative feed-backs designed to produce precisely the effect Hardy wanted" in themes and styles),[28] we may call the new trend in favour of Romanticism a positive feed-back.

The technical conservatism of the poets of the Movement is traced to the influence of Hardy. But it is likely that Yeats' use of traditional forms in poetry, commended by Davie,[29] had also some impact on them. The Hardyan tradionalism was indeed a matter of surface. It covered up an unorthodox mind. The leaders of the Movement were able to strike a rapport with him partly on that score. Eliot's experimentalism, on the contrary, coincided with a spiritual conservatism. The Movement poets could relish neither of them. But the modernist experimentalism was not an end in itself. Alvarez has pointed out that "the great moderns experimented not just to make their technique new formally, but to open poetry to new areas of experience."[30] The Movement poets went the other way about. Their conscious strategy narrowed down the scope of their poetry. Technical perfection, sure enough, is "a minor attraction", as D.J. Enright calls it.[31] But the Movement-poets exerted themselves overmuch for its sake. Their insistence on decorum prompted them to steer clear of strong emotions. Their realism represented "an obliteration of peak moments of becoming, of idealism, of creativity."[32]

26. Davie, Donald, "Personification", p. 103.
27. Davie, Donald, *AE.*, p. 61.
28. Alvarez, A., "English Poetry Today", p. 82.
29. Davie, Donald, *AE.*, p. 129.
30. Alvarez, A., "English Poetry Today", p. 83.
31. Enright, D.J., *Conspirators and Poets* (London: Chatto & Windus, 1966), p. 97.
32. Holbrook, David, *Lost Bearings*, p. 173.

The Movement-poetry thus developed an "anaemic quality".[33] The post-modernist attempt to restore clarity and good sense to poetry had been anticipated by Eliot's own later work published nearly simultaneously with the much-maligned poetry of Dylan Thomas and his imitators.

The anti-intellectual trend in the poetry of the century appears to have been signalled by D.H. Lawrence. The tendency to delve into the darker recesses of the human psyche was also initiated by him. It was the impact of Surrealism, which drew sustenance from the Freudian findings, that made those trends assume the dimensions of a disease in the later years. The intellectual strain in the work of Dylan Thomas, which accounted for its rhetorical and imagistic excesses, tended to be overlooked in the process. His followers used his work "as an excuse to kiss all meaning good-bye." And it was but natural that the pendulum then swung to the other extreme.

If the earlier poetry suffered from an obsessive exploration of individual experiences, the experience found expression in the Movement-poetry appears "empty". A poem, according to Yvor Winters, is "a statement in words, and about a human experience, and it will be successful insofar as it realizes the possibilities of that kind of statement."[34] The Movement-poetry sticks to that prescription. Winters also said that poetry had something "in common with music, namely rhythm".[35] Philip Larkin's early "infatuation" with the dangerously potent music of Yeats"[36] amounts to a response to that view. W.H. Auden has said that "Yeats' rhythm and the conversational power of his poetry had tremendous influence, but his vision none."[37] Auden's observation is exemplified by the early Larkin. Of course, a conversational power that is nearly Yeatsian is revealed by his later work too in poems such as "Lines on a Young

33. Fraser, G.S., *The Modern Writer and His World* (London : Penguin Books, A Pelican Book, 1953, Revised Edition, 1964), p. 353.

34. Winters, Yvor, *The Function of Criticism: Problems and Exercises* (Routledge & Kegan Paul, 1957), p. 103.

35. *Ibid.*, p. 104.

36. Larkin, Philip, Introduction to the 1966 edition of *The North Ship*, remarks quoted in Press, John, *A Map of Modern English Verse* (Oxford University Press, Paperback 1969), p. 254.

37. Auden, W.H., remarks quoted in Bayley, John, *RS.*, p. 92.

Lady's Photograph Album"[38] and "Old Fools".[39] Larkin seems to have developed a positive aversion to Yeats' heroic poses and gestures. He loved to face the cold realities of life as they are. It was then that he found out that the Hardyan concept of poetry was after his heart. It allowed him to "relapse" into his own life and write from it.[40] It also helped him to tighten up his poetic technique. Davie has observed how Hardy leads poets to mistrust "the claims of poetry to transcend the linear unrolling of recorded time".[41] He is not sure whether it is a strength or a limitation. Larkin in his early phase seems to have taken it for a strength. That is why the Yeatsian efforts at transcendence failed to impress him. But he was to realize soon enough that "The greatest poetry is not to live/In the physical world."[42] The fighting qualities of neither Yeats nor Hardy had any impact on him. He looked at the world with a closed mind, as it were. Keats has said:

> The only means of strengthening one's intellect is to make up one's mind about nothing – to let the mind be a thoroughfare for all thoughts.[43]

The early Larkin was in no mood to heed that counsel. Along with the other Movement-poets he laboured under a dismal philosophy for quite some time. David Holbrook has called it "egoistical nihilism." He regards it as "the philosophy of our culture".[44] To him it is "a mark of lost bearings." But we have reason to hope that the loss of bearings in the case has not been more than a passing phase.

---

38. Larkin, Philip, *The Less Deceived* (Yorkshire : The Marvell Press, 1954). Henceforth cited as *The Less Deceived*.
39. Larkin, Philip, *High Windows* (London : Faber and Faber, 1974, 4th Impression 1976), pp. 19-20. Henceforth cited as *High Windows*.
40. Larkin, Philip, remarks quoted in Thwaite, Anthony, "The Poetry of Philip Larkin", *The Survival of Poetry : A Contemporary Survey*, (ed.) Martin Dodsworth (London: Faber and Faber, 1970), p. 43.
41. Davie, Donald, *Thomas Hardy and British Poetry* (London: Routledge & Kegan Paul, 1973), p. 4.
42. Stevens, Wallace, "Esthetique Du Mal", *The Collected Poems of Wallace Stevens*, p. 325, quoted in Whallen, Terry, "Philip Larkin's Imagist Bias: His Poetry of Observation", *Critical Quarterly* (Vol. 23, No. 2, Summer 1981), p. 30. Henceforth cited as *Terry Whallen*.
43. Keats, John, Letter to George and Georgiana Keats, September 24, 1819, *The Letters of John Keats*, ed., Maurice Buxton Forman, Oxford University Press, 1931, Fourth edition 1952, p. 425. Henceforth cited as *The Letters of John Keats*.
44. Holbrook, David, *Lost Bearings*, pp. 184-85.

The later poetry of Philip Larkin gives room for that hope. Having felt as helpless and inconsequential as the portraits of an album earlier, Larkin has developed "a hunger in himself to be more serious".[45] Thereafter the perspective revealed in his poetry often suggests a new dimension. He begins to look beyond the dry, drab stretches of life, "towards something more mysterious". A tension characteristic of the best poetry of the modernist phase thus seems to have stolen into a good number of his poems. It involves a straining after an intensity which is beyond the comprehension of the conscious mind. In Hulme's vocabulary it marks the intrusion of the infinite.

As observed by David Lodge, Larkin then begins to surprise us again and again in the closing lines of his poems, by "his ability to transcend – or turn ironically upon – the severe restraints he seems to have placed on authentic expression of feeling in poetry".[46]

Terry Whallen has drawn attention to the central importance of epiphanic moments in Larkin's work.[47] "The Whitsun Weddings" and "High Windows" are cited as examples. "Forget What Did",[48] "The Building",[49] "Sad Steps"[50] and "Explosion"[51] are among other poems recording his "struggle to transcend". The awareness in such cases is of the moments of light. But Larkin has been alive to certain moments of emptiness too. Terry Whallen calls them "epiphanics of void". They are exemplified by "Ambulances", "Absences" and "Aubade".[52] The integrity with which the poet has recorded his awareness of both the light and the void suggests what he has meant while maintaining that his "prime responsibility is to the experience itself".[53]

---

45. Larkin, Philip, "Church Going", *The Less Deceived*. See Watson, J.R., "The Other Larkin", *Critical Quarterly* (Vol. XVII, No. 4, Winter 1975), p. 354.
46. Lodge, David, *The Modes of Modern Writing, Metaphor, Metonymy and the Typology of Modern Literature* (New York: Cornell University Press), pp. 218-219.
47. Terry Whallen, p. 40.
48. *High Windows*, p. 16.
49. *Ibid.*, pp. 24-26.
50. *Ibid.*, p. 32.
51. *Ibid.*, p. 42.
52. Terry Whallen, p. 44.
53. Larkin, Philip, *Poets of the 1950s*, ed. D.J. Enright, p. 77. Remarks quoted in Timms, David, *Philip Larkin* (Edinburgh : Oliver & Boyd, 1973), p. 60.

The sceptical approach revealed by Larkin's poetry bears testimony to the authenticity of his perceptions. Terry Whallen has noted how it fails to erase his Romantic impulse.[54] It provides a Keatsian aspect to his imaginative flights and brings him abreast of the sceptical Romantics dealt with earlier.

Although Larkin learnt from Hardy "to feel" and "to have confidence in what he felt",[55] he would not have approved of the Hardyan tendency to colour the outer landscapes with the poet's own inner gloom. He realizes that

> Things are tougher than we are, just
> As earth will always respond
> However we mess it about;
> Chuck filth in the sea, if you must:
> The tides will be clean beyond.[56]

The attitude revealed here suggests a realism reminiscent of Edward Thomas. That realism makes Larkin true not only to his own inner nature, but to the outer universe as well.

The romantic ideal of sincerity tended to be equated to an intensity that implied a capacity on the part of the poet to feel the emotion expressed in a poem deeply at the time of writing it, though "he did not feel it ever before or after."[57] As noted already, Yeats held fast to that ideal. Of course, he brought to it a ring of authenticity and integrity typically Yeatsian.

The twentieth century has witnessed attempts to bridge the gap between poetic sincerity and personal honesty, without compromising on the intensity of emotions found expression in poetry. Sincerity thus signifies "both an utmost precision and a wide inclusiveness, an ability to catch both the exact shade and the whole scope of meaning."[58] The ring of sincerity and authenticity gained thus seems to have a profound appeal for the modern mind. The Yeatsian note of integrity, with all its intensity, seems to have suffered partly from the Romantic quality of his attitude to the realities of life. The kind

54. Terry Whallen, p. 42.

55. Larkin, Philip, remarks quoted in Bedient, Calvin, *Eight Contemporary Poets* (Oxford University Press, 1974), p. 74. Henceforth cited as Calvin Bedient.

56. *High Windows*, p. 21.

57. Perkins, David, *Wordsworth and the Poetry of Sincerity*, p. 3.

58. *Ibid.*, p. 6.

of realism, we have commented on earlier, was apparently beyond him. The poetry of Edward Thomas, the later Eliot and Philip Larkin may be said to have lived up to the new exacting ideal of sincerity.

The new concern for absolute integrity in poetic utterances, again, appears to have been influenced by the extreme self-consciousness of the modern mind. The change in the attitude towards the kind of sincerity found expression in poetry may testify to the movement of Romanticism closer to life in the century.

The last and truest humanism in art, according to Bernard Bergonzi, "is the truthful expression of emotion."[59] Judged by that standard, the sceptical Romantics of the century are all humanists. Larkin's poetry reveals a deep humanity, too. He feels much compassion for man. Indeed what the poet could do to help the pathetic human situation is pretty little, insofar as he allows himself to be fettered by a nihilistic philosophy. A great bulk of his poetry shows him "steeped in futility".[60] Calvin Bedient has rightly observed that "English poetry has never been so persistently out in the cold as it is with Philip Larkin."[61] The rescue of it from that cold must have been helped, marginally at least, by the example of Edward Thomas, whose mystical leanings gave him an edge over Hardy. Larkin has suggested, perhaps in a lighter vein, that his old age has also something to do with it.[62] This lighter vein appears to be a contribution of the sceptical approach of our time to the Romantic tradition. Murry Krieger says:

> The self-conscious humorless seriousness which characterizes the so-called romantic disposition is what bothers the modern critic most, since because of it the romantic becomes vulnerable to irony, not being able to supply his own.[63]

The sceptical Romantics of the century, dealt with earlier, would seem to have remedied the situation with a remarkable degree of success. The Romantic idealism is no longer allowed to hamper the

---

59. Bergonzi, Bernard, *The Turn of the Century : Essays on Victorian and Modern Literature* (Macmillan, 1973, reprint 1974), p. 181.
60. Calvin Bedient, p. 75.
61. *Ibid.*, p. 69.
62. See *High Windows*, pp. 19-20.
63. Krieger, Murry, *The New Apologists for Poetry* (Connecticut: Greenwood Press, Publishers, 1956, reprint 1977), p. 36.

functioning of the conscious mind, although it has often prompted poets to turn 'a cold eye' on the outer nature.

A shift of interest from nature to man has in fact been typical of the major Romantics, Wordsworth downward. Their attitude towards nature is put in a nutshell by Keats, when he says: "Scenery is fine, but human nature is finer."[64] The major poets of the present century, except Eliot, have thought highly of human nature. The Movement-poets also share that partiality for man.

The leading poet of the Group, Ted Hughes, has invited severe strictures from critics, as he tends to disparage human consciousness in his attempt to exalt the mysteries of the non-human nature. But the non-human creatures caught in the web of his nihilistic philosophy seem to develop certain sinister aspects. The violence attributed to them by the poet appears to emanate from his own self. Indeed, for the Romantics the primary function of the non-human nature has always been to provide symbols for projecting their inner awareness. But the great Romantics, while going "beyond what has been crystalized," guarded themselves against the tendency to distort the shape and substance of the physical nature. But the insights gained by Ted Hughes into the inner life of the lesser animals appear to involve the demolition of their identity. The pathetic fallacy revealed in the context suggests a disturbing new dimension as hinted at Robert Langbaum.[65]

Nevertheless, Ted Hughes' feeling for non-human mysteries is bound to make inroads into the egoistical and nihilistic approach afflicting the modern mind. And, along with the Romantic leanings of others like R.S. Thomas, Thom Gunn and the later Larkin, it seems to form a silver-lining in the cloud which casts a deep gloom on the modern arena.

The mystical pretensions of the Romantic poets are often discounted by men of positivist convictions. The distinction drawn by the clergyman-poet R.S. Thomas between the poet and the mystic may help us in the context:

> ...the *Deus absconditus* is immediate; to the poet he is mediated. The mystic fails to mediate God adequately insofar as he is not a poet. The

64. Keats, John, Quoted in *Poetry and Impersonality*, p. 53.
65. Langbaum, Robert, *The Modern Spirit*, p. 106.

> poet with possibly less immediacy of apprehension shows his spiritual nature through the medium of language, the supreme symbol.[66]

To give such mystical apprehensions verbal form is to express the inexpressible. The Eliotian "raid on the inarticulate" suggests a similar effort. It is the primary concern that distinguishes the major Romantics from their minor contemporaries. And, as observed by Robert Pinsky, "insofar as the poet uses language with conviction, he must be a philosophical realist."[67] It may be said that the ability of a poet to remain such a realist without losing touch with the mystical and mysterious aspects of his inner and outer universe may have a bearing on the success of his poetry in the modern world. In other words, it may be observed that a successful Romantic poet in the present century is the one who stresses his role as a 'maker' without ceasing to be a 'vehicle'.[68] A realist of the positivist mould, on the other hand, tends to lose sight of the mysteries of man's inner and outer lives and refuses to give credence to the poet's function as a 'vehicle'. Cleanth Brooks says:

> A renewed consciousness of a poem as an object – an artifact – and with that a renewed respect for craftsmanship, have been the salient traits of the twentieth century literary theory...[69]

The fact that such a consciousness need not necessarily nullify the Romantic urges of a poet is emphasized by the present study. The primary factor that has rendered the presence of that new consciousness imperative in our times is suggested by John Bayley when he says:

> The dispossessed imagination may suffer from the lack of an intellectual tradition to set in order the experiences which impinge upon it. The adolescent imagination does not so suffer, because it is not called upon to judge what it experiences by any other standard than its own intensity.[70]

In the modern world, this 'dispossession' – or shall we say the alienation of imagination from its traditional sources of strength – seems to have led to a situation in which the lack of a vigorous intellect to back up the function of the imagination is itself taken as

66. Thomas, R.S., Introduction to *Penguin Anthology of Contemporary Verse*. Quoted in *Christian Themes in Contemporary Poets*, p. 24.
67. Pinsky, Robert, *The Situation of Poetry : Contemporary Poetry and Its Traditions* (New Jersey : Princeton University Press, 1976), p. 58.
68. See Eliot, T.S., *SE.*, p. 405.
69. Brooks, Cleanth, *Literature and Belief*, p. 65.
70. Bayley, John, *Twentieth Century Views*, p. 63.

evidence of adolescence. This fact is borne out by the kind of treatment received by the Surrealists and the New Apocalypse group. A masterly analysis of the manner, in which the fortunes of the Romantic tradition have been affected by the changed environment, is offered by F.W. Bateson:

> The exploits of the subliminal self, which could do no wrong in Romantic eyes, are viewed by us in the sardonic light of a socially conscious science. Our Symbols are often identical with theirs, but the synthesis is not between the subconscious mind and human physical world, but between the two parts of the mind, the consciousness and the sub-consciousness. We are struggling towards the recovery of an integrated personality. Modern poetry is a record of that struggle; its warnings are of the dangers of a relapse.[71]

The Movement-poetry of the 1950s, as seen already, illustrates such a relapse. The extent of a Romantic poet's popularity in our midst seems to depend as much on the vigour of his conscious mind as on the power of his imagination. A vigorous mind in the context may mean a consciousness that is fully alive and alert. A sceptical leaning promoted by a scientific education and an approach that is humane and humanistic may form part of that consciousness. A proper co-ordination between such a consciousness and the sub-consciousness (or the "unconscious", as Eliot calls it, or "antiself-consciousness", as Hartman does) leads to the integration of the poetic personality. A self-conscious endeavour to enforce such an integration is evidenced in the insistence of the major poets of the century on Unity of Being and Unification of Sensibility. The absence of any evidence of such a coordinated effort in the work of a poet may account for his relative failure. Such an effort may be said to involve a healthy tension or a struggle. It seems to result in the making of an enduring type of Romantic poetry owing allegiance primarily to Keats. It may also be found to be largely in consonance with the Coleridgean aesthetic that insists on a "wrestle" between the creative power and the intellectual energy,[72] though poems such as "Kubla Khan" create a different impression. The affinity of poets like Kathleen Raine seems to be to the Coleridge of "Kubla Khan". Her belief in the existence of an unwritten poem "with which, words as they are written, must constantly be checked and rectified"[73] may

71. Bateson, F.W., *English Poetry : A Critical Introduction* (London : Longmans, Green, 1950), p. 89.

72. See *TVF*., p. 160.

73. Raine, Kathleen, Introduction to *The Collected Poems of Kathleen Raine*, p. XIII.

testify to that fact. Such a belief implies a dependence on the capacity of imagination to order its own perceptions. In the words of Bateson, it amounts to a belief – which has apparently been outmoded in our day – that the subliminal self "could do no wrong". The relative failure of Kathleen Raine to make a deep impact on the modern mind, in spite of the purity of the vision revealed in her poetry, may be ascribed to that fact.

The success of the Romantic poet in our midst does not seem to depend on his artistic skill either. The failure of Vernon Watkins to come to the limelight, in spite of the sheer excellence of his poems as works of art, may testify to that fact. On the other hand, the work of Dylan Thomas, particularly in its early phase, and of George Barker may illustrate the harm done to the Romantic tradition by extreme cerebral activity unaccompanied by matching emotional intensity.

Most of us hate, no less than Keats, "poetry that has a palpable design upon us."[74] Yet, it may be impossible for us to affirm, with Allen Tate, that "poetry finds its true usefulness in its perfect inutility."[75] We may be inclined to think that "expression has a definite therapeutic value" both for the author and his reader.[76] And it should be hard indeed to believe that a poetry revelling in a cynical nihilism – which is perhaps a sure enough symptom of the mind's fall off all sustaining hinges – can affect its readers favourably.

It is a faith in the imaginative faculty of the human mind which can possibly rescue both poets and readers in the context. Man's vision, we are told, "can redeem the world filling it with mystery, meaning and human gratitude for existence."[77] A belief in the possibility of mystical experiences may have a direct bearing on one's capacity for such a vision. T.S. Eliot has testified to the authenticity of such experiences in unambiguous terms:

> You may call it communion with the Divine, or you may call it a temporary crystallization of the mind. Until science can teach us to

---

74. Keats, John, Letter to J.H. Reynolds, February 3, 1818, *The Letters of John Keats*, p. 95.
75. Tate, Allen, On the Limits of Poetry, p. 113. Quoted in Abrams, Meyer H., "Belief and Suspension of Belief", *Literature and Belief*, p. 10.
76. Brooks, Cleanth, *A Shaping Joy : Studies in the Writer's Craft* (London : Methuen & Co. Ltd., 1971), p. 4.
77. *Lost Bearings*, p. 88.

> reproduce such phenomena at will, science cannot claim to have explained them; and they can be judged only by their fruits.[78]

In bringing such 'fruits', wrapped up, as it were, in realistic verbal forms, within the grasp of his fellow-men, the modern Romantic poet performs a function of supreme significance.

78. Eliot, T.S., *SE*., p. 405.

SELECT BIBLIOGRAPHY

(*a*) **Poems**

De la Mare, Walter, *Collected Poems*. London: Faber and Faber, 1942, Eleventh Impression, September, 1954. *Collected Rhymes and Verses*. London: Faber and Faber, 1944, Reprint, 1975.

Eliot, T.S., *The Complete Poems and Plays of T.S. Eliot*. London: Faber and Faber, 1969.

Thomas, Edward, *The Collected Poems of Edward Thomas*. (Ed.) R.G. Thomas, Oxford: Clarendon Press, 1978.

Yeats, W.B., *The Collected Poems of W.B. Yeats*. London: Macmillan and Co., Limited, 1933, Second Edition, Reprinted 1952.

(*b*) **Critical Works**

Abercrombie, Lascelles, *Romanticism* (London: High Hill Books, 1926, reprint 1963).

Abrams, Meyer H., (Ed.) *English Romantic Poets: Modern Essays in Criticism*. London, Oxford, New York: Oxford University Press, 1960, Second edition, 1975.

——, (Ed.) *Literature and Belief* – English Institute Essays, 1957. New York: Columbia University Press, 1958.

——, *The Mirror and the Lamp: Romantic Theory and the Critical Tradition*. London, Oxford, New York: Oxford University Press, 1953, Paperback, 1971.

——, *Natural Supernaturalism: Tradition and Revolution in Romantic Literature*. Oxford University Press, 1971.

——, "Structure and Style in the Greater Romantic Lyric", *From Sensibility to Romanticism*, Ed. Frederick W. Hilles and Harold Bloom. New York: Oxford University Press, 1965.

Aivaz, David, "The Poetry of Dylam Thomas", *Hudson Review*, Vol. VIII, No. 3, Autumn, 1950.

Alvarez, A., *The Shaping Spirit*. London: Chatto & Windus, 1969.

Arnold, Matthew, *Essays in Criticism*. London : Every Man's Library, 1906, New York : Dutton, 1966.

Auden, W.H., *Selected Essays*. London: Faber and Faber, 1956.

Barfield, Owen, *Poetic Diction: A Study in Meaning*. London : Faber and Faber Ltd., 1928, reprint. 1957.

——, *Saving the Appearances : A Study in Idolatry*. New York : Harcourt, Brace & World, Ind., A Harbinger Book.

——, *Worlds Apart*. London : Faber and Faber Ltd., 1963.

Bate, Jackson W., *The Burden of the Past and the English Poet*, London: Chatto & Windus, 1971.

Bateson, F.W., *English Poetry: A Critical Introduction*. London : Longmans, Green, 1950.

Batho, Edith C., *The Victorians and After, 1830-1914*. London: The Cresset Press, 1938, reprint 1962.

Bayley, John, *The Romantic Survival : A Study in Poetic Evolution*. London: Chatto & Windus, 1957.

Beach, Joseph Warren, *The Making of Auden Canon*. Minneapolis: University of Minnesota Press, 1957.

Bedient, Calvin, *Eight Contemporary Poets*. Oxford University Press, 1974.

Beer, J.B., *Coleridge the Visionary*. London: Chatto & Windus, 1970.

Bergonzi, Bernard, "Critical Situations: From the Fifties to the Seventies," *Critical Quarterly*, Vol. 15, No. 1, Spring 1973.

——, (Ed.) *T.S. Eliot: Four Quartets*: A Casebook. Macmillan, 1969, reprint 1975.

——, Masters of World Literature Series. New York: Macmillan, 1972.

——, *The Turn of the Century* : *Essays on Victorian and Modern Literature*. Macmillan, 1973, reprint 1974.

Bilan, R.P., "F.R. Leavis' Revaluation of T.S. Eliot". *University of Toronto Quarterly*. Winter 1977-78.

Blackmur, R.P. *Language as Gesture*. London: George Allen & Unwin Ltd., 1954.

Blamires, Harry, *Word Unheard: A Guide through Eliot's Four Quartets*. London: Methuen & Co. Ltd., 1969.

Bloom, Harold, (Ed.), *Romanticism and Consciousness: Essays in Criticism*. New York: W.W. Norton & Co., 1970.

——, *The Visionary Company : A Reading of English Romantic Poetry*. London: Faber and Faber, 1962.

——, *Yeats*. London; Oxford, New York: OUP., 1970.

Bodkin, Maud, *Archetypal Patterns in Poetry : Psychological Studies of Imagination*. Oxford University Press, 1963.

Bornstein, George, (Ed.), *Romantic and Modern Revaluations of Literary Tradition* (1977).

——, *Transformations of Romanticism in Yeats, Eliot and Stevens*. Chicago and London: The University of Chicago Press, 1976.

——, *Yeats and Shelley*. Chicago and London: University of Chicago Press, 1970.

Bowra, C.M., *The Heritage of Symbolism*, Macmillan, 1943. Paperback 1967.

Bowra, Sir Maurice, *The Romantic Imagination*. Oxford University Press, 1950, Paperback 1969.

Bradbury, John M., "Four Quartets : The Structural Symbolism", *The Sewanee Review*, Vol. LIX, No. 2, April-June, 1951.

Brenner, Rica, *Poets of Our Time*. New York: Harcourt, Brace & Company, 1941.

Brooks, Cleanth, *The Hidden God: Studies in Hemmingway, Faulker, Yeats, Eliot and Warren*. New Haven and London: Yale University Press, 1963.

——, *Modern Poetry and the Tradition*. New York: Oxford University Press, 1939 Revised edition reprint 1965.

——, *A Shaping Joy : Studies in the Writer's Craft*. London: Methuen & Co. Ltd., 1971.

——, *The Well Wrought Urn*. New York Reynal & Hitchcock, 1947.

Bullough, Geoffrey, *The Trend of Modern Poetry*. Edinburg: Oliver & Boyd, London: Tweedale Court, 1934, Third Edition, 1949.

Bush, Douglas, *English Poetry: The Main Currents from Chaucer to the Present*. New York: Oxford University Press, 1952, A Galaxy Book, 1963.

——, *Science and English Poetry : A Historical Sketch 1590-1950*. New York: Oxford University Press, 1950.

Butter, P.H., "Four Quartets : Some Yes-Buts to Dr. Leavis", *Critical Quarterly*, Vol. 18, No.1, Spring 1976.

Cahill, Audrey F., *T.S. Eliot and the Human Predicament.* Connecticut: Laurence Verry Incorporated, Mystic, and University of Natel Press, 1967.

Cohen, J.M., *Robert Graves*, Edinburg & Lodnon : Oliver and Boyd, Writers and Critics Series, 1960.

Coleridge, S.T., *Biographia Literaria,* Ed. Shawcross, J. London: Oxford University Press, 1907, reprint 1939.

Collins, A.S., *English Literature of the Twentieth Century.* London : University Tutorial Press, 1951, reprint 1960.

Coombes, H., *Edward Thomas : A Critical Study.* London : Chatto & Windus, 1956, reprint 1973.

Cowell, Raymond, *(Ed.) Critics on Yeats: Readings in Literary Criticism.* London: George Allen and Unwin Ltd., 1971.

——, *W.B. Yeats.* London: Evan Brothers Ltd., 1969.

Cox, C.B. (Ed.) *Dylan Thomas: A Collection of Critical Essays*. New York : Prentice Hall Inc., Twentieth Century Views Series, 1966.

Cox, C.B. and Dyson, A.E. (Eds.) *The Twentieth Century Mind,* Vols. I, II and III. Oxford University Press, paperback, 1972.

——, *Modern Poetry* : *Studies in Practical Criticism.* London: Edward Arnold (Publishers) Ltd., 1963.

Danby, John F., "Edward Thomas", *Critical Quarterly,* Vol. I, Winter 1959.

Davie, Donald, *Articulate Energy* : *An Enquiry into the Syntax of English Poetry.* London: Routledge and Kegan Paul, 1955.

——, "Personification". F.W. Bateson Memorial Lecture, *Essays in Criticism,* Vol. XXXI, No. 2, April 1981, pp. 91-104.

——, *Thomas Hardy and British Poetry.* London: Routledge & Kegan Paul, 1973.

Davies, Wilford, *Dylan Thomas: New Critical Essays,* London: J.M. Dent & Sons Ltd., 1972.

Donoghue, Denis, *The Sovereign Ghost: Studies in Imagination*. London: Faber and Faber Ltd., 1978.

——, *Yeats*. Fontana: Collins, 1971.

Draper, R.P. (Ed.), *D.H.Lawrence* – The Critical Heritage Series. London: Rout & Keg. Paul, 1970.

Drew, Elizabeth, *Poetry.* Dell Publishing Co., 1959.

Duffin, Henry Charles, *Walter de la Mare : A Study of His Poetry.* London: Sidwick and Jackbon Limited, 1949.

Durrell, Lawrence, *Key to Modern Poetry.* Reprint by Rupa & Co., Calcutta etc., 1961.

Eliot, T.S., *After Strange Gods : A Primer of Modern Heresy.* London: Faber and Faber Ltd., 1934.

——, *To Criticize the Critic and Other Writings.* London : Faber and Faber Ltd., 1965.

——, *The Idea of a Christian Society.* London : Faber and Faber Ltd., 1939.

——, *Notes Towards the Definition of Culture.* London: Macmillan & Co. Ltd., 1948.

——, *On Poetry and Poets.* London : Faber and Faber Ltd., 1957.

——, *The Sacred Wood.* London: Methuen, 1920. University paperback, 1966.

——, *The Use of Poetry and the Use of Criticism: Studies in the Relation of Criticism to Poetry in England.* London: Faber and Faber Ltd., 1933.

Ellmann, Richard, *The Identity of Yeats.* London: Macmillan and Co. Ltd., 1954.

——, *The Man and the Masks.* Macmillan and Co. Ltd., 1949.

Enright, D.J., *Conspirators and Poets.* London: Chatto & Windus, 1966.

Evans, Ifor, *English Poetry in the Later Nineteenth Century.* London: Methuen & Co. Ltd., 1933, reprint 1966.

Fairchild, Hoxie Neale, *Religious Trends in English Poetry,* Vol. III. New York: Morning Side Heights, Columbia University Press, 1949.

Faulkner, Peter, *William Morris and W.B. Yeats.* Dublin : The Dolmen Press, 1962. Distributed by Oxford University Press.

Foakes, R.A., *The Romantic Assertion : A Study in the Language of Nineteenth Century Poetry.* London: Methuen & Co. Ltd., 1958.

Ford, Boris (Ed.), *A Guide to English Literature,* Vol. 7. "The Modern Age". London: Cassel, 1961, reprint 1966.

Fraser, G.S. *The Modern Writer and His World.* Perguin Books, A Pelican Book, 1953, reprint 1964.

——, *Vision and Rhetoric : Studies in Modern Poetry.* London : Faber and Faber Ltd., 1959.

Frayne, John P. (Ed.), *The Uncollected Prose by W.B. Yeats,* Vol. I. Reviews and Articles, 1886-1896. Macmillan, 1970.

Frazier, Adrian, "The Ascendancy Poetry of W.B. Yeats". *The Sewanee Review,* Winter 1980.

Frye, Northrop, *Anatomy of Criticism.* Princeton, New Jersey : Princeton University Press, 1957.

——, *Fables of Identity : Studies in Poetic Mythology.* New York, Burlingame : Harcourt Brace & World, Inc., 1963.

——, (Ed.), *Romanticism Reconsidered* – Selected Papers from the English Institute. New York and London : Columbia University Press, 1963.

——, *The Stubborn Structures: Essays on Criticism and Society* London: Methuen & Co. Ltd., 1970.

Fuller, John, *A Reader's Guide to W.H. Auden.* London: Thames & Hudson, 1970.

Furst, Lilian R., *Romanticism.* Methuen Series, 1969. The Critical Idiom No. 2.

——, *Romanticism in Perspective.* Macmillan, 1969.

Gardner, Helen, *The Art of T.S. Ediot.* London: Faber & Faber Ltd., 1949.

——, *The Composition of Four Quartets.* London and Boston : Faber and Faber, 1978.

——, "The Landscapes of Eliot's Poetry" – The Robert Spence Watson Lecture, delivered to the Literary and Philosophical Society of New Castle, *Critical Quarterly*, Vol. 10, 1968.

Garrod, H.W., *Wordsworth : Lectures and Essays.* Oxford : at the Clarendon Press, 1923, reprint 1958.

Gillie, Christopher, *Movements in English Literature 1900-1940.* Cambridge University Press, 1975.

Gordon, Lyndall, *Eliot's Early Years.* New York: Oxford University Press, 1977.

Graff, Gerard, *Poetic Statement and Critical Dogma.* Chicago and London : The University of Chicago Press, 1970.

Grierson, Sir Herbert, *The Background of English Literature*. London: Chatto & Windus, 1925.

Grierson, H.J.C. and Smith, J.C., *A Critical History of English Poetry*. London: Chatto & Windus, 1944, reprint 1956.

Gutierrez, Donald, "Lapsing Out: Ideas of Mortality and Immortality in Lawrence, *Twentieth Century Literature : A Scholarly and Critical Journal,* Vol. 24, No. 2, Summer, 1978.

Hall, James and Steinmann, Martin, *The Permanence of Yeats*. New York: Collier Books, 1961.

Hamilton, Ian, *A Poetry Chronicle : Essays and Reviews*. London: Faber and Faber, 1973.

Harding, D.W., "The Character of Literature from Blake to Byron", *A Guide to English Literature* (Ed.), Boris Ford, Vol. 5, London: Cassel, 1957, reprint 1966.

——, *Experience into Words: Essays on Poetry*. London : Chatto & Windus, 1963.

——, "A Note on Nostalgia", *Scrutiny*, Vol. I, May 1932.

Harper, George Mills, *Yeats' Quest for Eden*, Being No. 9 of the Dolmen Press Yeats Centenary Papers, 1966.

Henn, T.R., *The Lonely Tower : Studies in the Poetry of W.B. Yeats*. London : Methuen & Co. Ltd., 1950, reprint 1965.

Hepburn, James, "Leda and the Dumbledore", *The Sewanee Review,* Vol. LXXXVIII, No. 1, Winter 1980.

Higinbotham, R.N. Objections to a Review of 'Little Gidding', *Scrutiny,* Vol. XI, No. 4, Summer 1943.

Hoffman, Daniel, *Barbarous Knowledge : Myth in the Poetry of Yeats, Graves and Muir*. Oxford University Press, 1967.

Hogarth, Herbert, *Notes on Some Figures Behind T.S. Eliot*. London: Chatto & Windus, 1965.

Holbrook, David, *Llareggub Revisited: Dylan Thomas and the State of Modern Poetry*. Bath: Cedric Chivers, Partway, 1962.

——, *Lost Bearings in English Poetry*. London : Vision Press Limited, Vision Critical Studies, 1977.

Holland, Norman N., "Freud on Shakespeare", *PMLA*., Vol. 75, 1960.

Hollander, John, (Ed.), *Modern Poetry : Essays in Criticism*. Oxford University Press, 1968.

Holloway, John, *The Colours of Clarity* : *Essays on Contemporary Literature*. London: Routledge & Kegan Paul, 1964.

Hone, Joseph, *W.B. Yeats, 1865-1939*. Macmillan, 1943.

Hopkins, Kenneth, *English Poetry* : *A Short History*. London : Phoenix House Ltd., 1962.

Hough, Graham, *The Dark Sun* : *A Study of D.H. Lawrence.* London : Gerald Duckworth & Co., 1956.

Hough, Graham, *Image and Experience: Studies in a Literary Revolution*. London: Gerald Duckworth & Co. Ltd., 1960.

Hough, Graham, *The Last Romantics.* London: Methuen, New York: Barnes & Noble, 1947.

——, *The Romantic Poets.* Hutchinson of London, 1953, reprint 1976.

——, *Selected Essays.* Cambridge University Press, 1978.

Housman, A.E., *The Name and Nature of Poetry*. The Leslie Stephen Lecture delivered at Cambridge on 9 May 1933. New York : The Macmillan Company; Cambridge, English, at the University Press, 1944.

Howarth, Herbert, *Notes on Some Figures Behind T.S. Eliot.* London: Chatto & Windus, 1965.

Hynes, Samuel, *The Pattern of Hardy's Poetry.* London: Oxford University Press, 1956, reprint 1961.

——, "The Hardy Tradition in Modern English Poetry", *The Sewanee Review*, Winter 1980, Vol. LXXXVIII, No. 1.

Jarrel, Randall, *Poetry and the Age.* London : Faber and Faber, 1955, paper covered edition 1973.

Jeffares, A. Norman, *W.B. Yeats* : *The Man and the Poet.* London : Routledge & Kegan Paul Ltd., 1949.

——, *W.B. Yeats* : *The Poems* – Studies in Literature Series. London: Edward Arnold (Publishers) Ltd., 1961.

——, *Commentary on the Poems of W.B. Yeats.* London: Macmillan 1968, reprint 1974.

——, *The Circus Animals: Essays on W.B. Yeats.* Macmillan, 1970.

——, & Cross, K.G. (Eds.) *In Excited Reverie* : *A Centenary Tribute to W.B. Yeats*, 1865-1939. Macmillan, 1965.

Johnson, R.V., *Aestheticism.* London : Mathuen & Co. Ltd., The Critical Idiom Series.

Johnston, John H., *English Poetry of the First World War.* Princeton University Press, 1964.

Keats, John, *The Letters of John Keats* (Ed.), Maurice Buxton Forman, Oxford University Press, 1931, Fourth edition, 1952.

Kenner, Hugh, *The Invisible Poet: T.S. Eliot.* London: Methuen & Co., 1960, University paperback, 1965.

Kermode, Frank, *Romantic Image.* London: Routledge and Kegan Paul, 1957, paperback 1961.

——, *Modern Essays.* London: Collins, Fontana Books, 1971.

——, *Puzzles and Epiphanies: Essays and Reviews, 1958-1961.* London: Routledge & Kegan Paul, 1962.

Kirkham, Michael, *The Poetry of Robert Graves.* London: University of London, Athlone Press, 1969.

——, "Edward Thomas' Other Self", *Ariel: A Review of International English Literature,* Vol. 6, No. 3, July 1975.

——, "The 'Desert Places' in Edward Thomas' Poetry", *University of Toronto Quarterly,* Summer 1979, Vol. XLVIII, No. 4.

Knights, L.C., *Explorations.* London: Chatto & Windus, 1946, reprint 1951.

Koch, Vivienne, *W.B. Yeats: The Tragic Phase.* London: Routledge & Kegan Paul, 1951.

Kostelanetz, Richard (Ed.), *On Contemporary Literature.* New York: Avon Books, 1964.

Krieger, Murray, *The New Apologists for Poetry.* Connecticut : Greenwood Press, Publishers, 1956, reprint by the University of Minnesota, 1977.

Kumar, Shiv. K., (Ed.), *British Romantic Poets : Recent Revaluations.* New York: New York University Press; London : University of London Press Ltd., 1966.

Langbaum, Robert, *The Modern Spirit : Essays on the Continuity of Nineteenth and Twentieth Century Literature.* New York: Oxford University Press, 1970.

——, *The Poetry of Experience : The Dramatic Monologue Literary Tradition.* London: Chatto & Windus, 1972.

Lawrence, D.H., Introduction to the American edition of New Poems (1918), reprinted in *The Complete Poems of D.H. Lawrence,* Vol. I, ed., Vivian de Sola Pinto & Warren Roberts. London: Heinemann, 1964, reprint 1972, pp. 181-186.

Leavis, F.R., *Education and the University : A Sketch for an English School* (1943), London: Chatto & Windus, 1965.

——, *Revaluation : Tradition and Development in English Poetry.* London: Chatto and Windus, 1962.

——, *English Literature in Our Time and the University.* London: Chatto & Windus, paperback 1969.

——, *New Bearings in English Poetry.* London: Chatto and Windus, 1932, reprint 1959.

Lehmann, John, "The Wain-Larkin Myth: Reply to John Wain", *The Sewanee Review,* Autumn, 1958.

Lewis, D. Day, *The Poetic Image* – The Clark Lectures given at Cambridge in 1946. London: Jonathan Cape, 1947.

Lewis., C.S., "Psycho-Analysis and Literary Criticism". *Selected Literary Essays.* Cambridge University Press, 1969.

Lodge, David, *The Modes of Modern Writing – Metaphor, Metonymy and the Typology of Modern Literature.* New York : Cornell University Press, 1977.

Lodge, David, (Ed.), *Twentieth Century Literary Criticism.* Longman, 1972.

Longley, Edna, (Ed.), *Poems and Last Poems.* Collins Annotated Student Texts, 1973.

——, (Ed.), *A Language Not to be Betrayed: Selected Prose of Edward Thomas.* Carcanet Press in Association with Mid Northumberland Arts Group, 1981.

Lowes, John Livinstone, *Convention and Revolt in Poetry.* Boston and New York: Houghton Mifflin Company; Cambridge: The Riverside Press, 1926.

Lucas, F.L., *The Decline and Fall of the Romantic Ideal.* Cambridge University Press, 1936, reprint 1963.

Lucas, F.L., *Literature and Psychology.* The University of Michigan Press, U.S.A., Ann Arbour Paperbacks, 1957.

Lucy, Sean, *T.S. Eliot and the Idea of Tradition.* London : Cohen & West, 1960.

MacNeice, Louis, *The Poetry of W.B. Yeats.* Oxford University Press, 1941.

Marcos, Phillip L., *Yeats and the Beginning of the Irish Renaissance,* Cornell University Press, 1970.

Marsden, Kenneth, *The Poems of Thomas Hardy : A Critical Introduction*. London : University of London, The Athlone Press, 1969.

Marsh, Jan, *Edward Thomas : A Poet for His Country.* London: Paul Felk, 1978.

Martin, Bruce K., *Philip Larkin.* Boston : Twayne Publishers, 1978.

Martz, Louis L., *The Poem of the Mind: Essays on Poetry, English and American*. Oxford University Press, 1966.

Matthiessen, F.O., *The Achievement of T.S. Eliot : An Essay on the Nature of Poetry.* New York: Oxford University, 1935; A Galaxy Book, 1958.

Maxwell, D.E.S., *Poets of the Thirties.* London : Routledge & Kegan Paul, 1969.

Megroz, R.L., *Modern English Poetry, 1882-1932.* Strand : Ivor Nicholson & Watson Ltd., 1933.

Melchiori, Girogio, *The Whole Mystery of Art: Pattern into Poetry in the Work of W.B. Yeats*. London : Routledge and Kegan Paul, 1960.

Mellor, Anne K., "On Romantic Irony, Symbolism and Allegory", *Criticism,* Vol. XXI, No. 3. Summer, 1979.

Menon. V.K. Narayana, *The Development of W.B. Yeats.* Edinburgh: Oliver & Boyd, 1942.

Miller, Jr., James E., *T.S. Eliot's Personal Waste Land.* Pennsylvania State University Press, 1977.

Molina, Davi Newton de, *The Literary Criticism of T.S. Eliot,* London: University of London, The Athlone Press, 1977.

Montgomery, Marion, *T.S. Eliot : An Essay on the American Magus.* Athens: University of Georgia Press, 1969.

Morgan, Kathleen E., *Christian Themes in Contemporary Poets : A Study of English Poetry of the Twentieth Century.* London : SCM Press Ltd., 1965.

Motion, Andrew, *The Poetry of Edward Thomas.* London, Boston and Henley : Routledge and Kegan Paul, 1980.

——, "Everlasting Moments: Review of Edward Thomas', *The Chess Player and Other Essays", The Times Literary Supplement* (August 21, 1981).

Moynihan, William T., *The Craft and Art of Dylan Thomas*. New York: University of Connecticut, Cornell paperback, 1968.

Muir, Edwin, *The Estate of Poetry*– The Charles Eliot Norton Lectures, 1955-56. London: Hogarth Press, 1962.

Nandakumar, Prema, *The Glory and the Good: Essays on Literature*. Bombay etc. : Asia Publishing House, 1965.

Nelson, Gerald, *Changes of Heart: A Study of the Poetry of W.H. Auden*. Berkeley and Los Angeles: University of California Press, 1969.

Newlin, Margaret, "The Suicide Bandwagon". *Critical Quarterly*, Vol. 14, No. 4, Winter, 1972.

Nicholson, Norman, *Writers of Today*, London : Sidwick and Jackson, 1946.

Olson, Elder, *The Poetry of Dylan Thomas*. Chicago : University of Chicago Press, 1954.

Parkinson, Thomas, *W.B. Yeats: Self-Critic* : *A Study of His Early Verse* (1951), and *The Later Poetry (1964)* – Two volumes in one. Berkeley and Los Angeles: University of California Press, 1971.

Partridge, A.C., *The Language of Modern Poetry* : *Yeats, Eliot, Auden*. London : The Language Library, Andre Deutsch Ltd., 1976.

Paulin, Tom, *Thomas Hardy the Poetry of Perception*. Macmillan, 1975.

Paz, Octavio, *Children of the Mire*: *Modern Poetry from Romanticism to the Avant-Garde,* The Charles-Eliot-Norton Lectures, translated by Rachel Phillips, 1971-72, Harward University Press, 1974.

Perkins, David, *A History of Modern Poetry* : *From the 1890s to the High Modernist Mode*. The Belknap Press of Harward University Press, 1976.

——, *Wordsworth and the Poetry of Sincerity*. The Belknap Press of Harward University Press, 1964.

Pettet, E.C., "Keats' Romanticism", *On the Poetry of John Keats*. Cambridge University Press, 1957.

Pikoulis, John, "Alun Lewis and Edward Thomas", *Critical Quarterly,* Vol. 23, No. 4, Winter 1981.

Pinsky, Robert, *The Situation of Poetry : Contemporary Poetry and Its Traditions*. Princeton, New Jersey : Princeton University Press, 1976.

Pinto, Vivian de Sola, *Crisis in English Poetry, 1880-1940*. London: Hutchinson University Library, 1951, reprint 1967.

Pinto, Vivian de Sola, "D.H. Lawrence : Poet Without a Mask", *The Complete Poems of D.H. Lawrence,* Vol. I, Ed., Vivian de Sola Pinto & Warren Roberts, London : Heinemann, 1964, reprint, 1972, pp. 1-21.

Praz, Mario, *The Romantic Agony* (translated from the Italian by Angus Davidson), Oxford University Press, 1933, reprint, 1954.

Press, John, *Rule and Energy : Trends in British Poetry Since the Second World War.* London : Oxford University Press, 1963.

——, *A Map of Modern English Verse.* Oxford University Press, Paperback, 1969.

Pritchard, William H., *Seeing Through Everything : English Writers 1918-1940.* London : Faber & Faber, 1977.

Quinn, Maire A. "The Personal Past in the Poetry of Thomas Hardy and Edward Thomas", *Critical Quarterly,* Vol. XVI, No. 1, Spring 1974.

Raine, Kathleen, "David Gascoyne and the Prophetic Role", *The Sewanee Review,* Spring 1967.

Rajan, Balachandra, (Ed.) *T.S. Eliot : A Study of His Writings by Several Hands,* London : Dennis Dobson Ltd., 1948, reprint 1971.

——, *W.B. Yeats : A Critical Introduction.* Hutchinson University Library, 1965.

——, *The Overwhelming Question: A Study of the Poetry of T.S. Eliot.* Toronto and Buffalo : University of Toronto Press, 1976.

Rayan, Krishna, *Suggestion and Statement in Poetry.* London: University of London, The Ahtlone Press, 1972.

Read, Herbert, *The True Voice of Feeling: Studies in English Romantic Poetry.* London : Faber and Faber Ltd., 1947, paper covered edition, 1968.

——, *The Cult of Sincerity.* London : Faber and Faber, 1968.

——, *A Coat of Many Colours.* London : Routledge & Kegan Paul Ltd., 1945, reprint 1956.

——, *Phases of English Poetry.* London : Leonard & Virginia Woolf at the Hogarth Press, 1928.

Reeves, James, *The Critical Sense.* London : Heinemann, 1956, reprint 1966.

——, *The Modern Poet's World.* London: Heinemann, 1957.

——, (Ed.), *Georgian Poetry.* Introduction by James Reeves. Penguin 1962.

——, *Commitment to Poetry.* London: Heinemann, 1969.

Reid, B.L., *William Butler Yeats : The Lyric of Tragedy.* Norman: University of Oklahoma Press, 1961.

Rexroth, Kenneth, "The Poetry of D.H. Lawrence", *D.H. Lawrence,* Ed. Leo Hamalian, McGraw-Hill Paperbacks, Contemporary Studies in Literature, U.S.A.

Richards, I.A., *Coleridge on Imagination.* London : Routeledge & Kegan Paul Limited, 1934.

——, *The Principles of Literary Criticism.* London : Routledge & Kegan Paul, 1924, reprint 1963.

Roberts, Michael (Ed.), *Faber Book of Modern Verse.* London: Faber & Faber Ltd., 1935, Introduction by Michael Roberts.

Robson, W.W., *Modern English Literature,* Oxford University Press, 1970.

——, "T.S. Eliot, the Noise of Life, and the Harmony of Poetry, *The Sewanee Review,* Winter 1980.

Rodway, Allan, *The Romantic Conflict.* London : Chatto & Windus, 1963.

Rogers, Timothy, (Ed.) *Georgian Poetry, 1911-1922.* The Critical Heritage Routledge & Kegan Paul, 1977.

Rosenthal, M.L., *The Modern Poets : A Critical Introduction.* New York: Oxford University press, 1960.

——, *The New Poets : American and British Poetry Since World War II.* London, Oxford, New York : Oxford University Press, 1967.

——, *Sailing into the Unknown.* New York : Oxford University Press, 1978.

Rowlinson, D.H., *The Practice of Criticism.* Cambridge University Press, 1971.

Rudd, Margaret, *Divided Image : A Study of William Blake and W.B. Yeats.* London : Routledge and Kegan Paul Ltd., 1953.

Sabin, Margery, *English Romanticism and the French Tradition.* Harward University Press, 1976.

Sagar, Keith, *The Art of D.H. Lawrence.* Cambridge University Press, 1966.

Scofield, Martin, "A Gesture and a Pose: T.S. Eliot's Images of Love", *Critical Quarterly*, Vol. 18, No. 3, Autumn, 1976.

Scott-James, R.A., *Fifty Years of English Literature, 1900-1950*. Longmans, Green & Co., 1951.

——, *The Making of Literature*. London: Secker & Warburg, 1930, reprint, 1958.

Serio, John N., "Landscape and Voice in T.S. Eliot's Poetry", *The Centennial Review*, Vol. XXVI, No.1. Winter 1982.

Shapiro, Karl, *In Defence of Ignorance*. New York : Random House Inc., 1955.

Sisson, C.H., *English Poetry -- 1900-1950 : An Assessment*. London: Rupert Hart-Davis, 1971.

Sitwell, Edith, *Aspects of Modern Poetry*. London : Duckworth, 1934.

Skelton, Robin, (Ed.) *Herbert Read : A Memorial Symposium*. London: Methuen & Co. Ltd., 1970.

Smith, Grover, *T.S. Eliot's Poetry & Plays : A Study in Sources of Meaning*. Chicago & London : The University of Chicago Press, 1950.

Smith, Stan, "A Public House and not a Hermitage : Nature, Property and Self in the Work of Edward Thomas", *Critical Quarterly*, Vol. 19, No. 1, Spring 1977.

Southam, B.C., *A Student's Guide to the Selected Poems of T.S. Eliot*. London: Faber and Faber, 1974.

Spears, Monroe K., The Dominant Symbols of Auden's Poetry, *The Sewanee Review*, Vol. LIX, No. 3, Summer 1951.

——, "Auden in the Fifties : Rites of Homage", *The Sewanee Review*, Summer, 1961.

——, *The Poetry of W.H. Auden : The Disenchanted Island*. New York: Oxford University Press, 1963.

——, *Dionysus and the City : Modernism in Twentieth Century Poetry*. New York: Oxford University Press, 1970.

Spender, Stephen, *The Destructive Element*. London, Toronto, Jonathan Cape, 1938.

——, "Poetry Since 1939", *Since 1939: Drama, Novel, Poetry, Prose Literature* by Robert Speaight et al. London : Phoenix House, by arrangement with the British Council, 1949.

——, *The Struggle of the Modern*. Berkeley and Los Angeles: University of California Press, 1963, reprint, 1965.

Spilka, Mark, *D.H. Lawrence*. N.J. : Prentice Hall, Inc., Twentieth Century Views Series, 1963.

Stallworthy, Jon, *Between the Lines: Yeats' Poetry in the Making*. Oxford University Press, 1963.

——, (Ed.), *Yeats – Last Poems*, A Casebook, Macmillan, 1968.

——, *Vision and Revision in Yeats' Last Poems*. Oxford: at the Clarendon Press, 1969.

——, "W.B. Yeats and Wilfred Owen", *Critical Quarterly*, Vol. 11, No. 3, Autumn, 1969.

Stead, C.K., *The New Poetic : Yeats to Eliot* (1964). Penguin Books by arrangement with Hutchinson of London, 1967.

Stewart, J.I.M., *Eight Modern Writers*. Oxford History of English Literature, Vol. XII, Clarendon Press, Oxford, 1963.

Stock, A.G., *W.B. Yeats : His Poetry and Thought*. Cambridge University Press, 1964.

Tate, Allen, *The Man of Letters in the Modern World : Selected Essays, 1928-1955*. London : Thames and Hudson, Meridian Books, 1957.

——, (Ed.), *T.S. Eliot : The Man and His Work*. London: Chatto & Windus, 1967.

Taylor, Estella Ruth, *The Modern Irish Writers*, University of Kansas Press, 1954.

Tedlock Jr., E.W., *Dylan Thomas : The Legend and the Poet*. London: Mercury Books, 1960.

Thomas, R. George, "Edward Thomas : Poet and Critic", *Essays and Studies*, 1968.

Thorburn, David, and Hartman, Geoffrey (Eds.), *Romanticism – Vistas, Instances, Continuities*. Itheca and London: Cornell University Press, 1973.

Thwaite, Anthony, *Contemporary English Poetry: An Introduction*. London etc.: Heinemann Educational Books Ltd., 1957.

Timms, David, *Philip Larkin*. Edinburgh: Oliver & Boyd, 1973.

Tolley, A.T., *The Poetry of the Thirties*. London: Victor Gollancz Ltd., 1975.

Tompkins, Jane P., *Reader Response Criticism: From Formalism to Post-structuralism*. Baltimore and London: The Johns Hopkins University Press, 1980.

Traversi, Derek, *T.S. Eliot : The Longer Poems*. London, Sydney, Toronto: The Bodley Head, 1976.

Treece, Henry, *Dylan Thomas : Dog Among the Fairies*. London: Ernest Been Ltd., 1949.

Underhill, Hough, "The Poetical Character of Edward Thomas, *Essays in Criticism*, Vol. XXIII, No. 3, July 1973.

Unger, Lennard, *T.S. Eliot : Moments and Patterns*. Minnespolis: University of Minnesota Press, 1956, reprint, 1966.

Unterecker, John, *A Reader's Guide to William Butler Yeats*. Thames & Hudson, 1959, Third Impression, 1965.

——, (Ed.), *Yeats : A Collection of Critical Essays*. N.J. : Prentice-Hall, Inc., Eaglewood Cliff, The Twentieth Century Views Series, 1963.

Vines, Sherad, *A Hundred Years of English Literature*. New York : Collier Books, 1950.

Viswanathan, S., "Eliot and Shelley: A Sketch of Shifts in Attitude", *Ariel : A Review of International English Literature*, Vol. II, No. 1, January, 1971.

Vivas, Eliseo, *Creation and Discovery : Essays in Criticism and Aesthetics*. New York : The Noonday Press, 1955.

Wain, John, "English Poetry: The Immediate Situation", *The Sewanee Review*, Vol. LXV, 1957.

——, "The New Puritanism, The New Academicism, The New, The New..." *Critical Quarterly*, Vol. 14, No. 1, Spring, 1972.

Watson, J.R., *Picturesque Landscape and English Romantic Poetry*. London: Hutchinson International, 1970.

——, "The Romantics", *Critical Quarterly*, Vol. 21, No. 1, Spring, 1979.

——, "The Other Larkin", *Critical Quarterly*, Vol. XVII, No. 4, Winter, 1975.

Webster, Brenda S., *Yeats : A Psycho-Analytical Study*. Macmillan, 1973.

Wellek, Rene and Warren, Austin, *Theory of Literature*, Penguin Books, 1942, reprint 1963.

Wellek, Rene, *A History of Modern Critcism, 1750-1950.* "The Romantic Age". London: Jonathan Cape, 1955.

—, "The Concept of Romanticism" and "Romanticism Re-examined," *Concepts of Criticism*, Ed. Stephen G. Nichols, Jr., New Haven and London: Yale University Press, 1963.

West, Anthony, *D.H. Lawrence*. London : Arthur Barker Ltd., 1950, reprint, 1957.

Whallen, Terry, "Philip Larkin's Imagist Bias : His Poetry of Observations", *Critical Quarterly*, Vol. 23, No. 2, Summer, 1981.

Whitaker, Thomas, *Swan and Shadow: Yeats' Dialogue with History*. Chapel Hill: University of Carolina Press, 1964.

Williams, Charles, *Poetry at Present*. Oxford: Clarendon Press, 1930.

Williamson, George, *A Reader's Guide to T.S. Eliot: A Poem by Poem Analysis*. London: Thames & Hudson, 1955, reprint, 1976.

Wilson, Edmund, *Axel's Castle: A Study in the Imaginative Literature of 1870-1930*. London, New York: Charles Scribner's Sons, 1935.

Wilson, F.A.C., *W.B. Yeats and Tradition*. London: Bollancz, 1958.

—, *Yeats' Iconography*. London: Victor Gollancz Ltd., 1960.

Wimsatt, W.K., *The Verbal Icon: Studies in the Meaning of Poetry*. London: Methuen & Co. Ltd., 1954.

Winters, Yvor, *In Defence of Reason*. The University of Denver Press, A Swallow Press Book, 1937.

—, *The Function of Criticism : Problems and Exercises*. London: Routledge & Kegan Paul, 1957.

—, *The Poetry of W.B. Yeats*. Denver : Allan Swallow, 1960.

Woodcock, George, "Romanticism : Studies and Speculations", *The Sewanee Review*, Spring 1980.

Wordsworth & Coleridge, *Lyrical Ballads*, Ed. R.L. Brett & A.R. Jones, London: Methuen & Co. Ltd., 1963, reprint 1968, Preface by Wordsworth.

Yeats, W.B., *Essays and Introductions*. London : Macmillan & Co. Ltd., 1961.

—, (Ed.), *The Oxford Book of Modern Verse, 1892-1935*. London: Oxford University Press, 1936, reprint 1972, Introduction.

Young, Alan "On Surrealism" – Reviews and Comment, *Critical Quarterly*, Vol. 15, No. 1, Spring 1973.

——, "Image as Structure: Dylan Thomas and Poetic Meaning", *Critical Quarterly*, Vol. 17, No. 4, Winter, 1975.

INDEX